1st Workshop on Causal Inference and Natural Language Processing (CI+NLP 2021)

Punta Cana, Dominican Republic
10 November 2021

ISBN: 978-1-7138-9187-1

Printed from e-media with permission by:

Curran Associates, Inc.
57 Morehouse Lane
Red Hook, NY 12571

Some format issues inherent in the e-media version may also appear in this print version.

Printed with permission by Curran Associates, Inc. (2024)

Association for Computational Linguistics
209 N. Eighth Street
Stroudsburg, Pennsylvania 18360

Phone: 1-570-476-8006
Fax: 1-570-476-0860

acl@aclweb.org

Additional copies of this publication are available from:

Curran Associates, Inc.
57 Morehouse Lane
Red Hook, NY 12571 USA
Phone: 845-758-0400
Fax: 845-758-2633
Email: curran@proceedings.com
Web: www.proceedings.com

EMNLP 2021

The First Workshop on Causal Inference and Natural Language Processing

Proceedings of CI+NLP

November 10, 2021

Introduction

Establishing causal relationships is a fundamental goal of scientific research. Quantifying the effectiveness of a vaccine, the persuasive power of a public health ad, or the effectiveness of a lockdown policy, all boil down to questions of causality: how would the treatment (vaccine, ad or policy) affect the outcome (infection rates) compared to a counterfactual world with no treatment? The strength and direction of causal relationships, once formally identified, play a key role in the formulation of clinical treatments, public policy and other long-standing prescriptive strategies.

Text plays an increasingly important role in the study of causal relationships across domains. In the setting of crowd lending, communication researchers have examined the impact of the language of funding requests on receiving loans, where text is the treatment. In the context of immigration policy, political scientists have studied the impact of knowing an illegal immigrant's criminal history on written justifications of whether they should be jailed, where text is the outcome. A growing body of literature studies the interplay between causal inference and NLP.

Despite the interdisciplinary interest in causal inference with text, several challenges remain. For example, it is unclear how deficiencies in NLP methods (such as their inaccuracy with low-resource languages, and their tendency to propagate biases in the data) affect downstream causal estimates. In addition, hyperparameter selection and modeling assumptions in NLP are motivated by accuracy and tractability considerations; how these choices affect downstream causal estimates remains unexplored.

The task of causal identification (linking unobservable causal quantities to observable data) is inherently a process of argument based on domain expertise. Hence, interaction between substantive experts (in medical research, the social sciences and other domains) and methodological experts (in computational linguistics, statistics and other disciplines) is crucial to make valid causal inferences with text. With the existing research in this space spanning several different academic communities, opportunities for such interaction have been lacking thus far.

The **CI+NLP** workshop aims to bring together substantive and methodological experts across academic communities, with an interest in the intersection of causal inference and NLP. It will explore how current and new NLP methodology can contribute to establishing and evaluating causal relationships, and how substantive expertise from different domains can contribute to answering causal questions with text. The CI+NLP workshop differs from prior interdisciplinary NLP workshops (such as the *Text as Data* conference series) in its focus on *causality*, both substantively and methodologically.

Main Workshop Topics. The broad themes of the workshop include, but are not restricted to:

1. *Causal inference theory for language:* Includes methodology for causal inference and optimal policy learning, with experimental or observational data, and text as a treatment, outcome, mediator, moderator or other causal identification device.

2. *Language processing systems and causality:* Includes research on counterfactual predictions with text, causal model interpretation and explanation, causal model bias estimation and debiasing, and methods and datasets to benchmark and analyze the sensitivity and robustness of causal inference and NLP systems.

3. *Society, language, influence and causality:* Includes research on language as a mechanism of influence and provocation, and causal questions related to linguistic framing, medical notes and clinical outcomes, and political messaging and propaganda.

CI+NLP would not have been possible without the dedication of its program committee. We would like to thank them for their invaluable effort in providing timely and high-quality reviews on a short notice. We are also grateful to our invited speakers and panelists for contributing to our program.

The CI+NLP workshop organizers,
Organizing Committee: Amir Feder, Katherine A. Keith, Emaad Manzoor, Reid Pryzant, Dhanya Sridhar, Zach Wood-Doughty

Steering Committee: Jacob Eisenstein, Justin Grimmer, Roi Reichart, Margaret E. Roberts, Uri Shalit, Brandon M. Stewart, Victor Veitch, Diyi Yang

Organizing Committee

- Amir Feder
- Katherine A. Keith
- Emaad Manzoor
- Reid Pryzant
- Dhanya Sridhar
- Zach Wood-Doughty

Steering Committee

- Jacob Eisenstein
- Justin Grimmer
- Roi Reichart
- Margaret E. Roberts
- Uri Shalit
- Brandon M. Stewart
- Victor Veitch
- Diyi Yang

Program Committee

- David Adelani
- Tim Althoff
- Elliott Ash
- Yonatan Belinkov
- Dallas Card
- Alexander D'Amour
- Naoki Egami
- Amir Feder
- Anjalie Field
- Peter Henderson
- Zhijing Jin
- Yohan Jo

- Shalmali Joshi
- Sarvnaz Karimi
- Divyansh Kaushik
- Vivek Kulkarni
- Adyasha Maharana
- Emaad Manzoor
- Huyen Nguyen
- Jekaterina Novikova
- Nadav Oved
- Yuval Pinter
- Matt Post
- Reid Pryzant
- Roi Reichart
- Maarten Sap
- Zeerak Talat
- Chenhao Tan
- Kellie Webster
- Liuyi Yao
- Justine Zhang

Invited Speakers

- Susan Athey
- David Blei
- Cristian Danescu-Niculescu-Mizil

Table of Contents

Conference Program

9:00–9:10 **Opening Remarks**

9:10–10:00 **Keynote 1**

10:00–10:30 **Coffee Break**

10:30–12:00 **Short Talks Session 1**

10:50–11:00 *Causal Augmentation for Causal Sentence Classification*
Fiona Anting Tan, Devamanyu Hazarika, See-Kiong Ng, Soujanya Poria and Roger Zimmermann

11:00–11:10 *Text as Causal Mediators: Research Design for Causal Estimates of Differential Treatment of Social Groups via Language Aspects*
Katherine Keith, Douglas Rice and Brendan O'Connor

11:10–11:20 *Enhancing Model Robustness and Fairness with Causality: A Regularization Approach*
Zhao Wang, Kai Shu and Aron Culotta

11:20–11:30 *What Makes a Scientific Paper be Accepted for Publication?*
Panagiotis Fytas, Georgios Rizos and Lucia Specia

12:00–13:00 **Lunch Break**

13:00–14:30 Short Talks Session 2

13:10–13:20 *Sensitivity Analysis for Causal Mediation through Text: an Application to Political Polarization*
Graham Tierney and Alexander Volfovsky

13:20–13:30 *A Survey of Online Hate Speech through the Causal Lens*
Antigoni Founta and Lucia Specia

13:30–13:40 *Identifying Causal Influences on Publication Trends and Behavior: A Case Study of the Computational Linguistics Community*
Maria Glenski and Svitlana Volkova

13:40–13:50 *It's quality and quantity: the effect of the amount of comments on online suicidal posts*
Daniel Low, Kelly Zuromski, Daniel Kessler, Satrajit S. Ghosh, Matthew K. Nock and Walter Dempsey

14:30–14:45 Mini Break

14:45–15:35 Invited Talk 2

15:35–16:25 Invited Talk 3

16:25–16:45 Coffee Break

No Day Set (continued)

16:45–17:30 Panel Discussion

17:30–18:30 Poster Session

Causal Augmentation for Causal Sentence Classification

Fiona Anting Tan[1], Devamanyu Hazarika[2], See-Kiong Ng[1], Soujanya Poria[3] and Roger Zimmermann[2]

[1]Institute of Data Science, National University of Singapore
[2]School of Computing, National University of Singapore
[3]Information Systems Technology and Design, Singapore University of Technology and Design
tan.f@u.nus.edu, hazarika@comp.nus.edu.sg, seekiong@nus.edu.sg,
sporia@sutd.edu.sg, rogerz@comp.nus.edu.sg

Abstract

Scarcity of annotated causal texts leads to poor robustness when training state-of-the-art language models for causal sentence classification. In particular, we found that models misclassify on augmented sentences that have been negated or strengthened with respect to its causal meaning. This is worrying since minor linguistic differences in causal sentences can have disparate meanings. Therefore, we propose the generation of counterfactual causal sentences by creating contrast sets (Gardner et al., 2020) to be included during model training. We experimented on two model architectures and predicted on two out-of-domain corpora. While our strengthening schemes proved useful in improving model performance, for negation, regular edits were insufficient. Thus, we also introduce heuristics like shortening or multiplying root words of a sentence. By including a mixture of edits when training, we achieved performance improvements beyond the baseline across both models, and within and out of corpus' domain, suggesting that our proposed augmentation can also help models generalize.

1 Introduction

Causality is an important concept for knowledge discovery as it conveys the idea of cause and effect. In the simplest sense, a causal relation exists between entities A and B through the statement "*A causes B*" or "*B is caused by A*". In recent years, causal relation extraction from text has garnered significant interest in Natural Language Processing (NLP) (Asghar, 2016; Xu et al., 2020; Yang et al., 2021).

Causal sentence classification (CSC) is the task of identifying sentences that contain causal meaning (Yu et al., 2019; Sumner et al., 2014; Mariko et al., 2020). Identification of causal sentences is often the first step in tasks like generating plot structures (Mirza and Tonelli, 2016a; Caselli and Vossen, 2017a) or constructing causal knowledge graphs (Heindorf et al., 2020) for further downstream Natural Language Understanding applications, like Question Answering (Dalal et al., 2021). Figure 1 demonstrates examples where similar claims are categorized by their causal strengths. CSC is challenging because the syntax of causality varies in context. Thus, it is difficult to exhaustively capture causal expressions, especially for implicit occurrences (Asghar, 2016). Negations and the absence of causality further complicate automatic causality identification (Heindorf et al., 2020).

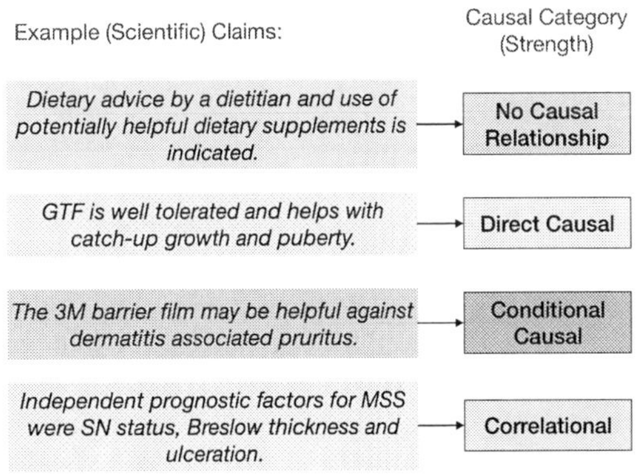

Figure 1: Causal sentence classification classifies textual claims into various categories of causal strengths.

Furthermore, there is a lack of good quality CSC datasets (Asghar, 2016; Xu et al., 2020). Most NLP datasets typically treat causal relation extraction as a subtask of relation extraction, where "Cause-Effect" is one of the many relation labels. However, we think that causality is a complex relation best learned using dedicated causal relation datasets. Such corpora that exist are mostly small in size (< 5000 sentences), except for AltLex (Hidey and McKeown, 2016) that has over 40000 sentences. Datasets also tend to label causal relations in an overly simplistic binary level (as 'causal' or 'not causal'). Only some works classify text by causal

Proceedings of CI+NLP: First Workshop on Causal Inference and NLP, pages 1–20
November 10, 2021.

strengths (Girju and Moldovan, 2002; Yu et al., 2019; Sumner et al., 2014).

Data augmentation is a natural avenue for handling small-sized datasets. Augments created must be meaningful to explain representation gaps in the current datasets. In causality, both the causal direction and strength matter. As such, we believe that models should be sensitive towards negations and semantics of words to avoid misclassification. For example, in Figure 1, the first three sentences include words related to *"help"*. However, the context of its usage and inclusion of modal words like *"may"* easily alters the intended causal strength of the sentence. This observation motivates us to artificially construct meaningful counterfactuals that would reflect the model's decision boundaries. We do so by applying rule-based schemes that negate causal relations or strengthen conditionally causal sentences. However, for negations, we notice that introducing edits is insufficient to improve model performance. Thus, we also explore adding heuristic edits.

We find that state-of-the-art (SOTA) language models, such as BERT (Devlin et al., 2019) with MLP or SVM classifiers, achieve improvements in classification performance when trained with our created counterfactuals. In addition, our evaluation on cross-domain datasets shows that training on augmented datasets (original plus edits) improves model generalization to out-of-domain (OOD) contexts. This is consistent with findings from (Kaushik et al., 2020a,b) in sentiment analysis and natural language inference contexts. In summary, we make the following contributions:

1. We show that current SOTA models are not robust to minimally perturbed sentences that differ in causal direction and strength. Therefore, we propose causal negation and strengthening schemes based on dependency and part-of-speech (POS) tags to augment causal sentences. To our knowledge, we are the first to study the effects of counterfactual augmentation in the context of causal claims classification.

2. We observe that simple heuristic edits on negated counterfactuals improve model effectiveness for the CSC task.

3. We show that a mixture of counterfactuals improves performance in the trained domain and also generalizes better to OOD corpora such as SCITE (Li et al., 2021) and AltLex (Hidey and McKeown, 2016).

Section 2 details related works in the literature and positions our work amongst them. Section 3 explains our methods for data augmentation, data processing and modeling. Section 4 presents and discusses our findings while Section 5 concludes.

2 Related Works

2.1 Causal Sentence Classification

Although causality is an important concept for knowledge discovery, benchmarking datasets and standardization of labeling rules have been limited, thus prohibiting empirical comparisons across methodologies (Asghar, 2016; Xu et al., 2020). Most NLP benchmarking datasets define causal relations as just one out of many class labels (e.g. Part-Whole) (Jurgens et al., 2012; Gábor et al., 2018; Caselli and Vossen, 2017b; Mirza et al., 2014; Mirza and Tonelli, 2016b). Others focus on causal relations and define such relations as a binary label (Li et al., 2021; Mariko et al., 2020; Hidey and McKeown, 2016). However, causality may not always occur at extremes in real-life statements, and correlation can get confused for causation (Buhse et al., 2018). As such, instead of using a binary model of causality, a better way is to classify varying "strengths" of causal relations in sentences. In fact, a seven-point scheme[1] was proposed by Sumner et al. (2014) to categorize causal statements from health-related news and academic press releases. Subsequently, Yu et al. (2019) adapted this for scientific texts into a four-level system. In this work, we adopt the four-level causality labeled corpus and classification model by Yu et al. (2019)[2].

There is also an often observed issue that NLP systems that perform well on task datasets do not generalize to "real-life scenarios", thereby misleading and overstating the accuracies and usefulness of their models. Ensuring model generalizability to other domains can be challenging. For example, Ramesh et al. (2012) showed discourse triggers are

[1]The seven levels of causal strengths are (1) no statement, (2) explicit statement of no relation, (3) correlational, (4) ambiguous (i.e., a relationship is present, but the direction and level is ambiguous), (5) conditional causal, (6) can cause, and (7) unconditionally causal.

[2]We were unable to work on Sumner et al.'s dataset as it was not publicly available and had very limited samples per class label.

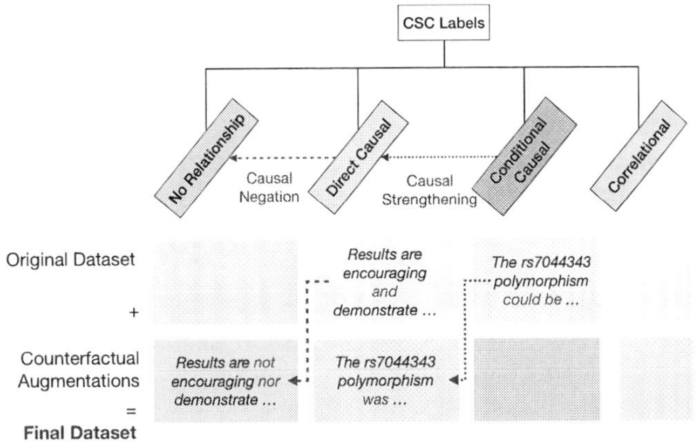

Figure 2: Strategies to generate counterfactual examples for CSC.

different between the biomedical and general domains. More focus has been placed on ensuring sufficient data representativeness and transferability of results onto OOD settings in recent years. In this work, we will also evaluate the generalizability of our models to classify causal sentences from other domains.

2.2 Counterfactuals in NLP

Counterfactual generation is a popular strategy for NLP researchers to test and improve model robustness via adversarial learning and attacks (Morris et al., 2020; Mahler et al., 2017) or for mitigating bias (Kaushik et al., 2020a; Maudslay et al., 2019).

Gardner et al. (2020) proposed using counterfactuals to fill local theoretical gaps in a model's decision boundary. They relied on expert judgments to generate similar but meaningfully different sentences and showed that SOTA models struggle on contrast sets compared to original test sets across multiple tasks. Recently, Wu et al. (2021) proposed a general-purpose counterfactual generator built on GPT-2 and also showed that the inclusion of realistic counterfactuals was useful across three different tasks. Their control codes included negation, delete, and restructure, amongst other options.[3] In our work, we generate counterfactuals purposefully for CSC, such as moving sentences across labels during Negation (*causal* $\rightarrow$ *no relationship*) and Strengthening (*conditional causal* $\rightarrow$ *causal*) strategies. We provide an automatic rule-based schema to negate and strengthen causal statements, focusing on precision over full coverage.[4]

Kaushik et al. (2020a) manually revised documents that would correspond to a counterfactual target label for sentiment analysis and natural language inference tasks. They showed that training with similar quantities of augmented data compared to the original improves generalization ability to OOD datasets. In this paper, we have also found that counterfactuals can help to improve model generalizability for CSC. Unlike their work, our linguistics-based augments do not rely on human intervention.

3 Methodology

3.1 Task Details

Our CSC task involved classifying a span of text with a causal label based on its intended meaning. We used the PubMed-based CSci corpus (Yu et al., 2019)[5] comprising of 3061 sentences, annotated with four levels of causal relation: *no relationship* (c_0), *causal* (c_1), *conditional causal* (c_2), and *correlational* (c_3).

3.2 Counterfactual Generation

In a low-resource setting, we propose creating counterfactuals that push causal sentences across labels to improve the robustness of models. Figure 2 demonstrates the two main strategies we employed to generate counterfactual examples for CSC: (1) Causal Negation ($c_1 \rightarrow c_0$) and (2) Causal

[3]Unfortunately, we did not investigate the negation and delete functions provided by Wu et al. (2021) but acknowledge this to be an important future work.

[4]Contemporaneously, we also contributed our rule-based algorithm to an open-source text augmentation effort at https://github.com/GEM-benchmark/NL-Augmenter under the transformation negate_strengthen.

[5]https://github.com/junwang4/causal-language-use-in-science

Strengthening ($c_2 \rightarrow c_1$). We discuss these strategies next.[6]

3.2.1 Causal Negation

In NEGATION, we negate the direction of causal statements from *causal* (c_1) to *no relationship* (c_0).

After obtaining POS tags and root words based on dependency trees[7], we performed negations around the root word. Our coding schema (Algorithm 1 in the Appendix) inserted negative words like *'no'*, *'not'*, *'nor'* or *'did not'* to negate the meaning of the sentence. 12 negation linguistic templates were used. Successfully negated sentences were termed as EDIT sentences. If no matching templates were found, the sentence was skipped. Of the 493 original (causal) sentences from the CSci corpus, 384 sentences had available negations.

To improve text flow, we used antonyms to replace negated edits where applicable. We did so by searching for antonyms of the original root word based on WordNet (Miller, 1995) and termed successful antonym edits as EDIT-ALT. To ensure a similar tense was used, we detected the original word's tense and applied the same tense onto the antonym word using the Pattern package (De Smedt and Daelemans, 2012). An example EDIT and EDIT-ALT sentence is shown in Table 1.

To decide between EDIT and EDIT-ALT versions, we calculated the Levenshtein edit distance of the original word versus the antonym. We selected EDIT-ALT only if the edit distance is less than or equal to 30% of the length of the longer word, rounded to the nearest integer. This allowed us to keep conversions like *'able'* $\rightarrow$ *'unable'* for more natural word flow, but discard bolder and more drastic changes like *'safe'* $\rightarrow$ *'dangerous'* and *'had'* $\rightarrow$ *'refused'* that suggested causality in the opposite direction (rather than *no relationship*) or were outright wrong. Finally, after dropping duplicates, we obtained 381 sentences that represented non-causality.

We were able to apply 11 out of the 12 linguistic templates to generate causal negation for the sentences in CSci. Most edits fell into the category where we negated the root verb or adjective of the sentence. Table A1 shows one randomly sampled example per available negation method when applied onto the CSci corpus. With respect to this table, Appendix A.1 briefly discusses the grammatical sanity of these sentences. We inspected these randomly sampled counterfactuals to verify that sentence flows were natural and desirable.

3.2.2 Causal Strengthening

For STRENGTHEN, we increased the strength of causal statements from *conditional causal* (c_2) to *causal* (c_1) by exploiting modal words. Similar to negation, we first obtained the POS tags and dependency trees for each sentence.

Algorithm 2 in the Appendix outlines the rule-based pseudo-code. To summarize, the 5 linguistic templates created converted modals based on the dictionary: *{'could', 'should', 'would'}* $\rightarrow$ *'would'* and *{'can', 'may', 'might', 'will'}* $\rightarrow$ *'will'*. If modals interacted with verbs with the lemma *'be'*, we replaced *'modal+be'* with *'was'* instead to convey certainty in the causal meaning. For special cases where the modal terms interacted with *'have'*, thereby forming conditional perfect tense, we converted the examples into simple past tense by replacing *'modal+have'* with *'had'*. When a modal was followed by an adverb (E.g. *"can possibly"*), the adverb was removed to avoid any deviation of the causal meaning from certainty.

Table A2 shows a randomly sampled example per causal strengthening method when applied onto the CSci corpus. Of the 213 available sentences, we successfully augmented 174 of them.

3.3 Dataset Processing

7 duplicated examples existed in the original CSci corpus and surfaced when we appended the edits with the original sentences. For such scenarios, we applied de-duplication based on priority rules discussed in Appendix A.2.

As our augmentations would increase the sample size for particular class labels, we randomly selected sentences to maintain the original class distribution. Our primary analysis focuses on randomly sampled datasets to eliminate the concern that any improved performance might result from increased data size or advantageous train set distribution.[8] As a side note, since the final dataset size is always slightly smaller than the original baseline

[6] Our edit schemes, model pipeline and augmented datasets are available at `https://github.com/tanfiona/CausalAugment`.

[7] We used NLTK (Wagner, 2010) to obtain POS tags in PennTreeBank format and spaCy (Honnibal et al., 2020) for dependency tree extraction.

[8] The aim of our paper is to demonstrate that any improvements in our scores are due to increased variations of examples per class label. These variations must be meaningful for any improvement in scores.

Conversion	Edit Type	Sentence
NEGATION	Original	TyG is effective to identify individuals at risk for NAFLD.
	REGULAR (EDIT)	TyG is not effective to identify individuals at risk for NAFLD.
	REGULAR (EDIT-ALT)	TyG is ineffective to identify individuals at risk for NAFLD.
	SHORTEN	TyG is ineffective
	MULTIPLES	is ineffective is ineffective is ineffective
STRENGTHEN	Original	Moreover, TT genotype may reduce the risk of CAD in diabetic patients.
	REGULAR (Edit)	Moreover, TT genotype will reduce the risk of CAD in diabetic patients.

Table 1: Examples of counterfactual causal sentence augments. *Notes.* Interventions are highlighted in green. Causal Strengthening can also have SHORTEN and MULTIPLES edits but is excluded due to space constrains.

due to the de-duplication step, the final distribution after random sampling slightly differs. The final sample counts across class labels per augmented dataset is reflected in Appendix Table A5.

3.4 Further Heuristics

Later in results Section 4.4.2, we observed that simple edits which highlight the main counterfactual phrase improved performance. Although these heuristics resulted in non-grammatical sentences, we believe that these edits explicitly emphasize augmented keywords for the model to learn the local syntactic changes better. Since we still trained the model with the original sentences (in fact, the majority), the model will not memorize on only non-grammatical examples.

An example sentence is detailed in Table 1 with the two heuristic options as follows:

- SHORTEN: We reduced the sentence length based on target/root word to cover a minimally interpretable phrase based on dependency parser. The final sentence might not be a consecutive slice from the original.

- MULTIPLES: We defined a phrase as one word before and after the target/root word (i.e. $PhraseLength = 3$). Phrases were then duplicated by a multiple of $OriginalSentenceLength/PhraseLength$ rounded to the nearest integer. This ensured that the final sentence was up to as long as the original length. Note that in the EDIT-ALT example of Table 1, *"is ineffective"* represents *"is not effective"*. Thus, although the actual phrase length was 2, the intended meaning is based off the latter phrase that had a length of 3. Hence, we maintained a fixed $PhraseLength$ for all sentences.

3.5 Out-of-domain Testing

In addition to training and validating on the CSci corpus, we also applied our trained models on two other datasets to demonstrate that exposing models to meaningful counterfactuals during training helps in OOD settings.

While the CSci corpus was constructed from scientific PubMed-based sentences, the SCITE (Li et al., 2021)[9] corpus comprised of general sentences extended from the SemEval 2010 Task 8 dataset (Hendrickx et al., 2010). On the other hand, AltLex (Hidey and McKeown, 2016)[10] contained sentences from English Wikipedia that included causal relations signaled by lexical markers. In AltLex, sentences can be duplicated if they have multiple relation markers and entities. Thus, we had to revise the corpus such that if a sentence had any causal relation, the sentence was labeled as *causal* and only one example was retained.

Additionally, because SCITE and AltLex have binary labels, we created two measures of accuracy. The first, 'Acc', considered only exact class labels (*no relationship* (c_0) and *causal* (c_1)) (i.e. predicting the other two labels is a misclassification). The second, 'Acc_{Group}', calculated accuracy after grouping [*no relationship, correlational*] into *no relationship* (c_0) and [*causal, conditional causal*] into *causal* (c_1) to align with the binary labels.

In total, we tested on 4439 sentences from SCITE and 37677 sentences from AltLex.

3.6 Modeling

In each setting, we trained and validated using $K = 5$ folds, with 5 epochs per fold. In both neural network set-ups, we used the standard cross-entropy loss for multi-class classification. For OOD testing, we took the majority prediction from

[9] https://github.com/Das-Boot/scite
[10] https://github.com/chridey/AltLex

the five trained models across the five folds. We implemented two models as follows:

3.6.1 BERT+MLP (MLP)

We replicated the best performing model on the CSci corpus (Yu et al., 2019) which was a BioBERT (Lee et al., 2020) plus multi-layer perceptron (MLP) pipeline. The default architecture used BioBERT embeddings fed through a single MLP layer serving as the classifier.

3.6.2 BERT+MLP+SVM (SVM)

Instead of applying LinearSVM based off unigrams and bigrams like the original authors (Yu et al., 2019), we believe a fairer comparison would be to use BERT embeddings as inputs into an SVM model. To allow for representation updates, for each sentence (s), the BioBERT encoder was first applied. Next, the BERT pooled output[11] (z) ran through two MLP layers (MLP_1 and MLP_2) to predict the class labels. After training, the second layer was discarded, and the hidden representation (r) was fed as fixed inputs into the SVM classifier. The equations below outlines this pipeline,

$$z = BERT(s), \quad z \in \mathbb{R}^{h_1} \tag{1}$$

$$r = MLP_1(z), \quad r \in \mathbb{R}^{h_2} \tag{2}$$

$$o = MLP_2(r), \quad o \in \mathbb{R}^{c} \tag{3}$$

$$p = SVM(r), \quad p \in \mathbb{R}^{1}, \tag{4}$$

where, p represents the final predicted label, and $h_1 = 768$, $h_2 = 24$, and $c = 4$.

4 Results & Discussion

4.1 Improvement over Baseline

Table 2 reports our performance on the CSci corpus. For the MLP baseline model, we were unable to exactly replicate the reported scores by Yu et al. (2019) of 90.1% accuracy and 88.1% macro F-score: We achieved slightly lower scores of 89.15% and 87.01% respectively. For SVM, our proposed implementation using updated BERT embeddings with a detached head was superior over Yu et al. (2019)'s unigram and bigrams method as we observed significant improvements of accuracy from 77.2% to 88.86% and macro F-score from 72.2% to 86.95%.

In our experiments, including a mixture of edits (NEGATION×SHORTEN with STRENGTHEN×REGULAR) during training returned the best performance across all metrics. Accuracy improved by 1.35% over our MLP baseline, achieving Acc_{Orig} of 90.60%.[12] Notice that we found improvements of accuracy and F-score beyond the original reported scores, even though our replicated scores were lower. The SVM model also demonstrated that including a mixture of edits during training improves performance, but in this setting, NEGATION×MULTIPLES with STRENGTHEN×REGULAR performed the best on average across metrics.

A possible explanation for our findings is that we successfully exposed our models to more sentence types of the real world. Furthermore, we intentionally created augments around label boundaries (i.e. the minor edits changes the sentences' labels). Therefore, the model learns better for the CSC task. Interestingly, for NEGATION, the heuristic edits improved performance against baseline more so than the REGULAR edits itself. Section 4.4.2 will expand on this finding.

4.2 Robustness on Edits

Table 3 highlights how current SOTA models are not robust to minimally altered sentences that changes in causal direction and strength.

To conduct the experiment, we randomly split the available negated edits (n=381) by half, keeping 191 negated sentences for training and the remaining 190 for testing. The 190 original sentences that correspond to the negated test set were removed from the original CSci corpus to avoid exposing models to highly similar sentences during training.[13] Models trained with this base train set dangerously predicted 157 out of 190 test sentences in the opposite direction as *causal* instead of *no relationship*. A shockingly dismal test accuracy of 12.63% was attained at best, and prediction counts are available in Appendix Table A6.

Our finding surfaces the problem that the models were likely memorizing key causal terms instead of understanding sentence structure and flow.

[11] Pooled output takes the hidden state from the first token.

[12] The full original set achieved 90.33% accuracy if we were to include the subset that is dropped out due to random sampling. To arrive at this value, we predicted the labels for this dropped-out subset like an OOD dataset, i.e. taken across 5-folds after training completes.

[13] In experiments not shown, the models trained on the full original CSci corpus almost certainly wrongly predicts the 190 negated sentences as *causal* To prove our point that models are memorizing causal terms, we removed the overlapping sentences to eliminate the possibility of the models memorizing similar sentences in train and test set instead.

Conversion	Edit Type	MLP				SVM			
		F1	Acc	$F1_{Orig}$	Acc_{Orig}	F1	Acc	$F1_{Orig}$	Acc_{Orig}
Yu et al. (2019)		88.10	90.10	88.10	90.10	72.20	77.20	72.20	77.20
Ours (Base)		87.01	89.15	87.01	89.15	86.95	88.86	86.95	88.86
NEGATION	REGULAR	-1.55	-1.92	-0.19	-0.95	-2.33	-1.99	-1.18	-1.28
NEGATION	SHORTEN	+1.06	+0.89	+0.57	-0.04	+0.95	+1.19	+0.38	+0.18
NEGATION	MULTIPLES	+1.46	+1.45	+0.93	+0.49	+1.14	+1.28	+0.60	+0.32
STRENGTHEN	REGULAR	+1.75	+1.14	+0.80	+0.84	+0.73	+0.49	-0.28	+0.20
STRENGTHEN	SHORTEN	+1.08	+0.91	+0.16	+0.62	+0.86	+1.08	-0.24	**+0.71**
STRENGTHEN	MULTIPLES	+0.98	+0.98	-0.05	+0.57	+0.62	+0.82	-0.50	+0.38
NEGATION×SHORT, STRENGTHEN×REGU		**+2.80**	**+2.33**	**+1.73**	**+1.35**	+1.45	+1.38	+0.14	+0.19
NEGATION×MULTI, STRENGTHEN×REGU		+1.81	+1.35	+0.09	-0.10	**+1.95**	**+1.81**	**+0.62**	+0.61

Table 2: Performance on CSci corpus. *Notes.* BioBERT models trained on variations of CSci corpus (Original plus edits), with edits matching existing labels and randomly sampled to match base class distribution. Results are for validation set when trained and predicted over 5-folds. Macro F-score (F1) and accuracy (Acc) are in %. Columns with lowerscript "Orig" are calculated for original sentences only (i.e. Edits are ignored). Rows below "Ours (Base)" report relative changes to it. Best performance per column is **bolded**. Precision and Recall scores are available in Appendix Tables A7 and A8.

Conversion	n	MLP	SVM
Original	190	12.63	10.53
NEGATION	190	**+61.05**	**+62.63**
Original	87	77.01	73.56
STRENGTHEN	87	**+11.49**	**+13.79**

Table 3: Accuracy (in %) of BioBERT models trained on a subset of CSci corpus and predicted on a fully augmented difference set. *Notes.* The best performance per section per column is **bolded**.

Therefore, they were unable to discern the negation involved. Inclusion of counterfactual examples helped to fill this representation gap. We created augmented sets by combining the base train set with the 191 negated train sentences for retraining. Once we exposed the models to these negated examples during training, the same models could predict the right label with up to 73.68% accuracy.

We also tested the models' efficacy on strengthened sentences converted from *conditional causal* to *causal*. Once counterfactual examples were included in the train set, improvements on test accuracy was obtained to a significant, but smaller, extent of +13.79% improvement at best.

4.3 Improving Generalization

In Table 4, we show that inclusion of edits during training also helps to improve generalization in cross-domain applications. Although our train dataset was an academic and scientific-based text represented by a BioBERT language model, we show that when we applied the same model to the general-based SCITE and Wikipedia-based AltLex corpora, inclusion of edits improved classification performance. For SCITE, we found improvements in generalization for the SVM model but not the MLP model. This could be due to our limited edit schemes that might not complement SCITE's sentence types. Nevertheless, for AltLex, consistent improvements for almost all edit combinations were obtained across both models. Overall, the mixture of edits with both conversion types once again reported the best average performance, demonstrating how such augments can indeed aid help models generalize.

4.4 Ablations

4.4.1 NEGATION vs. STRENGTHEN

While analyzing both result Tables 2 and 4, one might wonder why the REGULAR edit schemes helped improve performance for STRENGTHEN, but not for NEGATION conversions. One possible explanation for this phenomenon is as such – Since any sentence that did not represent any form of correlational or causal meaning falls under c_0, sentences that could fall under *no relationship* are lexically diverse. In other words, it is challenging to create edits that exhaustively reflect all c_0 sentence types. By and large, our negation schemes only covered one category of *no relationship* sentences, namely, sentences that imply *not causal*. On the other hand, *conditional causal* sentences were relatively well-defined in the original corpus. Therefore, STRENGTHEN did successfully represent most of the sentence types under c_2. Inclusion

Conversion	Edit Type	SCITE				AltLex			
		MLP		SVM		MLP		SVM	
		Acc	Acc_{Group}	Acc	Acc_{Group}	Acc	Acc_{Group}	Acc	Acc_{Group}
Ours (Base)		**86.28**	**85.83**	85.04	84.50	85.57	84.64	85.91	84.68
NEGATION	REGULAR	-1.46	-1.67	-0.36	-0.41	-0.22	-0.44	+0.18	+0.41
NEGATION	SHORTEN	-0.20	-0.27	+0.02	+0.02	+0.61	+0.54	+0.74	+1.05
NEGATION	MULTIPLES	-0.18	-0.16	-0.38	-0.38	+0.89	+0.95	**+1.19**	**+1.58**
STRENGTHEN	REGULAR	-0.27	-0.14	**+1.01**	**+1.10**	+0.51	+0.69	+0.54	+0.84
STRENGTHEN	SHORTEN	-3.40	-3.36	-0.11	-0.05	+0.30	+0.37	+0.99	+1.38
STRENGTHEN	MULTIPLES	-1.31	-1.28	-0.90	-0.90	+0.88	**+0.99**	+0.07	+0.29
NEGATION×SHORT, STRENGTHEN×REGU		-0.02	-0.05	+0.79	+0.63	**+0.94**	+0.84	+0.31	+0.41
NEGATION×MULTI, STRENGTHEN×REGU		-0.18	-0.16	+0.56	+0.56	+0.74	+0.88	+1.11	+1.33

Table 4: Performance on OOD datasets. *Notes.* BioBERT models trained on variations of CSci corpus (Original plus edits), with edits matching existing labels and randomly sampled to match base class distribution. For SCITE and AltLex, predictions are from takes mode class over 5-folds. Accuracies (Acc) are reported in %. Columns 'Acc' considers exact class labels, while 'Acc_{Group}' calculates accuracy after converting the four class labels into binary labels. Rows below "Ours (Base)" report relative changes to it. The best performance per column is **bolded**.

of these edits during training thus proved useful in highlighting the syntax that makes a sentence *causal* or *conditional causal* to the models.

4.4.2 Need for Heuristic Edits

Earlier in Table 2, we noted that models exposed to NEGATION×REGULAR edits were unable to effectively learn the label boundaries: Acc_{Orig} fell by 0.95% for the MLP model and 1.28% for the SVM compared to our baselines. However, when we performed simple heuristics like MULTIPLES, accuracy improved by +0.49% and +0.32% respectively. As for SHORTEN, accuracy rose by +0.18% for the SVM model, while the MLP model had a negligible reduction of -0.04%.

We study the net change in classification counts per model per label in Table 5 to explore this phenomenon. Given class labels i and j predicted by a model and our baseline respectively, we report the model's $NetChange_i = Right_i - Wrong_i = \sum_{j \neq i} n_{(i=true)j} - \sum_{i \neq j} n_{i(j=true)}$, where $i, j = c_0, c_1, c_2, c_3$ and n refers to the number of observations. $Right_i$ ($Wrong_i$) is the number of observations where a model predicts correctly (wrongly) for class label i but baseline predicts wrongly (correctly). When either MLP or SVM model is trained with the augmented NEGATION×REGULAR dataset, the model became confused and predicted poorly for *causal* (c_1) and *no relationship* (c_0) classes. Once the edits were presented in the heuristic forms, this situation improved.

We offer two plausible explanations for our findings: (1) It could be the case that highlighting the model to the short spans of (non-)causality aids its identification of the exact borders it needs to be sensitive to. (2) In the REGULAR form, non-causal sentences are linguistically very similar to causal ones. As mentioned in Section 4.4.1, these non-causal sentences only represent one out of many possible sentence types from c_0. Therefore, feeding some non-grammatical examples of c_0 might help make it more explicit to the model that c_0 can take a wide variety of sentences types. More work is needed to confirm either hypotheses.

Interestingly, we observed improvements in classification for labels we did not edit (c_3) in the majority of settings. This highlights the possibility that exposing models to minimally perturbed sentences around label boundaries might also improve comprehension beyond the introduced edits.

4.4.3 Capturing Causal Strengths

One benefit of capitalizing on CSci's four-label format is that our methodology is now able to identify causal strengths in SCITE and AltLex corpora beyond the original binary labels. For SCITE, the baseline MLP model originally labeled five sentences as *conditional causal.* When training the model with STRENGTHEN×REGULAR edits, four remained as *conditional causal* (c_2) while one of the sentence[14] correctly switched label to *causal* (c_1). For the baseline SVM model, seven sentences were tagged as c_2, of which four remained, and the same one as MLP's converted to c_1. One[15] cor-

[14]"In the present recession, which has been triggered by a collapse in land prices, land-value taxation would reverse the collapse - not by re-inflating a temporary speculative bubble, but by inducing investment in infrastructure that permanently enhances the utility of the land."

[15]"The glass tealight holder appears to float inside the metal spiral as it spins in the gentle breeze."

Conversion	Edit Type	MLP					SVM				
		c_0	c_1	c_2	c_3	**Total**	c_0	c_1	c_2	c_3	**Total**
NEGATION	REGULAR	-13	-18	+10	0	-21	-9	-21	+1	-2	-31
NEGATION	SHORTEN	-15	+9	+9	+2	+5	-4	+7	+1	+6	+10
NEGATION	MULTIPLES	-5	+9	+5	+9	+18	-1	+8	+3	+3	+13
STRENGTHEN	REGULAR	-7	+12	+10	+9	+24	+1	+1	+5	-4	+3
STRENGTHEN	SHORTEN	-7	+11	+6	+6	+16	0	+8	+3	+5	+16
STRENGTHEN	MULTIPLES	-14	+13	+7	+10	+16	-12	+11	+6	+3	+8
NEGATION×SHORT, STRENGTHEN×REGU		+2	+20	+10	+9	+41	-2	+12	+1	-4	+7
NEGATION×MULTI, STRENGTHEN×REGU		-16	+6	+5	+7	+2	+2	+9	+2	+5	+18

Table 5: Net change in correct classification counts on CSci corpus compared to "Ours (Base)" for original examples. Note that NEGATION is the conversion of $c_1 \rightarrow c_0$ and STRENGTHEN is the conversion of $c_2 \rightarrow c_1$;

rectly switched to *no relationship* (c_0) as labeled, while the last sentence[16] converted to *correlational* (c_3), which is surprising because we did not edit any sentences to or from class c_3. Unfortunately, the authors of SCITE tagged this sentence as causal, which means this is considered to be mislabeled. However, the sentence contains signals like *'corresponds to'*, which we believe should be correlational, not causal. Our short qualitative analysis again supports the earlier quantitative study that exposing models to meaningfully augmented sentences across labels could improve classification even for the other uninvolved labels.

4.4.4 Other Experiments

We also explored other popular methodologies but did not obtain consistent and significant improvements from baseline. These include, *(i)* creating more edit types (using masking, synonyms and paraphrasers), *(ii)* extending to a five-way classification problem (by labelling negated edits as a new class label representing *not causal*, separate from *no relationship* (c_0)), and *(iii)* experimenting with some contrastive learning loss functions. Appendix Section A.3 details these experiments further for interested readers.

5 Conclusion & Future Work

We explored the task of CSC in a low-resource setting. Following recent literature, we generated counterfactual sentences via rule-based edits that change sentences' causal direction and strength. We showed that SOTA CSC models worryingly misclassifies on such augmented sentences. This concern can be mitigated by including of our edits during training. We demonstrated that our proposal improves classification performance both on original and edit sentences, and within and outside of the corpus' domain. However, for NEGATION, we found that the regular format was insufficient to teach effective decision boundaries given limited data size and augmentation templates. Therefore, proposed heuristic edits and found performance improvements for both training and OOD contexts.

For future work, Yu et al. (2020)'s recent corpus using scientific press statements annotated with the same four class labels of causality is a promising dataset to replicate our findings upon. Additionally, we utilized rule-based augment schemes which have a finite number of working templates. Thus, our augmentations might not be lexically diverse. Therefore, our subsequent steps would be to explore SOTA NLP augmentation and generation tools, like from Wu et al. (2021) and Ross et al. (2021). Furthermore, it might be worthwhile to find alternative models that can learn directly from the augmented datasets without the need for heuristics.

Lastly, our work did not go beyond the "correctness" of the claims. However, in reality, one has to distinguish between causal effects as factual events of real-world or at the level of "meta-causality" (Andersson et al., 2020). Hence, grounding the claims to world knowledge will be an important research avenue to pursue.

Acknowledgements

This research is supported by Singapore Ministry of Education Academic Research Fund Tier 1 under MOE's official grant number T1 251RES2029.

[16]"The increase of the signal might correspond to formation of the high-density excitons, while the reduction of the signal originates from the relaxation."

References

Marta Andersson, Murathan Kurfalı, and Robert Östling. 2020. A sentiment-annotated dataset of English causal connectives. In *Proceedings of the 14th Linguistic Annotation Workshop*, pages 24–33, Barcelona, Spain. Association for Computational Linguistics.

Nabiha Asghar. 2016. Automatic extraction of causal relations from natural language texts: A comprehensive survey. *CoRR*, abs/1605.07895.

Susanne Buhse, Anne Christin Rahn, Merle Bock, and Ingrid Mühlhauser. 2018. Causal interpretation of correlational studies–analysis of medical news on the website of the official journal for german physicians. *PLoS One*, 13(5):e0196833.

Tommaso Caselli and Piek Vossen. 2017a. The event StoryLine corpus: A new benchmark for causal and temporal relation extraction. In *Proceedings of the Events and Stories in the News Workshop*, pages 77–86, Vancouver, Canada. Association for Computational Linguistics.

Tommaso Caselli and Piek Vossen. 2017b. The event storyline corpus: A new benchmark for causal and temporal relation extraction. In *Proceedings of the Events and Stories in the News Workshop@ACL 2017, Vancouver, Canada, August 4, 2017*, pages 77–86. Association for Computational Linguistics.

Ting Chen, Simon Kornblith, Mohammad Norouzi, and Geoffrey E. Hinton. 2020. A simple framework for contrastive learning of visual representations. In *Proceedings of the 37th International Conference on Machine Learning, ICML 2020, 13-18 July 2020, Virtual Event*, volume 119 of *Proceedings of Machine Learning Research*, pages 1597–1607. PMLR.

Dhairya Dalal, Mihael Arcan, and Paul Buitelaar. 2021. Enhancing multiple-choice question answering with causal knowledge. In *Proceedings of Deep Learning Inside Out (DeeLIO): The 2nd Workshop on Knowledge Extraction and Integration for Deep Learning Architectures*, pages 70–80, Online. Association for Computational Linguistics.

Tom De Smedt and Walter Daelemans. 2012. Pattern for python. *J. Mach. Learn. Res.*, 13(1):2063–2067.

Jacob Devlin, Ming-Wei Chang, Kenton Lee, and Kristina Toutanova. 2019. BERT: pre-training of deep bidirectional transformers for language understanding. In *Proceedings of the 2019 Conference of the North American Chapter of the Association for Computational Linguistics: Human Language Technologies, NAACL-HLT 2019, Minneapolis, MN, USA, June 2-7, 2019, Volume 1 (Long and Short Papers)*, pages 4171–4186. Association for Computational Linguistics.

Kata Gábor, Davide Buscaldi, Anne-Kathrin Schumann, Behrang QasemiZadeh, Haïfa Zargayouna, and Thierry Charnois. 2018. Semeval-2018 task 7: Semantic relation extraction and classification in scientific papers. In *Proceedings of The 12th International Workshop on Semantic Evaluation, SemEval@NAACL-HLT 2018, New Orleans, Louisiana, USA, June 5-6, 2018*, pages 679–688. Association for Computational Linguistics.

Matt Gardner, Yoav Artzi, Victoria Basmova, Jonathan Berant, Ben Bogin, Sihao Chen, Pradeep Dasigi, Dheeru Dua, Yanai Elazar, Ananth Gottumukkala, Nitish Gupta, Hannaneh Hajishirzi, Gabriel Ilharco, Daniel Khashabi, Kevin Lin, Jiangming Liu, Nelson F. Liu, Phoebe Mulcaire, Qiang Ning, Sameer Singh, Noah A. Smith, Sanjay Subramanian, Reut Tsarfaty, Eric Wallace, Ally Zhang, and Ben Zhou. 2020. Evaluating models' local decision boundaries via contrast sets. In *Proceedings of the 2020 Conference on Empirical Methods in Natural Language Processing: Findings, EMNLP 2020, Online Event, 16-20 November 2020*, pages 1307–1323. Association for Computational Linguistics.

Roxana Girju and Dan I. Moldovan. 2002. Text mining for causal relations. In *Proceedings of the Fifteenth International Florida Artificial Intelligence Research Society Conference, May 14-16, 2002, Pensacola Beach, Florida, USA*, pages 360–364. AAAI Press.

Stefan Heindorf, Yan Scholten, Henning Wachsmuth, Axel-Cyrille Ngonga Ngomo, and Martin Potthast. 2020. Causenet: Towards a causality graph extracted from the web. In *CIKM '20: The 29th ACM International Conference on Information and Knowledge Management, Virtual Event, Ireland, October 19-23, 2020*, pages 3023–3030. ACM.

Iris Hendrickx, Su Nam Kim, Zornitsa Kozareva, Preslav Nakov, Diarmuid Ó Séaghdha, Sebastian Padó, Marco Pennacchiotti, Lorenza Romano, and Stan Szpakowicz. 2010. SemEval-2010 task 8: Multi-way classification of semantic relations between pairs of nominals. In *Proceedings of the 5th International Workshop on Semantic Evaluation*, pages 33–38, Uppsala, Sweden. Association for Computational Linguistics.

Christopher Hidey and Kathy McKeown. 2016. Identifying causal relations using parallel wikipedia articles. In *Proceedings of the 54th Annual Meeting of the Association for Computational Linguistics, ACL 2016, August 7-12, 2016, Berlin, Germany, Volume 1: Long Papers*. The Association for Computer Linguistics.

Matthew Honnibal, Ines Montani, Sofie Van Landeghem, and Adriane Boyd. 2020. spaCy: Industrial-strength Natural Language Processing in Python.

David Jurgens, Saif Mohammad, Peter D. Turney, and Keith J. Holyoak. 2012. Semeval-2012 task 2: Measuring degrees of relational similarity. In *Proceedings of the 6th International Workshop on Semantic Evaluation, SemEval@NAACL-HLT 2012, Mon-*

tréal, Canada, June 7-8, 2012, pages 356–364. The Association for Computer Linguistics.

Divyansh Kaushik, Eduard H. Hovy, and Zachary Chase Lipton. 2020a. Learning the difference that makes A difference with counterfactually-augmented data. In *8th International Conference on Learning Representations, ICLR 2020, Addis Ababa, Ethiopia, April 26-30, 2020*. OpenReview.net.

Divyansh Kaushik, Amrith Setlur, Eduard H. Hovy, and Zachary C. Lipton. 2020b. Explaining the efficacy of counterfactually-augmented data. *CoRR*, abs/2010.02114.

Prannay Khosla, Piotr Teterwak, Chen Wang, Aaron Sarna, Yonglong Tian, Phillip Isola, Aaron Maschinot, Ce Liu, and Dilip Krishnan. 2020. Supervised contrastive learning. *arXiv preprint arXiv:2004.11362*.

Jinhyuk Lee, Wonjin Yoon, Sungdong Kim, Donghyeon Kim, Sunkyu Kim, Chan Ho So, and Jaewoo Kang. 2020. Biobert: a pre-trained biomedical language representation model for biomedical text mining. *Bioinform.*, 36(4):1234–1240.

Zhaoning Li, Qi Li, Xiaotian Zou, and Jiangtao Ren. 2021. Causality extraction based on self-attentive bilstm-crf with transferred embeddings. *Neurocomputing*, 423:207–219.

Taylor Mahler, Willy Cheung, Micha Elsner, David King, Marie-Catherine de Marneffe, Cory Shain, Symon Stevens-Guille, and Michael White. 2017. Breaking NLP: Using morphosyntax, semantics, pragmatics and world knowledge to fool sentiment analysis systems. In *Proceedings of the First Workshop on Building Linguistically Generalizable NLP Systems*, pages 33–39, Copenhagen, Denmark. Association for Computational Linguistics.

Dominique Mariko, Hanna Abi-Akl, Estelle Labidurie, Stephane Durfort, Hugues De Mazancourt, and Mahmoud El-Haj. 2020. The financial document causality detection shared task (FinCausal 2020). In *Proceedings of the 1st Joint Workshop on Financial Narrative Processing and MultiLing Financial Summarisation*, pages 23–32, Barcelona, Spain (Online). COLING.

Rowan Hall Maudslay, Hila Gonen, Ryan Cotterell, and Simone Teufel. 2019. It's all in the name: Mitigating gender bias with name-based counterfactual data substitution. In *Proceedings of the 2019 Conference on Empirical Methods in Natural Language Processing and the 9th International Joint Conference on Natural Language Processing, EMNLP-IJCNLP 2019, Hong Kong, China, November 3-7, 2019*, pages 5266–5274. Association for Computational Linguistics.

George A. Miller. 1995. Wordnet: A lexical database for english. *Commun. ACM*, 38(11):39–41.

Paramita Mirza, Rachele Sprugnoli, Sara Tonelli, and Manuela Speranza. 2014. Annotating causality in the TempEval-3 corpus. In *Proceedings of the EACL 2014 Workshop on Computational Approaches to Causality in Language (CAtoCL)*, pages 10–19, Gothenburg, Sweden. Association for Computational Linguistics.

Paramita Mirza and Sara Tonelli. 2016a. CATENA: CAusal and TEmporal relation extraction from NAtural language texts. In *Proceedings of COLING 2016, the 26th International Conference on Computational Linguistics: Technical Papers*, pages 64–75, Osaka, Japan. The COLING 2016 Organizing Committee.

Paramita Mirza and Sara Tonelli. 2016b. CATENA: causal and temporal relation extraction from natural language texts. In *COLING 2016, 26th International Conference on Computational Linguistics, Proceedings of the Conference: Technical Papers, December 11-16, 2016, Osaka, Japan*, pages 64–75. ACL.

John X. Morris, Eli Lifland, Jin Yong Yoo, Jake Grigsby, Di Jin, and Yanjun Qi. 2020. Textattack: A framework for adversarial attacks, data augmentation, and adversarial training in NLP. In *Proceedings of the 2020 Conference on Empirical Methods in Natural Language Processing: System Demonstrations, EMNLP 2020 - Demos, Online, November 16-20, 2020*, pages 119–126. Association for Computational Linguistics.

Adam Paszke, Sam Gross, Francisco Massa, Adam Lerer, James Bradbury, Gregory Chanan, Trevor Killeen, Zeming Lin, Natalia Gimelshein, Luca Antiga, Alban Desmaison, Andreas Köpf, Edward Yang, Zachary DeVito, Martin Raison, Alykhan Tejani, Sasank Chilamkurthy, Benoit Steiner, Lu Fang, Junjie Bai, and Soumith Chintala. 2019. Pytorch: An imperative style, high-performance deep learning library. In *Advances in Neural Information Processing Systems 32: Annual Conference on Neural Information Processing Systems 2019, NeurIPS 2019, December 8-14, 2019, Vancouver, BC, Canada*, pages 8024–8035.

Balaji Polepalli Ramesh, Rashmi Prasad, Tim Miller, Brian Harrington, and Hong Yu. 2012. Automatic discourse connective detection in biomedical text. *J. Am. Medical Informatics Assoc.*, 19(5):800–808.

Alexis Ross, Tongshuang Wu, Hao Peng, Matthew E. Peters, and Matt Gardner. 2021. Tailor: Generating and perturbing text with semantic controls. *CoRR*, abs/2107.07150.

Petroc Sumner, Solveiga Vivian-Griffiths, Jacky Boivin, Andy Williams, Christos A Venetis, Aimée Davies, Jack Ogden, Leanne Whelan, Bethan Hughes, Bethan Dalton, Fred Boy, and Christopher D Chambers. 2014. The association between exaggeration in health related science news and academic press releases: retrospective observational study. *BMJ*, 349.

Wiebke Wagner. 2010. Steven bird, ewan klein and edward loper: Natural language processing with python, analyzing text with the natural language toolkit - o'reilly media, beijing, 2009, ISBN 978-0-596-51649-9. *Lang. Resour. Evaluation*, 44(4):421–424.

Tongshuang Wu, Marco Tulio Ribeiro, Jeffrey Heer, and Daniel Weld. 2021. Polyjuice: Generating counterfactuals for explaining, evaluating, and improving models. In *Proceedings of the 59th Annual Meeting of the Association for Computational Linguistics and the 11th International Joint Conference on Natural Language Processing (Volume 1: Long Papers)*, pages 6707–6723, Online. Association for Computational Linguistics.

Jinghang Xu, Wanli Zuo, Shining Liang, and Xianglin Zuo. 2020. A review of dataset and labeling methods for causality extraction. In *Proceedings of the 28th International Conference on Computational Linguistics, COLING 2020, Barcelona, Spain (Online), December 8-13, 2020*, pages 1519–1531. International Committee on Computational Linguistics.

Jie Yang, Soyeon Caren Han, and Josiah Poon. 2021. A survey on extraction of causal relations from natural language text. *CoRR*, abs/2101.06426.

Bei Yu, Yingya Li, and Jun Wang. 2019. Detecting causal language use in science findings. In *Proceedings of the 2019 Conference on Empirical Methods in Natural Language Processing and the 9th International Joint Conference on Natural Language Processing, EMNLP-IJCNLP 2019, Hong Kong, China, November 3-7, 2019*, pages 4663–4673. Association for Computational Linguistics.

Bei Yu, Jun Wang, Lu Guo, and Yingya Li. 2020. Measuring correlation-to-causation exaggeration in press releases. In *Proceedings of the 28th International Conference on Computational Linguistics, COLING 2020, Barcelona, Spain (Online), December 8-13, 2020*, pages 4860–4872. International Committee on Computational Linguistics.

A Appendix

A.1 Negation Examples

Appendix Table A1 shows one randomly sampled example per available negation method when applied onto the CSci corpus. As shown, most examples fell into 'VB_3.1', 'VB_5.1', 'JJ_1.3' and 'VB_1.2' types, for which the templates in Algorithm 1 worked well for[17]. For rarer method types, like 'VB_2.1', the templates seemed to work poorly. Further investigation shows that the error arose from the POS tagging step: *"Both"* was tagged as a VB but should have been a DT or CC, for which, we have no template for at the moment, so the example would have been correctly skipped. As for 'VB_4.1', the negated example was unnatural but not grammatically wrong.

A.2 De-duplication

After appending original sentences with edits, we conducted de-duplication. Appendix Table A3 shows problematic duplicates that had differing labels. The original CSci corpus contained 7 duplicate sentences instances which were removed. 6 of them were exact duplicates (same label, same sentence), while the last one (sentence S/N 1) was duplicated with different labels (c_0 and c_2). We manually changed this to retain only the c_0-labeled example. The total data size thus reduced from 3061 to 3054. This explains the differences in data size and distribution when comparing the original versus augmented sets shown in Table A5. We also take this chance to highlight concerns that some sentences in CSci were labeled contrary to how we understood them.

Subsequent duplicates were handled via rule-based removal. The motivation was to ensure identical sentences do not have different labels which adds noise to our training. Our assumption was that if an edit was performed but remained identical to the original, the original must have been mislabeled. We note that our rule-based de-duplication cannot accommodate multi-label cases, as there was one sentence (S/N 4) that correctly reflected both c_0 and c_1 labels in different parts of the sentence, but due to de-duplication, we only kept the c_0 label.

[17]We highlight the main POS tags used and mentioned: VB (verbs, e.g. *'eating'*), JJ (adjective, e.g. *'big'*), IN (preposition or subordinating conjunction, e.g. *'by'*), DT (determiner, e.g. *'he'*), CC (coordinating conjunction, e.g. *'and'*), MD (modal, e.g. *'should'*).

A.3 Other Experiments

Other experiments that were conducted but did not produce significant improvements are mentioned here.

Other Edit Types Three were explored:

- MASK: Based on POS, all nouns were replaced by the token *"[MASK]"*.
- SYNONYMS: Using WordNet synonyms, we skipped common words[18] and randomly substituted up to 5 words. Synonyms matched the tense and plurality of original words using Pattern package, which we note, had imperfections.
- T5PARA: We ran the sentence through a pretrained T5-paraphraser model[19] to generate paraphrased sentences.

Appendix Table A4 shows an example sentence with the above edits for the same causal sentence of Table 1. With the SVM model, only STRENGTHEN×SYNONYMS appended with original increased accuracy on CSci by 1.01% while STRENGTHEN×T5PARA increased accuracy by 0.39%. However, these findings could not be replicated across to the MLP model nor for NEGATION.

Extending to a Five-way Classification In our main set up, we focused on edits that matched the original labels and were randomly sampled such that the unified train set matches base class distribution for fairer comparison to baseline. Successful NEGATION examples were labeled *no relationship* (c_0). However, to the extent that we believe negated causal statements deserve a class of their own, we also explore the event when negations were labeled with a new level *not causal* (c_4) instead. Based on the set up for Table 3, we obtained even higher improvements in accuracy of +70.53% and +74.74% for the MLP and SVM model respectively. This could be due to the clearer distinction of a *not causal* sentence structure compared to if we were to combine them with other *no relationship* statements. When we extended the MLP and SVM model to work with such a five-way classification set up, we did observe improvements in Acc_{Orig}

[18]We do not try to find synonyms for common words with these POS types: 'DT','IN', 'EX', 'CC', 'MD', 'WP', 'WD', 'WR', 'UH', 'RP', 'SY', 'PO'

[19]`https://huggingface.co/ramsrigouthamg/t5_paraphraser`

for SHORTEN, MULTIPLES and SYNONYMS edit types. However, because we cannot truly balance the dataset (random sampling does not apply here because we have a whole new class), we cannot be certain if the improvements were due to the larger dataset or the model picking up on the boundaries. Furthermore, the improvements did not generalize on our OOD set ups.

Other Training Setups In addition to standard cross-entropy based supervised learning, we also explored contrastive learning schemes. In particular, we trained with Supervised Contrastive Loss (SupCon) (Khosla et al., 2020; Chen et al., 2020) and Triplet Margin Loss (Paszke et al., 2019). In the contrastive setup, we introduced counterfactuals as the negative examples for each anchor sentence. For positive samples, we used SHORTEN, SYNONYMS and T5PARA augmentation strategies derived from the original anchor sentence. However, our results did not provide performance improvements in either CSci or OOD datasets, highlighting the challenge in building a generalized scheme of counterfactual generations. Exploring avenues in contrastive learning remains a critical future work.

A.4 Reproducibility Checklist

We include additional details about our main experiment not highlighted in other parts of the paper.

- **Computing Infrastructure:** Tesla V100 SXM2 32 GB
- **MLP Hyperparameters:** "attention_probs_dropout_prob": 0.1, "hidden_act": "gelu", "hidden_dropout_prob": 0.1, "hidden_size": 768, "initializer_range": 0.02, "intermediate_size": 3072, "layer_norm_eps": 1e-12, "max_position_embeddings": 512, "num_attention_heads": 12, "num_hidden_layers": 12, "type_vocab_size": 2, "vocab_size": 28996
- **SVM Hyperparameters:** kernel: "linear", "C": 1e-2
- **Average Runtime:** For 5 epochs and 5 folds, our baseline MLP model took approximately 22 minutes 51 seconds to train and validate for the CSci dataset.

A.5 Additional Figures & Tables

Algorithm 1: NegationRules – Causal negation scheme

```
Input: edit_id, text_ids, text, pos, sentid2tid, max_try=2, curr_try=0
Output: text, method, edit_id
curr_try ← curr_try + 1
curr_pos, curr_word ← pos[edit_id], text[edit_id]
prev_pos, prev_word ← pos[edit_id − 1], text[edit_id − 1] if valid else None
next_pos, next_word ← pos[edit_id + 1], text[edit_id + 1] if valid else None
while curr_try <= max_try do
    if curr_pos = VB then
        if curr_word = AuxilliaryType then
            if edit_id = max(text_ids) then
                Insert *not* in front of curr_word                    // Method "VB_1.1'
            else if next_word = DeterminerType then
                Replace next_word with *no*                           // Method 'VB_1.2'
                edit_id ← edit_id + 1
            else if next_word = NounType then
                Insert *not* behind of curr_word                      // Method 'VB_1.3'
            else if next_pos = VB then
                Insert *no* behind of curr_word                       // Method 'VB_1.4'
        else if edit_id = min(text_ids) then
            Replace curr_word with *Not* + lowercased curr_word       // Method 'VB_2.1'
        else if prev_word = NounType then
            Replace curr_word with *did not* + lemma(curr_word)       // Method 'VB_3.1'
        else if edit_id = max(text_ids) then
            Insert *not* in front of curr_word                        // Method 'VB_4.1'
        else if prev_word = AuxilliaryType next_pos = IN|TO then
            Insert *not* in front of curr_word                        // Method 'VB_5.1'
    else if curr_pos = NN then
        Get head_id of head word of curr_word based on dependency tree
        text, method, edit_id ← NegationRules(head_id, text_ids, text, pos, sentid2tid,
          curr_try)
    else if curr_pos = JJ then
        if edit_id = max(text_ids) then
            Insert *not* in front of curr_word                        // Method 'JJ_1.1'
        else if next_word = PositiveConjuctionType then
            Insert *not* in front of curr_word                        // Method 'JJ_1.2'
        Replace next_word with *nor* else
            Insert *not* in front of curr_word                        // Method 'JJ_1.3'
    else if curr_pos = IN then
        Insert *not* in front of curr_word                            // Method 'IN_1.1'
Define method as method name if applicable edit occurs
return text, method, edit_id
```

Method	REGULAR (EDIT)	REGULAR (EDIT-ALT)	n
VB_1.2	Eyes with better vision at baseline had no more favorable prognosis, whereas eyes with initial macular detachment, intraoperative iatrogenic break, or heavy SO showed more unfavorable outcomes.	Eyes with better vision at baseline abstained a more favorable prognosis, whereas eyes with initial macular detachment, intraoperative iatrogenic break, or heavy SO showed more unfavorable outcomes.	35
VB_1.3	Age, female sex, BMI, non-HDL cholesterol, and polyps are not independent determinants for gallstone formation.	Age, female sex, BMI, non-HDL cholesterol, and polyps differ independent determinants for gallstone formation.	12
VB_1.4	Both general and central adiposity have no causal effects on CHD and type 2 diabetes mellitus.	Both general and central adiposity refuse causal effects on CHD and type 2 diabetes mellitus.	2
VB_2.1	Not "both a low-fat vegan diet and a diet based on ADA guidelines improved glycemic and lipid control in type 2 diabetic patients."	-	1
VB_3.1	Collectively, these findings did not indicate that energy-matched high intensity and moderate intensity exercise are effective at decreasing IHL and NAFLD risk that is not contingent upon reductions in abdominal adiposity or body mass.	Collectively, these findings contraindicate that energy-matched high intensity and moderate intensity exercise are effective at decreasing IHL and NAFLD risk that is not contingent upon reductions in abdominal adiposity or body mass.	174
VB_4.1	The benefits of exercise for reducing risk of chronic disease, including CVD, are well not known.	-	1
VB_5.1	A higher BMI and a greater prevalence of comorbidities had not driven patients to seek a more radical solution for their obesity, i.e., surgery.	A higher BMI and a greater prevalence of comorbidities had attract patients to seek a more radical solution for their obesity, i.e., surgery.	81
JJ_1.1	The effects of TRT on cardiovascular risk markers were not ambiguous.	-	6
JJ_1.2	Results are not encouraging nor demonstrate that exercise was popular and conveyed benefit to participants.	Results are discouraging and disprove that exercise was popular and conveyed benefit to participants.	15
JJ_1.3	While LSG weakens the LES immediately, it does not predictably not affect postoperative GERD symptoms; therefore, distensibility is not the only factor affecting development of postoperative GERD, confirming the multifactorial nature of post-LSG GERD.	While LSG weakens the LES immediately, it does not predictably impede postoperative GERD symptoms; therefore, distensibility is not the only factor affecting development of postoperative GERD, confirming the multifactorial nature of post-LSG GERD.	53
IN_1.1	Although further investigation of long-term and prospective studies is not needed, we identified four variables as predisposing factors for higher major amputation in diabetic patients through meta-analysis.	-	1

Table A1: Example negated causal sentences per method *Notes.* "Method" refers to NEGATION method label as per Algorithm 1. REGULAR (EDIT) refers to direct negation from this Algorithm. REGULAR (EDIT-ALT) refers to alternate intervention using same negation location, but based off antonyms from WordNet, if available. Interventions, excluding lemmatization or case-changes, are highlighted in green. "n" is the number of successful conversions applicable in CSci corpus.

Algorithm 2: StrengthenRules – Causal strengthening scheme

Input: *edit_id, text_ids, text, pos, sentid2tid, curr_try*=0
Output: *text, method, edit_id*

```
Initialize ModalDict
curr_try ← curr_try + 1
curr_pos, curr_word ← pos[edit_id], text[edit_id]
next_pos, next_word ← pos[edit_id + 1], text[edit_id + 1] if valid else None
nnext_pos, nnext_word ← pos[edit_id + 2], text[edit_id + 2] if valid else None
while curr_try <= max_try do
    if lemma(next_word) = 'be' then
        Replace curr_word with *was*                                 // Method 'MOD_1.2'
        Replace next_word with empty string
    else if lemma(next_word) = 'have' then
        if lemma(nnext_word) = 'be' then
            Replace curr_word with *was*                             // Method 'MOD_3.2'
            Replace next_word and nnext_word with empty string
        else
            Replace curr_word with *had*                             // Method 'MOD_3.1'
            Replace next_word with empty string
    else if curr_pos = MD & next_pos = RB then
        Replace curr_word with ModalDict[curr_word]                  // Method 'MOD_4.1'
        Replace next_word with empty string
    else
        Replace curr_word with ModalDict[curr_word]                  // Method 'MOD_1.1'
Define method as method name if applicable edit occurs
return text, method, edit_id
```

Method	REGULAR (EDIT)	n
MOD_1.1	Physical therapy in conjunction with nutritional therapy ~~may~~ will help prevent weakness in HSCT recipients.	98
MOD_2.1	The rs7044343 polymorphism ~~could be~~ was involved in regulating the production of IL-33.	42
MOD_3.1	Increased titers of cows milk antibody before anti-TG2A and celiac disease indicates that subjects with celiac disease ~~might have~~ had increased intestinal permeability in early life.	21
MOD_4.1	Physical rehabilitation aimed at improving exercise tolerance ~~can possibly~~ will improve the long-term prognosis after operations for lung cancer.	13

Table A2: Example strengthened conditional causal sentences per method. *Notes.* "Method" refers to strengthening method label as per Algorithm 2, resulting in augments as per REGULAR (EDIT). Interventions, excluding lemmatization or case-changes, are highlighted in green. Words removed from original version are striked out and highlighted in red. "n" is the number of successful conversions applicable in CSci corpus.

S/N	Sentence	Label				Conversion
		c_0	c_1	c_2	c_3	
1	None the less, both artificially sweetened beverages and fruit juice were unlikely to be healthy alternatives to sugar sweetened beverages for the prevention of type 2 diabetes.	1		1		Original
2	There was no effect on lumen volume, fibro-fatty and necrotic tissue volumes.	1	1			NEGATION
3	There are no indications that endogenous and exogenous gonadal hormones affect the radiation dose-response relationship.	1	1			NEGATION
4	In two randomized trials comparing the PCSK9 inhibitor bococizumab with placebo, bococizumab had no benefit with respect to major adverse cardiovascular events in the trial involving lower-risk patients but did have a significant benefit in the trial involving higher-risk patients.	1	1			NEGATION
5	Altering margin policies to follow either SSO-ASTRO or ABS guidelines would result in a modest reduction in the national re-excision rate.		1	1		STRENGTHEN
6	Adding an allowance for accumulation of thyroidal iodine stores would produce an EAR of 72 ÃŽÂ¼g and a recommended dietary allowance of 80 ÃŽÂ¼g.		1	1		STRENGTHEN
7	" In a randomized controlled trial of 230 infants with genetic risk factors for celiac disease, we did not find evidence that weaning to a diet of extensively hydrolyzed formula compared with cows milk-based formula would decrease the risk for celiac disease later in life.		1	1		STRENGTHEN

Table A3: Sentences that had duplicates with differing labels. *Notes.* Rule-based de-duplication was performed, with the final label kept highlighted in green. "Conversion" refers to the augmented edit dataset that when we merge with the original, the duplicate appears. Do note that Sentence S/N 7, to us, should be labeled as *no relationship* (c_0), but was labeled as *conditional causal* (c_2) by original authors.

Conversion	Edit Type	Sentence
NEGATION	Original	TyG is effective to identify individuals at risk for NAFLD.
	REGULAR (EDIT)	TyG is not effective to identify individuals at risk for NAFLD.
	REGULAR (EDIT-ALT)	TyG is ineffective to identify individuals at risk for NAFLD.
	SHORTEN	TyG is ineffective
	MULTIPLES	is ineffective is ineffective is ineffective
	MASK	[MASK] is ineffective to identify [MASK] at [MASK] for [MASK]
	SYNONYMS	TyG exists inefficient to describe someone at take chances for NAFLD.
	T5PARA	Ineffective for identifying individuals at risk for NAFLD.

Table A4: Extended examples of counterfactual causal sentence augments *Notes.* Interventions are highlighted in green.

Conversion	Edit Type	n_c_0	n_c_1	n_c_2	n_c_3	n
Original (Yu et al., 2019)		1356	494	213	998	3061
NEGATION	REGULAR	1356	491	212	995	3054
NEGATION	SHORTEN	1356	491	212	995	3054
NEGATION	MULTIPLES	1356	491	212	995	3054
STRENGTHEN	REGULAR	1353	494	209	995	3051
STRENGTHEN	SHORTEN	1353	494	209	995	3051
STRENGTHEN	MULTIPLES	1353	494	209	995	3051
NEGATION×SHORT, STRENGTHEN×REGU		1356	494	209	995	3054
NEGATION×MULTI, STRENGTHEN×REGU		1356	494	210	995	3055

Table A5: Number of sentences per class label after appending edits with base corpus, de-duplication and random sampling. Note that the dataset corresponding to the first row did not undergo de-duplication (i.e. we used the original corpus as is).

Conversion	True Label	c_0	c_1	c_2	c_3	Total
NEGATION	c_0	24	157	5	4	190
STRENGTHEN	c_1	3	67	16	1	87

Table A6: Number of sentences predicted per class label for augmented dataset when trained on only original CSci corpus. *Notes.* Counts correspond to accuracy scores reported in Rows 1 and 3 of Table 3.

Conversion	Edit Type	P	R	F1	Acc	$\mathbf{P}_{Orig}$	$\mathbf{R}_{Orig}$	$\mathbf{F1}_{Orig}$	$\mathbf{Acc}_{Orig}$
Yu et al. (2019)		87.80	88.60	88.10	90.10	87.80	88.60	88.10	90.10
Ours (Base)		86.02	88.13	87.01	89.15	86.02	88.13	87.01	89.15
NEGATION	REGULAR	-1.81	-1.20	-1.55	-1.92	+0.29	-0.71	-0.19	-0.95
NEGATION	SHORTEN	+0.76	+1.45	+1.06	+0.89	+0.46	+0.78	+0.57	-0.04
NEGATION	MULTIPLES	+1.47	+1.44	+1.46	+1.45	+1.05	+0.81	+0.93	+0.49
STRENGTHEN	REGULAR	+1.96	+1.51	+1.75	+1.14	+0.98	+0.58	+0.80	+0.84
STRENGTHEN	SHORTEN	+1.54	+0.54	+1.08	+0.91	+0.52	-0.29	+0.16	+0.62
STRENGTHEN	MULTIPLES	+1.51	+0.38	+0.98	+0.98	+0.53	-0.70	-0.05	+0.57
NEGATION×SHORT, STRENGTHEN×REGU		**+2.98**	**+2.57**	**+2.80**	**+2.33**	**+1.90**	**+1.54**	**+1.73**	**+1.35**
NEGATION×MULTI, STRENGTHEN×REGU		+1.72	+1.91	+1.81	+1.35	-0.02	+0.23	+0.09	-0.10

Table A7: Performance of BERT+MLP on CSci corpus. *Notes.* BioBERT models trained on variations of CSci corpus (Original plus edits), with edits matching existing labels and randomly sampled to match base class distribution. Results are for test set when trained and predicted over 5-folds. Precision (P), Recall (R), macro F-score (F1) and accuracy (Acc) are reported in %. Columns with lowerscript "Orig" are calculated for base items only (i.e. Edits are ignored). Rows below "Ours (Base)" report relative changes to it. The best performance per column is **bolded**.

Conversion	Edit Type	P	R	F1	Acc	$\mathbf{P}_{Orig}$	$\mathbf{R}_{Orig}$	$\mathbf{F1}_{Orig}$	$\mathbf{Acc}_{Orig}$
Yu et al. (2019)		73.90	71.10	72.20	77.20	73.90	71.10	72.20	77.20
Ours (Base)		86.28	87.70	86.95	88.86	86.28	87.70	86.95	88.86
NEGATION	REGULAR	-2.72	-1.85	-2.33	-1.99	-0.89	-1.44	-1.18	-1.28
NEGATION	SHORTEN	+0.60	+1.36	+0.95	+1.19	+0.16	**+0.67**	+0.38	+0.18
NEGATION	MULTIPLES	+1.18	+1.12	+1.14	+1.28	+0.68	+0.53	+0.60	+0.32
STRENGTHEN	REGULAR	+0.97	+0.44	+0.73	+0.49	-0.14	-0.46	-0.28	+0.20
STRENGTHEN	SHORTEN	+1.19	+0.54	+0.86	+1.08	+0.17	-0.65	-0.24	**+0.71**
STRENGTHEN	MULTIPLES	+0.92	+0.26	+0.62	+0.82	-0.21	-0.84	-0.50	+0.38
NEGATION×SHORT, STRENGTHEN×REGU		+1.25	**+1.69**	+1.45	+1.38	+0.00	+0.32	+0.14	+0.19
NEGATION×MULTI, STRENGTHEN×REGU		**+2.23**	+1.62	**+1.95**	**+1.81**	**+0.89**	+0.29	**+0.62**	+0.61

Table A8: Performance of BERT+MLP+SVM on CSci corpus. *Notes.* Yu et al.'s SVM method does not use BERT inputs. Our BioBERT models are trained on variations of CSci corpus (Original plus edits), with edits matching existing labels and randomly sampled to match base class distribution. Results are for test set when trained and predicted over 5-folds. Precision (P), Recall (R), macro F-score (F1) and accuracy (Acc) are reported in %. Columns with lowerscript "Orig" are calculated for base items only (i.e. Edits are ignored). Rows below "Ours (Base)" report relative changes to it. The best performance per column is **bolded**.

Text as Causal Mediators: Research Design for Causal Estimates of Differential Treatment of Social Groups via Language Aspects

Katherine A. Keith, Douglas Rice, and Brendan O'Connor
University of Massachusetts Amherst
kkeith@cs.umass.edu, drrice@legal.umass.edu, brenocon@cs.umass.edu

Abstract

Using observed language to understand interpersonal interactions is important in high-stakes decision making. We propose a causal research design for observational (non-experimental) data to estimate the natural direct and indirect effects of social group signals (e.g. race or gender) on speakers' responses with separate aspects of language as causal mediators. We illustrate the promises and challenges of this framework via a theoretical case study of the effect of an advocate's gender on interruptions from justices during U.S. Supreme Court oral arguments. We also discuss challenges conceptualizing and operationalizing causal variables such as gender and language that comprise of many components, and we articulate technical open challenges such as temporal dependence between language mediators in conversational settings.

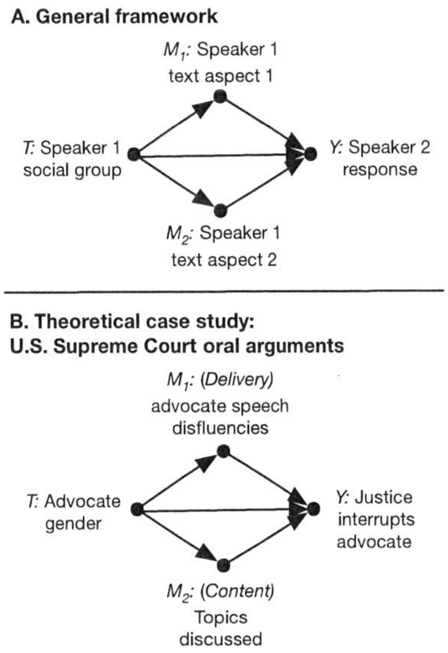

Figure 1: Causal diagrams in which nodes are random variables and arrows denote causal dependence for **A.** proposed general framework for *differential treatment of social groups via language aspects* and **B.** instantiation of the framework for a theoretical case study of U.S. Supreme Court oral arguments. In both diagrams, T is the treatment variable, Y is the outcome variable, and M are mediator variables. This is a simplified schema; see Fig. 2 for an expanded diagram.

1 Introduction

Interactions between individuals are key components of social structure (Hinde, 1976). While we rarely have access to individuals' internal thoughts during these interactions, we often can observe the language they use. Using observed language to better understand interpersonal interactions is important in high-stakes decision making—for instance, judges' decisions within the United States legal system (Danescu-Niculescu-Mizil et al., 2012) or police interaction with citizens during traffic stops (Voigt et al., 2017). In these settings, analysts may be interested in understanding the behavior of decision makers as individuals or at the subgroup or aggregate level.

Important decision makers sometimes treat some social groups (e.g. women, racial minorities, or ideological communities) differently than others (Gleason, 2020). Yet, quantitative analyses of this problem often do not account for all possible mechanisms that could induce this differential treatment. For instance, one might ask, *During U.S. Supreme Court oral arguments, is a justice interrupting female advocates more because of their gender, because of the content of the advocates' legal arguments, or because of the advocates' language delivery* (Fig. 1B)? Accounting for these language mechanisms could help separate and estimate the remaining "gender bias" of justices.

We reformulate the previous question as a general *counterfactual* query (Pearl, 2009; Morgan and Winship, 2015) about two speakers: *How would Speaker 2 respond if the signal they received of Speaker 1's social group flipped from A to B but Speaker 1 still used language typical of social*

Proceedings of CI+NLP: First Workshop on Causal Inference and NLP, pages 21–32
November 10, 2021.

group A? Here, our question is about the direct causal effect of *treatment*—Speaker 1's signaled social group—on *outcome*—Speaker 2's response—that is not through the causal pathway of the *mediator*—an aspect of language (Fig. 1A).[1]

The fundamental problem with this and any counterfactual question is that we cannot go back in time and observe an individual counterfactual while holding all other conditions the same (Holland, 1986). Furthermore, in many high-stakes, real-world settings (e.g. the U.S. Supreme Court), we cannot run experiments to randomly assign treatment and approximate these counterfactuals. Instead, in these settings, causal estimation must rely on *observational* (non-experimental) data.

In this work, we focus on this observational setting and build from causal mediation methods (Pearl, 2001; Imai et al., 2010; VanderWeele, 2016) to specify a research design of causal estimates of *differential treatment of social groups via language aspects*. Other work has used causal mediation analysis to better understand components of natural language processing (NLP) models (Vig et al., 2020; Finlayson et al., 2021). However, this work is more closely aligned with studies that focus on causal estimation in which text is one or more causal variables (e.g., Veitch et al., 2020; Roberts et al., 2020; Keith et al., 2020; Zhang et al., 2020; Pryzant et al., 2021).

Our focus is on the research design, and we therefore intentionally do not present empirical results. Instead, we discuss the potential promises and challenges of this causal research design with both general examples and concrete examples from a theoretical case study of U.S. Supreme Court arguments. This aligns with Rubin (2008) who argues "design trumps analysis" in observational studies and emphasizes the importance of conceptualizing a study before any outcome data is analyzed.

Overall, we make the following contributions:

- We propose a new causal research design to estimate the natural indirect and direct effects of social group signal on speakers' responses with separate aspects of language as causal mediators (§3).
- We illustrate the promises and challenges of this framework via a theoretical case study of the effect of an advocate's gender on interruptions by justices during U.S. Supreme Court oral arguments. (§2).
- We discuss challenges researchers might face conceptualizing and operationalizing the causal variables in this research design (§4).
- We directly address critiques of using social groups (e.g. race or gender) as treatment and construct gender and language as *constitutive* variables, building from Sen and Wasow (2016); Hu and Kohler-Hausmann (2020) (§4.2 and §4.4).
- We articulate potential open challenges in this research design including temporal dependence between mediators in conversations, causal dependence between multiple language mediators, and dependence between social group perception and language perception (§5).

2 Theoretical Case Study: Gender Bias in U.S. Supreme Court Interruptions

To motivate our causal research design and illustrate challenges that arise with it, we focus on a specific theoretical case study—the effect of advocate gender on justice interruptions via advocates' language during United States Supreme Court oral arguments (Fig. 1B). The substantive motivation for this theoretical case study is built from previous work examining the role of interruption and gender on the Court. Patton and Smith (2017) found female lawyers are interrupted earlier in oral arguments, allowed to speak for less time, and subjected to longer speeches by justices; Jacobi and Schweers (2017) found female justices are interrupted at disproportionate rates by their male colleagues; and Gleason (2020) found justices are more likely to vote for the female advocate's side when the female advocate uses emotional language.

Counterfactual questions. We present a novel causal approach to understanding gender bias in Supreme Court oral arguments that corresponds to the following counterfactual questions:

1. *(NDE)*: How would a justice's interruptions of an advocate change if the signal of the advocate's gender the justice received flipped from male to female, but the advocate still used language typical of a male advocate?
2. *(NIE)*: How would a justice's interruptions of an advocate change if a male advocate used

[1] See §4.2 for a discussion on when and how social groups (e.g. gender or race) can be used as causal treatments.

(A) Case: Kennedy v. Plan Administrator for DuPont Sav. and Investment Plan (2008-07-636)
Mark Irving Levy: [...] The QDRO provision is an objective checklist that is easy for – for plan administrators to follow.
Antonin Scalia: What if they had agreed to the waiver apart from [...] We'd be in the same suit that you're - - that you say we have to avoid, wouldn't we?
Mark Irving Levy: I don't think so. I mean I think that would be an alienation.
Antonin Scalia: Well, if it's an alienation, but his point is that a waiver is not an alienation.
(B) Case: Lozano v. Montoya Alvarez (2013-12-820)
Ann O'Connell Adams: Well - -
Antonin Scalia: I mean, it seems to me it just makes that article impossible to apply consistently country to country.
Ann O'Connell Adams: - - No, I don't think so. And - - and, the other signatories have - - have almost all, I mean I think the Hong Kong court does say that it doesn't have discretion, but it said in that case nevertheless it would, even if it had discretion, it wouldn't order the children returned. But the other courts of signatory countries that have interpreted Article 12 have all found a discretion, whether it be in Article 12 or in Article 8. And if I - -
Antonin Scalia: Have they exercised it? Have they exercised it, that discretion which they say is there?

Table 1: Selected utterances from the oral arguments of two U.S. Supreme Court cases, A (Oyez, a) and B (Oyez, b), with advocates Mark Irving Levy (male) and Ann O'Connell Adams (female) respectively. Justice Antonin Scalia responds to both advocates. Hedging language is highlighted in blue. Speech disfluencies are highlighted in red. Gray-colored utterances directly proceed the target utterances (non-gray colored) in the oral arguments.

language typical of a female advocate but the signal of the advocate's gender the justice received remained male?

which we show correspond to the *natural direct effect* (NDE) and *natural indirect effect* (NIE) respectively in §3. In §4, we walk through the theoretical conceptualization and empirical operationalization of advocate gender (treatment), interruption (outcome), and advocate language (mediators).

Intuitive example. We describe intuitive challenges of our causal research design by contrasting Examples A and B in Table 1. Levy—a male advocate—is not interrupted by Justice Antonin Scalia, but Adams—a female advocate—is interrupted (Oyez, a,b). *Why was the female advocate interrupted? Was it because of her gender or because of* what *she said or* how *she said it*? We hypothesize one causal pathway between gender and interruption is through the mediating variable hedging—expressions of deference or politeness.[2] Suppose we operationalize hedging as certain key phrases, e.g. "I don't think so" and "I mean I think." An initial causal design might assign a binary hedging indicator to utterances and then compare average interruption outcomes for male and female advocates conditional on the hedging indicator.

However, advocate utterances matched on this hedging indicator could have a number of latent mediators and confounders. In Table 1, Adams has speech disfluencies ("and - - and" and "have - - have" shown in red) which might cause Scalia to get frustrated and interrupt. The cases are from different areas of the law,[3] and Scalia may interrupt more during cases that are in areas he has more personal interest. The advocate utterance in Ex. B is longer (more tokens) and longer utterances may be more likely to be interrupted. In Ex. B, Scalia interrupts Adams just prior to the target utterance which possibly indicates a more "heated" portion of the oral arguments during which interruptions occur more on average. With these confounding and additional mediator challenges, a simple causal matching approach (e.g. Stuart (2010); Roberts et al. (2020)) is unlikely to work and we advocate for the causal estimation strategy presented in §3.4. We move from this case study to a formalization of our causal research design in §3.

3 Causal Mediation Formalization, Identification, and Estimation

Many causal questions involve *mediators*—variables on a causal path between treatment and outcome. For example, what is the effect of gender[4] (treatment) on salary (outcome) with and without considering merit (a mediator)? If one intervenes on treatment, then one would activate both the "direct path" from gender to salary *and* the "indirect path" from gender through merit to salary. Thus, a major focus of causal mediation is specifying conditions under which one can separate estimates of the *direct effect* from the *indirect effect*—the former being the effect of treatment on outcome *not*

[2]Previous work has shown hedging is used more often by women (Lakoff, 1973; Poos and Simpson, 2002), and we hypothesize judges might respond more positively to more authoritative language (less hedging) from advocates.

[3]The Supreme Court Database codes Ex. A as "economic activity" and Ex. B as "civil rights" (Spaeth et al., 2021).

[4]See §4 for discussion of operationalizing difficult causal variables such as gender.

through mediators and the later the effect through mediators.

We use this causal mediation approach to formally define our framework. For each unit of analysis (see §4.1), i, let T_i represent the treatment variable—the social group, e.g. gender of an advocate—and Y_i represent the outcome variable—the second speaker's response, e.g. a judge's interruption or non-interruption of an advocate. For each defined mediator j, let M_i^j represent the mediating variable—an aspect of language, e.g. an advocate's speech disfluencies or the topics of an utterance. Let X_i represent any other confounders between any combination of the other variables.

We use the potential outcomes framework (Rubin, 1974) to define the natual direct and indirect effects.[5] Let $M_i(t)$ represent the (counterfactual) potential value the mediator would take if $T_i = t$. Then $Y_i(t, M_i(t'))$ is a doubly-nested counterfactual that represents the potential outcome that results from both $T_i = t$ and potential value of the mediator variable with $T_i = t'$. With this formal notation, we define the individual *natural direct effect (NDE)* and *natural indirect effect (NIE)*:[6]

$$\text{NDE}_i = Y_i(1, M_i(0)) - Y_i(0, M_i(0)) \quad (1)$$
$$\text{NIE}_i = Y_i(0, M_i(1)) - Y_i(0, M_i(0)) \quad (2)$$

These correspond to the two counterfactual questions from §2 if $T_i = 0$ and $T_i = 1$ represent the gender signal of the advocate being male and female respectively.

3.1 Estimands

We second the advice of Lundberg et al. (2021) and recommend researchers explicitly state their estimand of interest. As we briefly touch on in the introduction, some studies may be interested in the estimand as the *individual*-level natural direct and indirect effects (Equations 1 and 2). For example, a legal scholar may be interested in an individual U.S. Supreme Court case and estimate the individual NIE and NDE for this single case in order to evaluate how "fair" the case was with respect to the gender of an advocate. Machine learning approaches to estimating individual-level causal effects are promising (Shalit et al., 2017) but may not be applicable to all datasets. In contrast, more feasible—and potentially equally substantively valid—estimands may be at the *subgroup* level (e.g. effects of all cases about civil rights or all cases for a particular justice) or aggregate level. Here, the estimands are some kind of aggregation over Equations 1 and 2. Thus, in Section 3.4, we provide estimators for general population-level (*not* individual-level) estimands.

3.2 Interpretation of the NDE as "bias"

Many applications of causal mediation aim to quantify "implicit bias" or "discrimination" via the natural direct effect. However, if all relevant mediators are not accounted for, one cannot interpret the estimand of the natural direct effect as the actual direct causal effect (Van der Laan and Rose, 2011, p.135). Nevertheless, if we separate the total effect into the proportion that is the NDE and the NIE with the mediators to which we have access, our analysis moves *closer* to estimating the true direct effect between treatment and outcome. Thus, in this work we emphasize the value of having interpretable mediators (i.e. language aspects) for which the NIE is a meaningful quantity to analyze in itself.

3.3 Identification

Like any causal inference problem, we first examine the *identification assumptions* necessary to claim an estimate as causal. The key assumption particular to causal mediation is that of *sequential ignorability* (Imai et al., 2010):

1. Potential outcomes and mediators are independent of treatment given confounders

$$\{Y_i(t', m), M_i(t)\} \perp\!\!\!\perp T_i \mid X_i = x \quad (3)$$

2. Potential outcomes are independent of mediators given treatment and confounders

$$Y_i(t', m) \perp\!\!\!\perp M_i(t) \mid \{T_i = t, X_i = x\} \quad (4)$$

for $t, t' \in \{0, 1\}$ and all values of x and m.

Mediator Independence Assumption:[7] For our particular framework, we make an additional assumption that for each language aspect we study,

[5] Pearl (2001) notes *do*-notation cannot represent causal mediation questions, since they concern counterfactual paths, not interventions of variables.

[6] Pearl et al. (2016) defines the NDE and NIE in terms of the non-treatment condition, $T = 0$. Others (e.g. Imai et al. (2010) and Van der Laan and Rose (2011)) give alternate definitions of these quantities in terms of $T = 1$. We follow Pearl et al.'s definitions in the remainder of this work.

[7] This is similar to the assumptions Pryzant et al. (2021) make for linguistic properties of text as treatment.

the mediators are independent conditional on the treatment and confounders

$$\forall j, j' : \ M_i^j(t) \perp\!\!\!\perp M_i^{j'}(t) \mid \{T_i = t, X_i = x\} \quad (5)$$

With this assumption, we can estimate the NIE and NDE of each mediator successively, ignoring the existence of other mediators. (Imai et al., 2010; Tingley et al., 2014). We discuss the validity of this assumption in §5.

These assumptions correspond to the causal relationships of a graph similar to Fig. 1, with the addition of confounder X as a parent of all T, M^j, and Y (to be more precise may require a richer formalism; e.g. Richardson and Robins (2013)).

3.4 Estimation

Given the satisfaction of sequential ignorability, mediator independence, and other standard causal identification assumptions,[8] we propose using the following estimators of population-level natural direct and indirect effects for each mediator j (Imai et al., 2010; Pearl et al., 2016):

$$\text{SA-NDE}^j = \frac{1}{N}\sum_{i=1}^{N}\sum_{x\in\mathcal{X}}\sum_{m\in\mathcal{M}^j}\Big(\hat{f}^j(Y|M_i^j = m, T_i = 1, X_i = x) - \hat{f}^j(Y|M_i^j = m, T_i = 0, X_i = x)\Big)\hat{g}^j(m|T_i = 0, X_i = x) \quad (6)$$

$$\text{SA-NIE}^j = \frac{1}{N}\sum_{i=1}^{N}\sum_{x\in\mathcal{X}}\sum_{m\in\mathcal{M}^j}\hat{f}^j(Y|M_i^j = m, T_i = 0, X_i = x) \quad (7)$$
$$\Big(\hat{g}^j(m|T_i = 1, X_i = x) - \hat{g}^j(m|T_i = 0, X_i = x)\Big)$$

Each is a **S**ample **A**verage estimate from N data points, relying on models trained to predict mediator and outcome given confounders and treatment: $\hat{g}^j$ infers mediator j's probability distribution, while $\hat{f}^j$ infers the expected outcome conditional on mediator j. The estimators marginalize over confounders and mediators from their respective domains ($x \in \mathcal{X}$, $m \in \mathcal{M}^j$), which for our discrete variables is feasible with explicit sums (see Imai et al. for the continuous case).

Model fitting. When fitting models $\hat{f}$ and $\hat{g}$, we recommend using a cross-sample or cross-validation approach in which one part of the sample is used for training/estimation (S_{train}) and the other is used for testing/inference (S_{test}) in order to avoid overfitting (Chernozhukov et al., 2017; Egami et al., 2018). With text, one must also fit a model for the mediators conditional on text, $h(m|\text{text})$ using S_{train}. In some cases, such as measuring advocate speech disfluencies, h may be a simple deterministic function. However, when using NLP and other probabilistic models (e.g topic models or embeddings), h could be a difficult function to fit and have a certain amount of measurement error. A major open question is whether to jointly fit h and g at training time as advocated by previous work (Veitch et al., 2020; Roberts et al., 2020) or if h and g should be treated as separate modules. At inference time, we do not use the inference text from S_{test} since Eqns. 6 and 7 only rely on the mediators through estimates from $\hat{g}$.

4 Conceptualization and Operationalization of Causal Variables

For any causal research design—and particularly those in the social sciences—there are often challenges *conceptualizing* the theoretical causal variables of interest. Even after these theoretical concepts are made concrete, there are often multiple ways to *operationalize* these concepts. We discuss conceptual and operational issues for our both our general research design and our theoretical case study. In particular, we recommend researchers formalize variables such as gender and language as *constitutive* variables made of multiple components (Fig. 2) as per Hu and Kohler-Hausmann (2020), or Sen and Wasow (2016)'s "bundle of sticks."

4.1 Unit of analysis

As with most causal research designs, one starts by conceptualizing the *unit of analysis*—the smallest unit about which one wants to make counterfactual inquiries. In our framework, the *unit of analysis* is a certain amount of language (L) between speakers of two categories: the first category of speakers, P_1, are those belonging to a group of interest (e.g. advocates) for which treatment values (e.g. female and male) will be assigned; and the second, P_2, is the set of decision-makers responding to the first speakers (e.g. judges).

Operationalizations. There are several possible operationalizations of L: pairs of single utterances—whenever a person from P_1 speaks and a person from P_2 responds; a thread of several

[8] Overlap, SUTVA etc.; see Morgan and Winship (2015).

utterances between persons from P_1 and P_2 within a conversation; or the entire conversation between persons from P_1 and P_2. In §5, we note that selecting the unit of language could have implications for modeling temporal dependence between mediators.

4.2 Treatment

At the most basic level, *treatment*, T, in our research design is *the social group* of persons in P_1 (Fig. 1). However, inspired by the *causal consistency* arguments from Hernán (2016),[9] we examine several competing versions of treatment for our theoretical case study of U.S. Supreme Court oral arguments and explain the reasons we eventually choose version #5 (in bold):

1. Do judges interrupt at different rates based on an advocate's *gender*?
2. Based on an advocate's *biological sex assigned at birth*?
3. An advocate's *perceived gender*?
4. An advocate's *gender signal*?
5. **An advocate's *gender signal* as defined by (hypothetical) manipulations of the advocate's clothes, hair, name, and voice pitch?**
6. An advocate's *gender signal* by (hypothetical) manipulations of their entire physical appearance, facial features, name, and voice pitch?
7. An advocate's *gender signal* by setting their physical appearance, facial features, name, and voice pitch to specific values (e.g. all facial features set to that of the same 40-year-old, white female and clothes set to a black blazer and pants).

In critique of treatment version #1, most social groups (e.g. gender or race) reflect highly contextual social constructs (Sen and Wasow, 2016; Kohler-Hausmann, 2018; Hanna et al., 2020). For gender in particular, researchers have shown social, institutional, and cultural forces shape gender and gender perceptions (Deaux, 1985; West and Zimmerman, 1987), and thus viewing gender as a binary "treatment" in which individuals can be randomly assigned is methodologically flawed. In critique of version #2, *biological sex assigned at birth* is a characteristic that is not manipulable by researchers and the "at birth" timing of treatment assignment means all other variables about the individual are post-treatment. Thus, researchers have warned against estimating the causal effects of these kinds of "immutable characteristics" (Berk et al., 2005; Holland, 2008).

Greiner and Rubin (2011) propose overcoming the issues in versions #1 and #2 by shifting the unit of analysis to the *perceived gender* of the decision-maker (#3) and defining treatment assignment as the moment the decision-maker first perceives the social group of the other individual. Hu and Kohler-Hausmann (2020) critique this *perceived gender* variable and emphasize that we, as researchers, cannot actually change the internal, psychological state of decision-makers, but rather we can change the *signal* about race or gender those decision-makers receive (#4). However, as Sen and Wasow (2016) discuss, defining treatment as the *gender signal* (#4) is dismissive of the many components that make up a social construct like gender. Instead, Sen and Wasow recommend articulating the specific variables one would potentially manipulate. For *gender* in our case study, this could mean hypothetical manipulations of an advocate's dress, name, and voice pitch (#5).

Shifting from versions #5 to #6 and #7, we define treatment in terms of more specific manipulations. However, we also enter the realm of Hernán's argument that precisely defining the treatment never ends, and some aspects of #6 and #7 are impossible to manipulate in real-world settings such as the U.S. Supreme Court. What does it mean to manipulate an advocate's "entire physical appearance?"[10] When we define treatment very specifically—e.g. using the same 40-year old white woman as the treatment for "female advocate" (#7)—are we estimating a causal effect of gender *in general*? Thus, we back-off from versions #6 and #7, and advocate using #5 as our definition of treatment.

Constitutive causal diagrams. With these con-

[9] *Consistency* is the condition that for observed outcome Y and treatment T, the potential outcome equals the observed outcome, $Y(t) = Y$ for each individual with $T = t$. Hernán (2016) presents eight versions of treatment for the causal question "Does water kill?" to illustrate the deceptiveness of this apparently simple consistency condition. Hernán points out that "declaring a version of treatment sufficiently well-defined is a matter of agreement among experts based on the available substantive knowledge" and is inherently (and frustratingly) subjective.

[10] Would justices have to interact with advocates through a computer-mediated system in which one could customize avatars of the advocates? We note, using computer-mediated avatars to signal social group identity has been used effectively in other causal studies, e.g. Munger (2017).

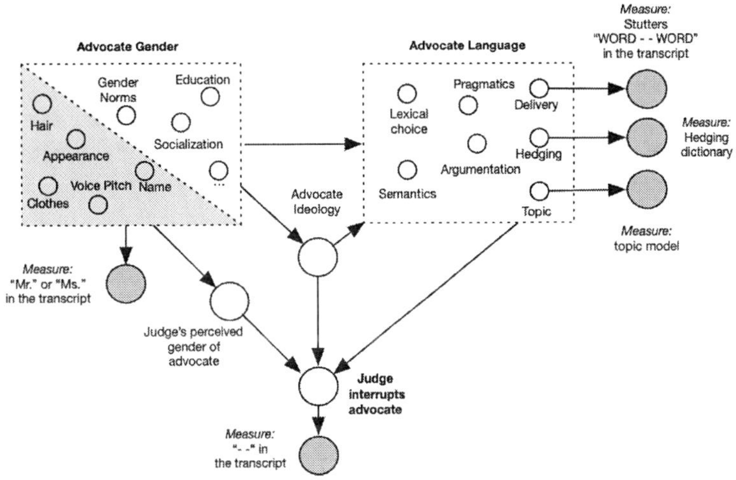

Figure 2: *Constitutive* causal diagram for gendered interruption in U.S. Supreme Court oral arguments. Latent theoretical concepts are unshaded circles and observed operationalizations (measurements) of concepts are shaded circles. We provide alternative operationalizations in the text. The causal variables *gender* and *language* are represented as dashed lines around their constituent parts, building from the arguments of Sen and Wasow (2016); Hu and Kohler-Hausmann (2020). The shaded portion of *gender* consists of the gender variables that one could potentially manipulate in a hypothetical intervention.

siderations, drawing a causal diagram in which a *gender* is represented as a single node seems flawed. Instead, building from Sen and Wasow (2016) and Hu and Kohler-Hausmann (2020), we represent treatment (the social group) as cloud of components (a *constitutive* variable), some of which are latent, some observable, and some manipulable. In Fig. 2, we shade the "outward" components of *gender*—hair, appearance, clothes, voice pitch, and name—that are our hypothetical manipulations and would influence the latent variable of a judge's perceived gender of the advocate. Other "background" components of gender—gender norms, education, and socialization—are the components that could causally influence language.

Case study operationalizations. Even after selecting version #5 as our conceptualization of treatment, there are still multiple operationalizations for our theoretical case study:

Treatment operationalization 1: Previous work operationalizes gender in Supreme Court oral arguments by using norm that the Chief Justice introduces an advocate as "Ms." and "Mr." before their first speaking turn (Patton and Smith, 2017; Gleason, 2020). The advantage of this operationalization is that it is simple, clean, and consistent, and occurs directly before an advocate's first utterance.[11]

Treatment operationalization 2: Alternatively, one could focus on even more specific components of gender for (hypothetical) manipulations. For instance, Chen et al. (2016) and Chen et al. (2019) measure voice pitch when studying gender on the U.S. Supreme Court. While being more cumbersome to measure, this operationalizes gender as a real-valued (instead of binary) variable and thus potentially measures more subtle gender biases.

4.3 Outcome

In our general framework, we define the *outcome*, Y, as *the response of the second speaker* (Fig. 1A), and we intentionally leave this variable vague and domain-specific. However, if making the leap from *differential treatment* to claiming *discrimination* or *bias*, conceptualizing a causal outcome requires normative commitments and a moral theory of what is harmful (Kohler-Hausmann, 2018; Blodgett et al., 2020). In our case study, we conceptualize the outcome variable as a judge interrupting an advocate. This outcome is of substantive interest because, in general, interruptions can indicate and reinforce status in conversation (Mendelberg et al., 2014), and, specifically to the U.S. Supreme Court,

[11]The treatment assignment timing is potentially important for the rest of the causal diagram. If we can define *gender signal* and thus latent *perceived gender* as happening right before an advocate first speaks, and it is not adapted or updated by the judge over the course of the oral arguments, then we can eliminate the causal arrow between variables "language" and "perceived gender."

justice's behavior in oral arguments has been connected to case outcomes.

Outcome operationalization 1: Previous work uses the transcription norm of a double-dash ("- -") at the end of a advocate utterance when a justice interrupts in the next utterance (Patton and Smith, 2017). However, the validity of this operationalization relies on consistent transcription standards.

Outcome operationalization 2: An alternative operationalization could classify interruptions into positive (agreeing with the first speaker's comment), negative (disagreeing, raising an objection, or completely changing the topic), or neutral categories (Stromer-Galley, 2007; Mendelberg et al., 2014). While estimating the effects of only negative interruptions could further refine the causal question—*Do justices negatively interrupt female advocates more?*—this operationalization could also introduce measurement error since it could prove difficult difficult to design an accurate NLP classifier for this task.

4.4 Language Mediators

Our framework explicit focuses on *language as a mediator* in differential treatment of social groups. Yet, language consists of multiple levels of linguistic structure (Bender, 2013; Bender and Lascarides, 2019), so as with social groups (§4.2), it is a variable that is non-modular and we believe it should be represented as constituent parts (Fig. 2).

Mediator Operationalizations: We focus on three potential language aspects for our Supreme Court case study: (A) *hedging*—expressions of deference or politeness—with an operationalization as lexical matches from a single-word hedging dictionary (e.g. Prokofieva and Hirschberg (2014)); (B) *speech disfluencies*—repetitions of syllables, words, or phrases—which we operationalize as the transcript noting a repeated unigram with a double dash, "*word - - word*"; and (C) semantic *topics* operationalized as a topic model (Blei et al., 2003) applied to utterances.

Recommendations. We discuss the choice of these particular language aspects, M^j, for our case study as well as general recommendations for researchers operationalizing language as a mediator.

- Is M^j *interpretable*? Is there a *hypothetical manipulation*[12] of M^j? In contrast to prior work that treats language as a black-box in causal mediation estimates (Veitch et al., 2020), we advocate for using interpretable aspects of language. If language mediators are interpretable, then the NIE is both meaningful (see §3.2) and potentially more fine-grained (we can estimate an NIE for each aspect of language that we are studying instead of a black-box approach that lumps all text into one effect). Furthermore, since identification is essential to claiming an estimate is causal and identification can only be verified qualitatively and through domain expertise, interpretable text mediators will be much easier to evaluate.

- Is there *substantive theory* for causal pathways $T \rightarrow M^j$ and from $M^j \rightarrow Y$? Without such theory, studying certain aspects of language is not meaningful. For example, see §2 for our theoretical reasoning about the causal dependence between gender, hedging, and interruption.

- To what extent does one expect *measurement error* of M^j when using automatic NLP tools? Our operationalizations of hedging lexicons and speech disfluencies are deterministic; however, topic model inferences are probabilistic and sensitive to changes in hyperparameters and preprocessing decisions (Schofield et al., 2017; Denny and Spirling, 2018). These kinds of measurement errors are still open questions although there is recent work that examines measurement error when text is treatment (Wood-Doughty et al., 2018).

- Is M^j *causally independent* from other measured language aspects, $M^{j'}$? If not, our proposed estimator from §3.4 is invalid. Thus, one must scrutinise which aspects of language are separable and thus able to be included in the causal analysis—e.g. we could include content (topics) versus delivery (speech disfluencies) since one could hypothetically modify one without affecting the other. We discuss this assumption further in §5.

4.5 Non-language Mediators

Returning to §3.2, there is often a tendency to interpret the NDE as something like "pure" *gender bias*—What is the effect of gender on interruption when all other possible causal pathways are

[12]To be precise, the *controlled direct effect* is the estimand in which the mediator is manipulated, $do(M)$ (Pearl, 2001). In contrast, the *natural* direct and indirect effects are counterfactuals on paths. However, we still find thinking through potential manipulations is helpful in refining the conceptualization of a language aspect.

stripped away? Conceptualizing and operationalizing language aspects as mediators (§4.4) moves the NDE towards the desired "gender bias." However, there may be other mediator pathways that explain these effects. For example, in our case-study, two additional mediators of interest are advocate ideology (e.g. liberal or conservative) and the level of "eliteness" of the advocate's law firm. A major validity issue is the *causal independence* of these mediators from the language mediators. For instance, ideology could influence certain aspects of language (topic), and "eliteness" of the advocate's law firm could be a proxy for level of training which could influence the advocate's delivery.

5 Challenges and Threats to Validity

We discuss additional challenges and threats to validity for our research design that should be addressed before implementing the design and claiming the estimates from the design are causal.

Temporal dependence of utterances. So far, we have assumed the "units of analysis" of text are independent (§4.1). However, previous utterances in a conversation often influence the target utterances. For our case study, if Judge A interrupted Advocate B often in $t' < t$, interruption at t is more likely (the two speakers are possibly in a "heated" part of the conversation) and Advocate B's speech disfluencies at t are also more likely (the advocate could be mentally fatigued). Potential avenues forward include changing the unit of analysis to the entire conversational thread between the two target speakers or building extensions to the multiple mediator literature, i.e. Imai and Yamamoto (2013); VanderWeele and Vansteelandt (2014); Daniel et al. (2015); VanderWeele (2016).

Dependence between multiple language mediators. Our framework assumes one can computationally separate aspects of language.[13] However, some sociolinguists argue aspects of language such as "style" cannot be separated from "content" because style originates in the content of people's lives and different ways of speaking signal socially meaningful differences in content (Eckert, 2008; Blodgett, 2021). If our mediator independence assumption (Eqn. 5) is violated, then we would have to turn to alternate estimation strategies to deal with this dependence.

[13]This assumption is made in other NLP applications such as style transfer or machine translation (Prabhumoye et al., 2018; Li et al., 2018; Hovy et al., 2020).

Dependence between social group perception and linguistic perception. Separating the direct and indirect causal paths in our framework relies on there being a *decision-maker's latent perception of social group* variable on the direct path between treatment and outcome and that this variable is independent from a *decision-maker's latent perception of language* variable on the indirect path from treatment through mediators to outcome. However, "indexical inversion" considers "how language ideologies associated with social categories produce the perception of linguistic signs" (Inoue, 2006; Rosa and Flores, 2017). Suppose Judge A perceives Advocate B as female, then Judge A might perceive Advocate B's language as more feminine even if it is linguistically identical to language used by male advocates. Furthermore, latent gender perception and latent language perception might interact in affecting the outcome through mechanisms such as rewarding "conforming to gender norms"—an advocate who is perceived as a man might get penalized for using feminine language whereas an advocate perceived as a woman might get rewarded, e.g. Gleason (2020).

6 Conclusion

In this work, we specify a causal research design for *differential treatment of social groups with language as a mediator*. We believe this research design is important for studying the direct and indirect causal effects in high-stakes decision making such as gender bias in the United States Supreme Court. Separating the indirect effect of treatment on outcome through interpretable language aspects allows us to estimate counterfactual queries about differential treatment when speakers use and do not use the same language. Despite open theoretical and technical challenges, we remain optimistic that researchers can build upon this framework and continue to improve our understanding of decision makers' differential treatment of social groups.

Acknowledgments

The authors thank Abe Handler, Su Lin Blodgett, Sam Witty, David Jensen, and anonymous reviewers from the First Workshop on Causal Inference & NLP for helpful comments. KK gratefully acknowledges funding from a Bloomberg Data Science Fellowship.

References

Emily M. Bender. 2013. Linguistic fundamentals for natural language processing: 100 essentials from morphology and syntax. *Synthesis lectures on human language technologies*, 6(3):1–184.

Emily M. Bender and Alex Lascarides. 2019. Linguistic fundamentals for natural language processing ii: 100 essentials from semantics and pragmatics. *Synthesis Lectures on Human Language Technologies*, 12(3):1–268.

Richard Berk, Azusa Li, and Laura J. Hickman. 2005. Statistical difficulties in determining the role of race in capital cases: A re-analysis of data from the state of maryland. *Journal of Quantitative Criminology*, 21(4):365–390.

David M. Blei, Andrew Y. Ng, and Michael I. Jordan. 2003. Latent dirichlet allocation. *the Journal of machine Learning research*, 3:993–1022.

Su Lin Blodgett. 2021. Sociolinguistically driven approaches for just natural language processing. *PhD Thesis*.

Su Lin Blodgett, Solon Barocas, Hal Daumé III, and Hanna Wallach. 2020. Language (Technology) is Power: A Critical Survey of "Bias" in NLP. In *Proceedings of the 58th Annual Meeting of the Association for Computational Linguistics*, pages 5454–5476.

Daniel Chen, Yosh Halberstam, and Alan CL Yu. 2016. Perceived masculinity predicts us supreme court outcomes. *PloS one*, 11(10):e0164324.

Daniel L Chen, Yosh Halberstam, Manoj Kumar, and Alan Yu. 2019. Attorney voice and the us supreme court. *Law as Data, Santa Fe Institute Press, ed. M. Livermore and D. Rockmore*.

Victor Chernozhukov, Denis Chetverikov, Mert Demirer, Esther Duflo, Christian Hansen, and Whitney Newey. 2017. Double/debiased/neyman machine learning of treatment effects. *American Economic Review*, 107(5):261–65.

Cristian Danescu-Niculescu-Mizil, Lillian Lee, Bo Pang, and Jon Kleinberg. 2012. Echoes of power: Language effects and power differences in social interaction. In *WWW*.

Rhian M. Daniel, Bianca L. De Stavola, SN Cousens, and Stijn Vansteelandt. 2015. Causal mediation analysis with multiple mediators. *Biometrics*, 71(1):1–14.

Kay Deaux. 1985. Sex and gender. *Annual review of psychology*, 36(1):49–81.

Matthew J. Denny and Arthur Spirling. 2018. Text preprocessing for unsupervised learning: Why it matters, when it misleads, and what to do about it. *Political Analysis*, 26(2):168–189.

Penelope Eckert. 2008. Variation and the indexical field 1. *Journal of sociolinguistics*, 12(4):453–476.

Naoki Egami, Christian J. Fong, Justin Grimmer, Margaret E. Roberts, and Brandon M. Stewart. 2018. How to make causal inferences using texts. *arXiv preprint arXiv:1802.02163*.

Matthew Finlayson, Aaron Mueller, Stuart Shieber, Sebastian Gehrmann, Tal Linzen, and Yonatan Belinkov. 2021. Causal analysis of syntactic agreement mechanisms in neural language models. In *ACL-IJCNLP*.

Shane A. Gleason. 2020. Beyond mere presence: Gender norms in oral arguments at the us supreme court. *Political Research Quarterly*, 73(3):596–608.

D. James Greiner and Donald B. Rubin. 2011. Causal effects of perceived immutable characteristics. *Review of Economics and Statistics*, 93(3):775–785.

Alex Hanna, Emily Denton, Andrew Smart, and Jamila Smith-Loud. 2020. Towards a critical race methodology in algorithmic fairness. In *Proceedings of the 2020 conference on fairness, accountability, and transparency*, pages 501–512.

Miguel A. Hernán. 2016. Does water kill? a call for less casual causal inferences. *Annals of epidemiology*, 26(10):674–680.

R. A. Hinde. 1976. Interactions, relationships and social structure. *Man*, 11(1):1–17.

Paul W. Holland. 1986. Statistics and causal inference. *Journal of the American statistical Association*, 81(396):945–960.

Paul W. Holland. 2008. Causation and race. *White logic, white methods: Racism and methodology*, pages 93–109.

Dirk Hovy, Federico Bianchi, and Tommaso Fornaciari. 2020. "You Sound Just Like Your Father" Commercial Machine Translation Systems Include Stylistic Biases. In *Proceedings of the 58th Annual Meeting of the Association for Computational Linguistics*, pages 1686–1690.

Lily Hu and Issa Kohler-Hausmann. 2020. What's sex got to do with machine learning? In *Proceedings of the 2020 Conference on Fairness, Accountability, and Transparency*, pages 513–513.

Kosuke Imai, Luke Keele, and Dustin Tingley. 2010. A general approach to causal mediation analysis. *Psychological methods*, 15(4):309.

Kosuke Imai and Teppei Yamamoto. 2013. Identification and sensitivity analysis for multiple causal mechanisms: Revisiting evidence from framing experiments. *Political Analysis*, 21(2):141–171.

Miyako Inoue. 2006. *Vicarious language*. University of California Press.

Tonja Jacobi and Dylan Schweers. 2017. Justice, interrupted: The effect of gender, ideology, and seniority at supreme court oral arguments. *Va. L. Rev.*, 103:1379.

Katherine Keith, David Jensen, and Brendan O'Connor. 2020. Text and Causal Inference: A Review of Using Text to Remove Confounding from Causal Estimates. In *Proceedings of the 58th Annual Meeting of the Association for Computational Linguistics*, pages 5332–5344.

Issa Kohler-Hausmann. 2018. Eddie Murphy and the dangers of counterfactual causal thinking about detecting racial discrimination. *Nw. UL Rev.*, 113:1163.

Robin Lakoff. 1973. Language and woman's place. *Language in society*, 2(1):45–79.

Juncen Li, Robin Jia, He He, and Percy Liang. 2018. Delete, retrieve, generate: a simple approach to sentiment and style transfer. In *Proceedings of the 2018 Conference of the North American Chapter of the Association for Computational Linguistics: Human Language Technologies, Volume 1 (Long Papers)*, pages 1865–1874.

Ian Lundberg, Rebecca Johnson, and Brandon M Stewart. 2021. What is your estimand? defining the target quantity connects statistical evidence to theory. *American Sociological Review*, 86(3):532–565.

Tali Mendelberg, Christopher F. Karpowitz, and J. Baxter Oliphant. 2014. Gender inequality in deliberation: Unpacking the black box of interaction. *Perspectives on Politics*, 12(1):18–44.

Stephen L. Morgan and Christopher Winship. 2015. *Counterfactuals and causal inference*. Cambridge University Press.

Kevin Munger. 2017. Tweetment effects on the tweeted: Experimentally reducing racist harassment. *Political Behavior*, 39(3):629–649.

Oyez. a. Kennedy v. Plan Administrator for DuPont Sav. and Investment Plan. Accessed 15 Jul. 2021.

Oyez. b. Lozano v. Montoya Alvarez. Accessed 15 Jul. 2021.

Dana Patton and Joseph L. Smith. 2017. Lawyer, interrupted: Gender bias in oral arguments at the US Supreme Court. *Journal of Law and Courts*, 5(2):337–361.

Judea Pearl. 2001. Direct and indirect effects. In *Proceedings of the Seventeenth conference on Uncertainty in artificial intelligence*, pages 411–420.

Judea Pearl. 2009. *Causality*. Cambridge university press.

Judea Pearl, Madelyn Glymour, and Nicholas P. Jewell. 2016. *Causal inference in statistics: A primer*. John Wiley & Sons.

Deanna Poos and Rita Simpson. 2002. Cross-disciplinary comparisons of hedging. *Using corpora to explore linguistic variation*, pages 3–23.

Shrimai Prabhumoye, Yulia Tsvetkov, Ruslan Salakhutdinov, and Alan W. Black. 2018. Style transfer through back-translation. In *Proceedings of the 56th Annual Meeting of the Association for Computational Linguistics (Volume 1: Long Papers)*, pages 866–876.

Anna Prokofieva and Julia Hirschberg. 2014. Hedging and speaker commitment. In *5th Intl. Workshop on Emotion, Social Signals, Sentiment & Linked Open Data, Reykjavik, Iceland.*

Reid Pryzant, Dallas Card, Dan Jurafsky, Victor Veitch, and Dhanya Sridhar. 2021. Causal effects of linguistic properties. In *Proceedings of the 2021 Conference of the North American Chapter of the Association for Computational Linguistics: Human Language Technologies*, Online. Association for Computational Linguistics.

Thomas S. Richardson and James M. Robins. 2013. Single world intervention graphs (SWIGs): A unification of the counterfactual and graphical approaches to causality. *Center for the Statistics and the Social Sciences, University of Washington Series. Working Paper 128.*

Margaret E. Roberts, Brandon M. Stewart, and Richard A. Nielsen. 2020. Adjusting for confounding with text matching. *American Journal of Political Science*, 64(4):887–903.

Jonathan Rosa and Nelson Flores. 2017. Unsettling race and language: Toward a raciolinguistic perspective. *Language in society*, 46(5):621–647.

Donald B. Rubin. 1974. Estimating causal effects of treatments in randomized and nonrandomized studies. *Journal of educational Psychology*, 66(5):688.

Donald B Rubin. 2008. For objective causal inference, design trumps analysis. *The Annals of Applied Statistics*, 2(3):808–840.

Alexandra Schofield, Måns Magnusson, and David Mimno. 2017. Pulling out the stops: Rethinking stopword removal for topic models. In *Proceedings of the 15th Conference of the European Chapter of the Association for Computational Linguistics: Volume 2, Short Papers*, pages 432–436.

Maya Sen and Omar Wasow. 2016. Race as a bundle of sticks: Designs that estimate effects of seemingly immutable characteristics. *Annual Review of Political Science*, 19:499–522.

Uri Shalit, Fredrik D Johansson, and David Sontag. 2017. Estimating individual treatment effect: generalization bounds and algorithms. In *International Conference on Machine Learning*, pages 3076–3085. PMLR.

Harold J. Spaeth, Lee Epstein, Andrew D. Martin, Jeffrey A. Segal, Theodore J. Ruger, and Sara C. Benesh. 2021. Supreme Court Database, Version 2021 Release 01. *Database at http://scdb.wustl.edu/.*

Jennifer Stromer-Galley. 2007. Measuring deliberation's content: A coding scheme. *Journal of public deliberation*, 3(1).

Elizabeth A. Stuart. 2010. Matching methods for causal inference: A review and a look forward. *Statistical science: a review journal of the Institute of Mathematical Statistics*, 25(1):1.

Dustin Tingley, Teppei Yamamoto, Kentaro Hirose, Luke Keele, and Kosuke Imai. 2014. Mediation: R package for causal mediation analysis.

Mark J. Van der Laan and Sherri Rose. 2011. *Targeted learning: causal inference for observational and experimental data.* Springer Science & Business Media.

Tyler VanderWeele and Stijn Vansteelandt. 2014. Mediation analysis with multiple mediators. *Epidemiologic methods*, 2(1):95–115.

Tyler J. VanderWeele. 2016. Mediation analysis: a practitioner's guide. *Annual review of public health*, 37:17–32.

Victor Veitch, Dhanya Sridhar, and David Blei. 2020. Adapting text embeddings for causal inference. In *Conference on Uncertainty in Artificial Intelligence*, pages 919–928. PMLR.

Jesse Vig, Sebastian Gehrmann, Yonatan Belinkov, Sharon Qian, Daniel Nevo, Yaron Singer, and Stuart M Shieber. 2020. Investigating gender bias in language models using causal mediation analysis. In *NeurIPS*.

Rob Voigt, Nicholas P. Camp, Vinodkumar Prabhakaran, William L. Hamilton, Rebecca C. Hetey, Camilla M. Griffiths, David Jurgens, Dan Jurafsky, and Jennifer L. Eberhardt. 2017. Language from police body camera footage shows racial disparities in officer respect. *Proceedings of the National Academy of Sciences*, 114(25):6521–6526.

Candace West and Don H. Zimmerman. 1987. Doing gender, gender and society. *Vol. 1, No. 2.(Jun*, page 125.

Zach Wood-Doughty, Ilya Shpitser, and Mark Dredze. 2018. Challenges of using text classifiers for causal inference. In *Proceedings of the Conference on Empirical Methods in Natural Language Processing. Conference on Empirical Methods in Natural Language Processing*, volume 2018, page 4586. NIH Public Access.

Justine Zhang, Sendhil Mullainathan, and Cristian Danescu-Niculescu-Mizil. 2020. Quantifying the causal effects of conversational tendencies. *Proceedings of the ACM on Human-Computer Interaction*, 4(CSCW2):1–24.

Enhancing Model Robustness and Fairness with Causality: A Regularization Approach

Zhao Wang
University of Chicago
zwang13@uchicago.edu

Kai Shu
Illinois Institute of Technology
kshu@iit.edu

Aron Culotta
Tulane University
aculotta@tulane.edu

Abstract

Recent work has raised concerns on the risk of spurious correlations and unintended biases in statistical machine learning models that threaten model robustness and fairness. In this paper, we propose a simple and intuitive regularization approach to integrate causal knowledge during model training and build a robust and fair model by emphasizing causal features and de-emphasizing spurious features. Specifically, we first manually identify causal and spurious features with principles inspired from the counterfactual framework of causal inference. Then, we propose a regularization approach to penalize causal and spurious features separately. By adjusting the strength of the penalty for each type of feature, we build a predictive model that relies more on causal features and less on non-causal features. We conduct experiments to evaluate model robustness and fairness on three datasets with multiple metrics. Empirical results show that the new models built with causal awareness significantly improve model robustness with respect to counterfactual texts and model fairness with respect to sensitive attributes.

1 Introduction

Modern machine learning models are becoming increasingly successful and are widely used in high-stake applications such as filtering loan applicants (Hassani, 2020), determining school admissions (Alvero et al., 2020), and medical diagnosis (Ahuja, 2019), etc. However, a big challenge for statistical machine learning is that the models are data-driven and usually built on statistical correlations that are sometimes spurious. For example, a sentiment classifier trained on IMDB movie reviews predicts *"the film directed by Spielberg is incredibly interesting"* as positive. While the prediction is correct, the model takes *"Spielberg"* as a highly predictive feature, that is learned to be strongly correlated with positive sentiment during model training. This is a spurious correlation

the film directed by	*Spielberg*	*is incredibly*	*interesting*	.
	0.712		0.576	
	0.290		0.874	

Table 1: The motivating example: the traditional classifier (1st row) learns spurious correlation between *Spielberg* and positive sentiment and assigns a large weight for the spurious feature. Our regularization approach (2nd row) encourages the model to assign a smaller weight for the spurious feature and a larger weight for the causal feature (*interesting*).

since an annotator won't label a review as positive just because it mentions *"Spielberg"*. A classifier built on this spurious correlation might perform well when the testing data has the same distribution as training data (i.e., positive reviews talking about *"Spielberg"*), however, it is very likely to fail when there's a distribution shift in testing data (i.e., negative reviews talking about *"Spielberg"*). For another example, a classifier trained on school admission data learns the *"gender"* attribute to be predictive of admission status. The classifier learns this correlation because the *"gender"* attribute happens to correlate with admission in the training data that might contain discrimination and societal bias. Such a biased classifier will raise issues of discrimination when deployed in the real world. In the above examples, the spurious correlations are built in the model because those features happen to correlate with a specific class in the training data, but model designers do not want such features to carry predictive power in the model because that will make the model suffer from robustness (e.g., fail on different distributions), fairness (e.g., bias towards specific groups), and trustworthiness (e.g., not convincing when explaining model performance).

Existing works have investigated multiple ways to deal with spurious correlations and improve model robustness and fairness, such as feature selection (Paul, 2017; Wang and Culotta, 2020), data augmentation (Kaushik et al., 2020; Wang

Proceedings of CI+NLP: First Workshop on Causal Inference and NLP, pages 33–43
November 10, 2021.

and Culotta, 2021), instance re-weighting (Zhang et al., 2020), counterfactual logit pairing (Garg et al., 2019), control for confounders (Landeiro and Culotta, 2018), apply constraints to design fair and robust objective functions (Dwork et al., 2012; Zhao et al., 2021). Recent works also explore causal inference for robust and fair models, such as leveraging human commonsense of causal reasoning (Srivastava et al., 2020), adapting text embeddings for causal inference (Veitch et al., 2020), and providing causal views on robustness of neural networks (Zhang and Li, 2020). While effective, most works only deal with either fairness or robustness, some works require significant human efforts, some have trade-offs between model robustness and overall performance on test set, and some are complex to deploy in real-world applications.

In this paper, we propose a simple and intuitive regularization approach to integrate causal knowledge in model training. We assign large regularization penalties on spurious features and small penalties on causal features (i.e., features that cause a sample to get a label). By doing so, we encourage the model to pay less attention to spurious features and more to causal features. Table 1 demonstrates a motivating example, where a traditional sentiment classifier (such as Logistic Regression) assigns a large weight for the spurious feature *"Spielberg (0.874)"* and a small weight for the causal feature *"interesting (0.576)"*. The new classifier built with our regularization approach decreases the weight of the spurious feature and increases the weight of the causal feature.

Specifically, we first manually identify causal and spurious features based on criteria motivated by the counterfactual framework of causal inference. Then, we incorporate regularization components to add different penalties for different types of features. By adjusting the strength of the penalty for each type of feature and optimizing the customized loss function, we build a model that assigns larger weights to causal features and smaller weights to non-causal features. Finally, we carry out experiments to test whether our approach improves model robustness and fairness. For model robustness, we experiment with IMDB movie reviews and Kindle book reviews text data. We evaluate the model performance on both the standard test set as well as a counterfactual test set. Results show that our models significantly improves robustness on the counterfactual test set compared to the traditional models (e.g., 12% increase in accuracy for the best model). For model fairness, we experiment with the law school admission dataset and evaluate with two metrics (i.e, equal opportunity and demographic parity). Our models show more fair performance than the traditional model (e.g., females and males almost get equal opportunity and demographic parity in the best model). With this framing, the main contributions of this paper are as follows:

Method: We propose a simple and novel regularization approach to integrate causality during model training. By constructing and optimizing the customized loss function that adjusts the penalty for causal and spurious features, we build predictive models that pay more attention to causal features and less to non-causal features.

Evaluation: We evaluate our proposed models on both robustness (with high-dimensional text data) and fairness (with low-dimensional tabular data). Our models outperform multiple baselines in terms of robustness to counterfactual texts and fairness to sensitive attributes, without sacrificing model performance on test set.

2 Related Work

As the main causes for fairness and robustness issues in ML, biases and spurious correlations can be introduced from multiple sources such as culture, data, and algorithm perspectives. Examples include societal discrimination and bias (Mehrabi et al., 2021; Yapo and Weiss, 2018), data imbalance, sampling bias, data poisoning (Zhao et al., 2018; Kiritchenko and Mohammad, 2018; Chen et al., 2017); covariate shift and confounders (Landeiro and Culotta, 2018), over-parameterization (Sagawa et al., 2020b,a).

Fairness in ML can be summarized as individual fairness (Lahoti et al., 2019), group fairness (Hardt et al., 2016), and max-min fairness (Lahoti et al., 2020). Related research typically falls into three categories based on the stage at which fairness is applied: (1) pre-processing: modify training data and revise sensitive attributes (Kamiran and Calders, 2011), generate balanced data, increase data diversity (Xu et al., 2018), instance reweighting (Zhang et al., 2020); (2) in-processing: apply fairness constraints (regularizations) to design objective functions (Dwork et al., 2012; Zhao et al., 2021), adversarially learn fair representations (Beutel et al., 2017); (3) post-processing: use active learning to collect feedbacks and correct predictions (Zaidan et al., 2007). Here we focus on group fairness with respect to sensitive attributes.

Robustness in ML-based NLP models: Ribeiro et al. (2020) propose CheckList to identify critical model failures with diverse types of test cases; Garg et al. (2019) introduce hard ablation, blindness, and counterfactual logit pairing to improve counterfactual token fairness. Kaushik et al. (2020) do counterfactual data augmentmentation to improve model robustness. Lu et al. (2020) create gender-balanced dataset to learn embeddings that mitigate gender stereotypes. Others explore robust optimization, adversarial training, and domain adaptation methods to improve model robustness (Namkoong and Duchi, 2016; Beutel et al., 2017; Ben-David et al., 2006).

Recent research draws connections between robustness and causal inference in text. Keith et al. (2020) and Wood-Doughty et al. (2018) provide detailed overviews. The works closely related to this paper include: achieving robustness by leveraging human commonsense and counterfactual reasoning (Srivastava et al., 2020), adopting active learning and feedback mechanism to highlight rationales (Zaidan et al., 2007), automatically generating counterfactuals with causal words (Wang and Culotta, 2021), applying causal inference for feature selection in text classification (Paul, 2017; Wang and Culotta, 2020), controlling for confounders (Landeiro and Culotta, 2018). Additional works integrate causal inference in text representation and deep learning, such as causal embedding (Veitch et al., 2020) and causal view on robustness of neural networks (Zhang and Li, 2020).

Our proposed approach is inherently different from the aforementioned approaches: (1) We propose a general regularization approach to achieve robustness and fairness with causality. While previous works have shown the ability to improve model fairness and robustness, most of them only deal with either fairness (to sensitive attributes) or robustness (to counterfactual examples); (2) Our proposed regularization approach is effective (with high prediction performance), efficient (requires little human annotation), and explainable (larger weights for causal features).

3 Problem Definition

Our primary task is given input x, where x is represented by a sequence of features $[x_1, x_2, ..., x_n]$, to predict an outcome y. We consider the case of a classifier f parameterized by w that produces a prediction $\hat{y} = f_w(x)$. The parameters w are learned during model training by optimizing (minimizing) the loss denoted by the error between y and $\hat{y}$.

To clearly illustrate the problem addressed in this paper, we first consider the simple approach of logistic regression classifier $f_w(x) = \frac{1}{1+e^{-\langle x,w\rangle}}$ (§6.2 discusses applying other complex models). We estimate the parameters w on labeled data $\mathcal{X}$ and then examine the (partial) correlations between features and labels by model coefficients (i.e., feature weights).

The goal is to train a model that performs well on test set and generalizes well on data from different distributions, so that the model maintains robustness to counterfactual data as well as fairness to sensitive attributes (e.g., gender, race).

3.1 Robustness to Counterfactuals

We measure model robustness on counterfactual samples. If a model is built on spurious correlations, its performance might not drop on a test set that has the same distribution as the training set, but the performance will drop sharply on the counterfactual set, which is created by editing samples from the test set towards a counterfactual label.

Taking text classification as an example, for a piece of text T, the corresponding counterfactual sample is created by editing T with minimum changes towards a counterfactual label (Kaushik et al., 2020). For example, for the positive review *"the film directed by Spielberg is incredibly interesting"*, the counterfactual negative review is *"the film directed by Spielberg is incredibly boring"*. If the classifier is built on spurious correlations such as the correlation between *"Spielberg"* and positive sentiment, it is very likely to make wrong predictions for the counterfactual sentences (e.g., negative reviews talking about *"Spielberg"*), which makes the classifier suffer from robustness on counterfactual data. However, if the classifier is built on causal associations such as the association between *"interesting"* and positive sentiment or *"boring"* and negative sentiment, the model will make right predictions for the counterfactual sentences and for datasets that have different distributions.

3.2 Fairness to Sensitive Attributes

Studies have shown that when there are patterns of previous discrimination and societal bias in the training data, the trained model is very likely to inherit the bias (Mehrabi et al., 2021; Yapo and Weiss, 2018). In this paper, we study group fairness with respect to sensitive attributes (e.g., gender, race). The goal is to train a model that ensures members of protected groups in the population (e.g., based on sensitive demographic attributes like gender or race) receive "fair share of beneficial outcomes" during model prediction (Hardt et al., 2016).

Taking the law school admission data as an example, we want to train a classifier that is fair to populations of different identity groups defined by sensitive attributes (e.g., gender, race). If the classifier is built on features such as test scores for the admission decision, the model should make fair predictions for applicants from different identity groups. However, if the classifier is built on biased correlations such as using *"gender"* as a predictive feature for the admission decision, it could potentially harm end-users who identify with those groups and cause ethical concerns.

In this work, we study group fairness with the low-dimensional law school admission data and it's possible to extend the proposed approach to high-dimensional text data with additional text processing. For example, in the task of toxicity prediction of online comments, we can first categorize the comments into different identity groups according to the sensitive attributes they describe (e.g., race, sexual orientation), and then improve classifier fairness with respect to the protected groups using our regularization approach. One big difference between studying fairness with low-dimensional tabular data (e.g., law school admission data) and high-dimensional text data is that for low-dimensional data, we directly identify the sensitive attributes as spurious features, but for text data, we need to identify keywords that are descriptive of sensitive attributes as spurious features (e.g., "black" and "white" are reflective of race, "gay" and "straight" are reflective of sexual orientation). We will take this as our future work.

4 Methods

To build a model that is robust to counterfactuals and fair to sensitive attributes, we need to deal with issues of spurious correlations and biases. Our solution is a two-stage process. We first manually identify causal and spurious features based on the criteria motivated by the counterfactual framework of causal inference. We then propose a regularization approach to build a loss function that adds small penalties for causal features and large penalties for spurious features. By doing so, the model is encouraged to rely more on meaningful causal associations and less on spurious correlations.

4.1 Annotate Causal and Spurious Features

Consider an instance x represented by a sequence of features $[x_1, x_2, ..., x_n]$ and having the label y. We identify causal and spurious features by using the counterfactual framework of causal inference (Winship and Morgan, 1999): if feature x_i were replaced with some other feature x_j, how likely is it that the label y would change? In this paper, we consider short texts (e.g., single sentences) and low-dimensional tabular data as the unit of analysis, and the following criteria is proposed for this type of data.

A *causal feature* is a feature x_i that causes the sample x to receive the label y. All else being equal, one would expect x_i to be a determining factor in assigning y to sample x. On the other hand, a *spurious feature* is a feature x_i that correlates with the target class y in a specific dataset, but replacing it with another feature x_j would be unlikely to change the instance label.

Taking a movie review sentence as an example, *"the film directed by Spielberg is incredibly interesting" (pos)*, "interesting" is a causal feature that is primarily responsible for the positive sentiment and replacing it with another word such as "boring" will change the sentiment to be negative. In contrast, "Spielberg" is a spurious feature as it does not convey positive sentiment nor cause a review to be positive, and replacing it with another word such as "Kevin" will not change the sentiment. Although "Spielberg" might correlate with positive sentiment due to its high frequency in positive movie reviews, this statistical correlation does not imply causality.

With the proposed criteria, we manually annotate causal and spurious features in §5.2. Table 2 shows examples of those features identified for sentiment classification and school admission tasks.

Prior works have explored methods that automatically identify causal and spurious features. For example, Wu et al. (2021) design Polyjuice as a general-purpose counterfactual generator that allows for control over multiple perturbation types and the generated counterfactuals are application agnostic. Wang and Culotta (2020) propose to fit a

	Causal	Spurious
Sentiment Classification	interesting boring wonderful inspiring enjoyed	movie story Spielberg definitely animated
School Admission	LSAT GPA	Gender Race

Table 2: Examples of causal and spurious features

classifier for auto-prediction of causal and spurious features using information such as word embeddings and individual treatment effects. Wang and Culotta (2021) propose a closest opposite matching approach for auto-identification of likely causal features. While these methods work well in general, each has its drawbacks. In this paper, we want to focus on the regularization effect and isolate the noises introduced by other procedures, so we manually annotate causal and spurious features as ground truth.

4.2 Regularization with Causal and Spurious Features

Our goal is to train a model that performs well on test data (that has the same distribution as training set) as well as maintains robustness to counterfactuals and fairness to sensitive attributes. Prior works (Kaushik et al., 2020; Wang and Culotta, 2021) have demonstrated the effectiveness of augmenting training data with counterfactuals to improve model robustness. Wang and Culotta (2021) conducted empirical analysis to compare the difference between a traditional model and a robust model, finding that the robust model assigns larger weights for causal features and smaller weights for spurious features.

While previous works have explored the effectiveness of adding L2/L1 penalty (regularization) to prevent over-fitting (Ng, 2004), the penalty is applied on all features. In this paper, we design a customized loss function that adds different penalties for different types of features (e.g, causal, spurious, and the remaining). The intuition is that when tuning a classifier, we want it to pay more attention to causal features (small penalty) and less attention to spurious features (large penalty). Below we consider three sets of features: causal (C), spurious (S), and remain (R, i.e., features except for those labeled as causal or spurious).

Let J be the loss function representing the error/difference between the truth and prediction. To add different penalties for causal, spurious, and remaining features separately, we design the loss function as:

$$\sum_{x \in X} J(f(x), y) + \frac{\lambda_c}{|C|} \sum_{c \in C} {w_c}^2 + \frac{\lambda_s}{|S|} \sum_{s \in S} {w_s}^2 + \frac{\lambda_r}{|R|} \sum_{r \in R} {w_r}^2 \tag{1}$$

where λ_c, λ_s, and λ_r refer to the strength of penalty for causal, spurious, and remaining features; $|C|$, $|S|$, and $|R|$ refer to the size of corresponding feature set; w_c, w_s, and w_r refer to the weights of features from each set.

There are many variations of this loss function. For example, we can set $\lambda_c = 0$ and $\lambda_r = 0$ to only penalize spurious features. We can also set $\lambda_c = 0$ to only penalize non-causal features (i.e., a combination of spurious and remain features).

The primary advantage of this approach is that it integrates causal knowledge into model training and provides the flexibility to penalize and address the importance of different types of features. By optimizing the proposed loss function, we seek to build classifiers that satisfy two desirable properties: (1) perform well on testing data and (2) pay more attention to causal features and less to spurious/non-causal features, which is the key to make the model robust and fair on data from different distributions.

5 Experiments

We conduct experiments with three datasets to evaluate the effectiveness of the proposed method from two aspects[1]: robustness to counterfactuals (evaluate on high-dimensional text data from IMDB movie reviews and Kindle book reviews) and fairness to sensitive attributes (evaluate on low-dimensional tabular data of law school admission).

5.1 Data

IMDB movie reviews: This dataset is collected and published by Kaushik et al. (2020). They first randomly sampled $2.5K$ reviews with balanced class distributions from the original large IMDB movie reviews dataset (Pang and Lee, 2005) and then instruct Amazon Mechanical Turk workers to

[1]Code and data available at: `https://github.com/tapilab/emnlp-2021-regularization`

edit each review with minimum changes towards a counterfactual label. In the final dataset, every review gets a corresponding counterfactual text. We apply the data splitting criteria from the paper and the train/validation/test sets contain 1,707/245/488 samples. The counterfactual test set is created by counterfactually editing samples from the test set.

Kindle book reviews: This dataset[2] contains book reviews from the Amazon Kindle store (He and McAuley, 2016) and each review is labeled as positive or negative based on its rating (ratings {4,5} as positive and ratings {1,2} as negative). To reduce noisy samples, we limit the reviews to those contain 5 to 40 words and the final dataset is split into train/validation/test sets containing 7,500/2,500/500 samples. For the 500 test samples, we manually edit each sample with minimum changes towards a counterfactual label (i.e., the same criteria used in (Kaushik et al., 2020) to edit counterfactuals for IMDB reviews above).

Law school admission data: This dataset contains admission data of 25 US law schools over 2005-2007[3]. Each sample is an admission record for a student and is represented by seven features: LSAT, GPA, resident, admission year, gender, race, URM (under-represented minority), with a binary label indicating the admission status. The dataset is split into train/validation/test sets containing 50%, 20%, and 30% samples.

For the IMDB and Kindle datasets, each sample x is a piece of text, represented by a binary, bag-of-words representation $x = [x_1, x_2, ..., x_v]$, where v is the vocabulary size and x_i is a binary value indicating the appearance of a word in the text. Compared with the high-dimensional text data, the law school admission data is low-dimension with each sample represented by seven numerical or categorical features. We process this dataset by first applying one-hot encoding for categorical features and then normalizing numerical features into range 0-1. In the experiments below, we show that our method works well on both high- and low-dimensional data.

5.2 Causal and Spurious Features

With the criteria proposed in 4.1, we ask two student annotators to manually label causal and spurious features from each dataset. Specifically,

[2]https://jmcauley.ucsd.edu/data/amazon/

[3]http://www.seaphe.org/databases.php

	IMDB	Kindle	Admission
#Instances	2.5k	10.5k	65.3k
#Features	2,388	2,041	7
#Causal(top)	65	76	2
#Spurious(top)	166	118	1
#Causal(vocabulary)	362	293	2

Table 3: Data summary

for each dataset, we first train an initial classifier and extract top coefficient features (e.g. coefficient magnitude > 1). For example, for logistic regression model, we would extract features with high magnitude coefficients. For more complex models, other transparency algorithms may be used (Martens and Provost, 2014).

For the IMDB and Kindle datasets, the annotators identified two sets of causal and spurious features: the first set is annotated from the top coefficient features and the second set is annotated from the whole vocabulary (the first set is a subset of the second set). While there is some subjectivity during annotation, we did a round of training to resolve disagreements prior to annotation and the final agreement was generally high for the experimental datasets (on average 96% raw agreement by fraction of labels that agree).

For the law school admission dataset, there are only seven features and the annotators directly identify *"LSAT"* and *"GPA"* as causal features and *"gender"* as a spurious feature (i.e., sensitive attribute). There are other spurious features such as *"race"* and *"URM"*, but for this paper, we only focus on model fairness with respect to gender (to have a direct comparison with previous work), so we identify *"gender"* as a spurious feature and take other potential spurious features as "remaining" features.

Table 3 summarizes the number of identified causal and spurious features for each dataset.

5.3 Experimental Settings

Among the numerous works focused on improving model robustness to counterfactuals, the ones most closely related to ours include: augmenting training data with counterfactuals to train a robust classifier (Kaushik et al., 2020; Wang and Culotta, 2021); a logit pairing strategy to penalize the norm of difference in logits of training examples and their counterfactuals (Garg et al., 2019); causal inference for feature selection (Paul, 2017); a feature selection strategy to remove spurious features and improve model robustness with respect to the worst-case accuracy (Wang and Culotta, 2020).

Method		IMDB Test	CTF		Kindle Test	CTF
Feature selection		0.835 ± 0.005	0.633 ± 0.012		0.850 ± 0.002	0.510 ± 0.017
Data augmentation		0.818	0.869		0.752	0.720
L2 with BOW		0.845 ± 0.005	0.567 ± 0.009		0.853 ± 0.027	0.412 ± 0.048
L2 with Glove		0.824 ± 0.002	0.619 ± 0.006		0.820 ± 0.004	0.553 ± 0.027
Regularization (*top*)	$\lambda_c, \lambda_s, \lambda_r$			$\lambda_c, \lambda_s, \lambda_r$		
causal+spurious	(0,10,0)	0.836 ± 0.006	0.632 ± 0.005	(0,10,0)	0.857 ± 0.007	0.545 ± 0.013
causal+non-causal	(0,100,100)	0.821 ± 0.011	0.658 ± 0.01	(0,10,10)	0.843 ± 0.003	0.557 ± 0.003
causal+spurious+remain	(0,100,0.1)	0.841 ± 0.007	0.635 ± 0.006	(0,100,1)	0.847 ± 0.003	0.571 ± 0.008
Regularization (*vocab*)						
causal+spurious	(0,10,0)	0.838 ± 0.004	0.634 ± 0.007	(0,100,0)	0.857 ± 0.003	0.545 ± 0.01
causal+non-causal	(0,100,100)	0.843 ± 0.005	0.700 ± 0.007	(0,10,10)	0.855 ± 0.005	0.641 ± 0.006
causal+spurious+remain	(0.01,100,100)	0.840 ± 0.004	0.697 ± 0.008	(0.001,1,10)	0.848 ± 0.006	0.636 ± 0.003

Table 4: Robustness evaluation for tuned classifiers. Accuracy reported for test and Counterfactual (CTF) data from IMDB and Kindle dataset. Results in 1st section are baseline and state-of-the-art methods, 2nd section shows regularization approach using causal features identified from top coefficient terms and 3rd section shows regularization approach using causal features identified from the whole vocabulary.

We compare our proposed regularization approach with the representative and state-of-the-art prior works:

- **Feature Selection** (Wang and Culotta, 2020): we explore whether directly removing spurious features is more effective than penalizing spurious features with regularization approach.
- **Data Augmentation** (Wang and Culotta, 2021): Augmenting original training data with corresponding counterfactual data (either automatically generated or manually edited). This method combines counterfactuals as part of the training data and changes data distribution and data size. It usually requires significant human efforts to generate/edit counterfactuals.

For our proposed regularization approach, we experiment with the LogisticRegression classifier and explore the following settings:

- **L2-regularization**: as representative of the traditional regularization approach.
- **Feature representation for text**: we explore Bag-Of-Words (BOW) and pre-trained Glove embedding (Pennington et al., 2014) representations to check whether complex representations help improve robustness.
- **The number of causal and spurious features**: we experiment with two sets of causal and spurious features: (a) a small set identified from top coefficient features and (b) a full set identified from the whole vocabulary. The goal is to check whether providing more causal features improves model robustness.

Hyper-parameter tuning: we use BinaryCrossEntropy as the basic loss function in all models and implement the regularization approach by customizing the loss function with penalties for causal, spurious, and remaining features as discussed in §4.2. The penalty strengths (i.e., $\lambda_c, \lambda_s, \lambda_r$) are explored in the range [0, 0.0001, 0.001, 0.01, 0.1, 1, 10, 100, 1000] with the constraint that $l_s \geq l_r > l_c$. We use Adam optimizer and set the initial learning rate to 0.001, and adjust the learning rate according to different λ values to avoid overshooting. We use early stopping criteria on validation data to determine the epoch to stop tuning (i.e., stop tuning if the validation loss hasn't decreased for 10 epochs). Among all the tuned models, we select the best model based on its performance on the counterfactual validation data.

After selecting the best model, we evaluate its performance on the test set and counterfactual set. We repeat the training process 10 times with different random seeds and report the model performance and corresponding hyper-parameter settings in Table 4. All experiments are conducted on a 64-bit machine with Nvidia GPU (Tesla V100, 1246MHz, 16 GB memory).

5.4 Robustness Evaluation

We evaluate model robustness on the counterfactual texts from IMDB and Kindle datasets. We train different models by optimizing the customized loss functions suggested in §4.2 and evaluate model performance on the test set and counterfactual set. The best model parameter setting and performance is reported in Table 4.

Results show that: (1) our proposed regularization approach outperforms feature selection on the counterfactual test set without sacrificing performance on the test set; data augmentation outperforms our regularization approach on the counterfactual set but sacrifices performance on the test set, which is expected because data augmentation approach increased training data size and changed training data distribution. And data augmentation usually requires more human efforts than our regularization approach. (2) separately penalizing causal, spurious, and remaining features is more effective than L2 regularization in terms of model robustness on counterfactual set. The best performance is achieved by assigning no/small penalty for causal features and large penalties for spurious and remaining features; (3) the more causal features provided, the better robustness on counterfactual set. For IMDB, the best model gives 9% improvement with top causal features and 13.3% with all causal features. For Kindle, the best model gives 15.9% improvement with top causal features and 22.9% with all causal features; (4) complex text representation (e.g., embedding) has limited improvements on model robustness.

Note that the results and parameter settings in Table 4 are based on the exploration of penalty strengths (i.e.,λ_c, λ_s, λ_r) in the range of [0, 0.0001, 0.001, 0.01, 0.1, 1, 10, 100, 1000]. The best parameter settings might change for different datasets and larger search space. According to our exploration about the effect of hyperparameter λ on model performance in §6.1, we recommend to set $\lambda_c <= 0.01$, $\lambda_s >= 1$, and $\lambda_r >= 1$ for experiments on new datasets that don't have counterfactual validation set to decide the best hyperparameter setting. As a reference, when we fix $\lambda_c = 0$, $\lambda_s = 100$, and $\lambda_r = 10$ for all datasets, the accuracy is within 97% of the best found setting.

We also show the percentage of causal features among top-n large coefficient features of each model in Fig 1. Top features are features that are most important and predictive of the classes, and a high percentage of causal features means that the model relies more on causal features and less on others. We can see that models tuned from our proposed loss functions have much higher percentage of causal features compared with the baselines (L2 and feature selection). The model that only considers causal and spurious features has a relative lower percentage compared with the other two models that consider causal, spurious, and remaining features. Taking the model that separately penalizes causal and non-causal features for an example (IMDB), all features in the top-10 and top-30 are causal features, and about 93% of top-50 and 70% of top-100 are causal features. The difference is even bigger for the Kindle dataset. However, for the baseline models, the percentage is much lower. The high percentage of causal features indicates that our regularization approach successfully makes the model rely more on causal features.

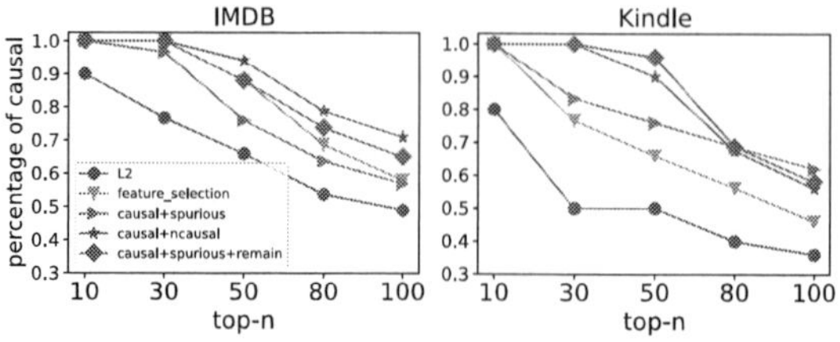

Figure 1: Percentage of causal features among the top-n features of each model. The three models tuned with penalties for causal, spurious, and remain features refer to the models shown in the last three lines in Table 4 (*best viewed with color*).

5.5 Fairness Evaluation

We experiment with law school admission dataset and ask the question:"does a model trained on this dataset makes fair admission predictions for female and male students?" We apply the same baseline and training procedure described in §5.4 with *"LSAT"* and *"GPA"* as causal features and *"gender"* as spurious feature (i.e., sensitive attribute). Following existing work on fairness evaluation (Zhao et al., 2021), we adopt two widely used evaluation metrics, equal opportunity and demographic parity.

Equal opportunity evaluates whether a classifier gives similar results for different sensitive groups in the positive class (Verma and Rubin, 2018; Hardt et al., 2016; Yan et al., 2020). We calculate equal opportunity difference Δ_{EO} to measure whether a classifier is fair for gender attribute:

$$\begin{aligned}\Delta_{EO} = |&Pr\{\hat{y} = 1|S = i, y = 1\} \\ &-Pr\{\hat{y} = 1|S = j, y = 1\}|\end{aligned} \tag{2}$$

where S is sensitive attribute, i and j are sensitive attribute values defined by S (e.g, male and female defined by gender), and y is the truth label.

In our experiment with law school admission data, if a model is fair, then the probability of an applicant being predicted to be admitted ($\hat{y} = 1$) should be the same for both male ($S = i$) and female ($S = j$) applicants that are actually being admitted ($y = 1$).

Penalty	$\lambda_c, \lambda_s, \lambda_r$	accuracy	f1	Δ_{EO}	Δ_{DP}
L2 (baseline)	N/A	0.796 ± 0.001	0.650 ± 0.012	0.102 ± 0.003	0.028 ± 0.001
causal+spurious	(0.0001,10,0)	0.795 ± 0.003	0.654 ± 0.011	0.023 ± 0.005	0.007 ± 0.001
causal + non-causal	(0.0001,0.001,0.001)	0.796 ± 0.001	0.655 ± 0.012	0.100 ± 0.006	0.027 ± 0.001
causal+spurious+remain	(0.0001,0.1,0.01)	0.794 ± 0.003	0.646 ± 0.01	0.028 ± 0.005	0.004 ± 0.002
FairRF (Zhao et al., 2021)	N/A	0.796 ± 0.002	N/A	0.023 ± 0.008	0.007 ± 0.004

Table 5: Tuned classifier performance on law school admission test set and fairness evaluation

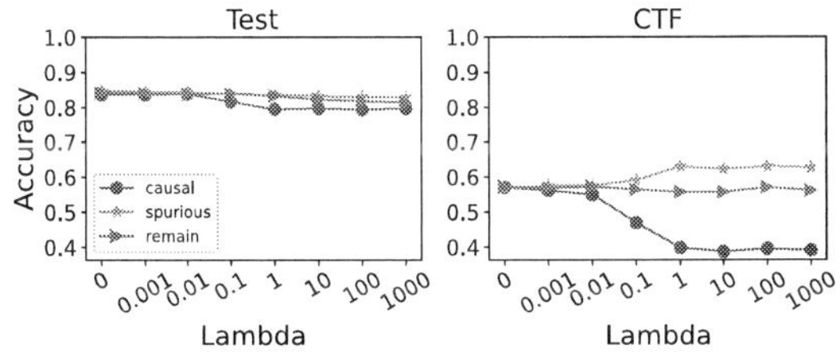

Figure 2: Model performance change with lambda (IMDB) (*best viewed with color*).

Demographic Parity measures non- discriminative performance of a classifier. We calculate demographic parity difference Δ_{DP} to check whether a classifier is fair for different sensitive groups:

$$\begin{aligned}\Delta_{DP} = Pr\{\hat{y} = 1 | S = i\} \\ - Pr\{\hat{y} = 1 | S = j\}\end{aligned} \tag{3}$$

We report the evaluation results from the best model and corresponding model parameters in Table 5. Results show that: (1) the model trained with our regularization approach is more fair with respect to the gender attribute and has comparable performance with previous work using complex models (Zhao et al., 2021); (2) model fairness is achieved by assigning small/no penalties for causal features and large penalties for non-causal features, which is similar as achieving robustness.

6 Discussion

6.1 The Effect of Hyperparameter λ

To understand the effect of λ_c, λ_s, and λ_r on model performance, we conduct experiments to first initialize λ to 0, and then change the value of each λ (Fig 2). We observe that: (1) model performance on test set is relatively stable with different λ parameters; (2) model performance on counterfactual set is mainly affected by λ_c. By increasing λ_c, we assign larger penalty on causal features and the model performance drops. In contrast, by increasing λ_s, we assign larger penalty on spurious features and the model performance increases. Penalizing causal features affects model performance more than penalizing spurious features, and penalizing remaining features has the least effect.

6.2 Extension in Deep Learning Framework

In the experiments, we use LogisticRegression as our basic classifier because it's intuitive to explain feature weights and penalties. But our main idea is to integrate causality in model training by adding small penalties to causal features and large penalties to non-causal features, and the loss function is not limited to any specific model, so we do think that our approach can be extended to more complex models. For example, possible ways to apply the idea to LSTM classifiers include: (1) assign different attentions for causal, spurious, and remaining features in the input; (2) specify different probabilities to mask out or drop out spurious and causal feature. We leave this part as our future work.

7 Conclusions

In this paper, we have introduced the idea of integrating causal knowledge through a regularization approach. We implement this by first identifying causal and spurious features and then assigning different penalties for causal and non-causal features in the loss function. The resulting model assigns larger weights for causal features and smaller weights for spurious features. Experiments have demonstrated that the tuned model is effective to improve robustness and fairness and it works well for both low- and high- dimensional data. The proposed idea is simple to implement, intuitive to explain, has the potential to be easily deployed to other frameworks and various tasks on model robustness and fairness. For future works, we will design automatic methods to identify causal and spurious features and extend the regularization approach to complex deep learning frameworks.

Acknowledgments

This research was funded in part by the National Science Foundation under grant #1618244. We would also like to thank the anonymous reviewers for useful feedbacks.

References

A. Ahuja. 2019. The impact of artificial intelligence in medicine on the future role of physician. *PeerJ*, 7.

A.J. Alvero, Noah Arthurs, anthony lising antonio, Benjamin W. Domingue, Ben Gebre-Medhin, Sonia Giebel, and Mitchell L. Stevens. 2020. Ai and holistic review: Informing human reading in college admissions. In *Proceedings of the AAAI/ACM Conference on AI, Ethics, and Society*, AIES '20, page 200–206, New York, NY, USA. Association for Computing Machinery.

Shai Ben-David, John Blitzer, K. Crammer, and Fernando C Pereira. 2006. Analysis of representations for domain adaptation. In *NIPS*.

Alex Beutel, Jilin Chen, Zhe Zhao, and Ed H. Chi. 2017. Data decisions and theoretical implications when adversarially learning fair representations. *ArXiv*, abs/1707.00075.

Xinyun Chen, Chang Liu, Bo Li, Kimberly Lu, and Dawn Song. 2017. Targeted backdoor attacks on deep learning systems using data poisoning. *arXiv preprint arXiv:1712.05526*.

C. Dwork, Moritz Hardt, T. Pitassi, O. Reingold, and R. Zemel. 2012. Fairness through awareness. *ArXiv*, abs/1104.3913.

Sahaj Garg, Vincent Perot, Nicole Limtiaco, Ankur Taly, Ed H. Chi, and Alex Beutel. 2019. Counterfactual fairness in text classification through robustness. In *Proceedings of the 2019 AAAI/ACM Conference on AI, Ethics, and Society*, AIES'19.

Moritz Hardt, EricPrice, and NathanSrebro. 2016. Equality of opportunity in supervised learning. In *NIPS*.

Bertrand Hassani. 2020. Societal biases reinforcement through machine learning: A credit scoring perspective.

Ruining He and Julian McAuley. 2016. Ups and downs. *WWW'16*.

F. Kamiran and T. Calders. 2011. Data preprocessing techniques for classification without discrimination. *Knowledge and Information Systems*, 33:1–33.

Divyansh Kaushik, Eduard Hovy, and Zachary Lipton. 2020. Learning the difference that makes a difference with counterfactually-augmented data. In *ICLR'20*.

Katherine Keith, David Jensen, and Brendan O'Connor. 2020. Text and causal inference: A review of using text to remove confounding from causal estimates. In *Proceedings of the 58th Annual Meeting of the Association for Computational Linguistics*, pages 5332–5344, Online. ACL.

Svetlana Kiritchenko and Saif Mohammad. 2018. Examining gender and race bias in two hundred sentiment analysis systems. In *Proceedings of the Seventh Joint Conference on Lexical and Computational Semantics*, New Orleans, Louisiana. ACL.

Preethi Lahoti, Alex Beutel, Jilin Chen, Kang Lee, Flavien Prost, Nithum Thain, Xuezhi Wang, and Ed H. Chi. 2020. Fairness without demographics through adversarially reweighted learning. *ArXiv*, abs/2006.13114.

Preethi Lahoti, K. Gummadi, and G. Weikum. 2019. Operationalizing individual fairness with pairwise fair representations. *Proc. VLDB Endow.*, 13:506–518.

Virgile Landeiro and Aron Culotta. 2018. Robust text classification under confounding shift. *Journal of Artificial Intelligence Research*, 63:391–419.

Kaiji Lu, Piotr Mardziel, Fangjing Wu, Preetam Amancharla, and Anupam Datta. 2020. Gender bias in neural natural language processing. In *Logic, Language, and Security*.

David Martens and Foster Provost. 2014. Explaining data-driven document classifications. *Mis Quarterly*, 38(1):73–100.

Ninareh Mehrabi, Fred Morstatter, Nripsuta Saxena, Kristina Lerman, and Aram Galstyan. 2021. A survey on bias and fairness in machine learning. 54(6).

Hongseok Namkoong and John C. Duchi. 2016. Stochastic gradient methods for distributionally robust optimization with f-divergences. In *NIPS*.

A. Ng. 2004. Feature selection, l1 vs. l2 regularization, and rotational invariance. *Proceedings of the twenty-first international conference on Machine learning*.

Bo Pang and Lillian Lee. 2005. Seeing stars: Exploiting class relationships for sentiment categorization with respect to rating scales. In *Proceedings of the 43rd annual meeting on association for computational linguistics*, pages 115–124. ACL.

Michael J. Paul. 2017. Feature selection as causal inference: Experiments with text classification. In *Proceedings of the 21st Conference on Computational Natural Language Learning (CoNLL 2017)*.

Jeffrey Pennington, Richard Socher, and Christopher D. Manning. 2014. Glove: Global vectors for word representation. In *Empirical Methods in Natural Language Processing (EMNLP)*, pages 1532–1543.

Marco Túlio Ribeiro, Tongshuang Wu, Carlos Guestrin, and Sameer Singh. 2020. Beyond accuracy: Behavioral testing of nlp models with checklist. In *ACL*.

Shiori Sagawa, Pang Wei Koh, Tatsunori B Hashimoto, and Percy Liang. 2020a. Distributionally robust neural networks for group shifts: On the importance of regularization for worst-case generalization. *ICLR*.

Shiori Sagawa, Aditi Raghunathan, Pang Wei Koh, and Percy Liang. 2020b. An investigation of why overparameterization exacerbates spurious correlations. *arXiv preprint arXiv:2005.04345*.

Megha Srivastava, Tatsunori B. Hashimoto, and Percy Liang. 2020. Robustness to spurious correlations via human annotations. In *ICML*.

Victor Veitch, Dhanya Sridhar, and David Blei. 2020. Adapting text embeddings for causal inference. In *Proceedings of the 36th Conference on Uncertainty in Artificial Intelligence (UAI)*, volume 124 of *Proceedings of Machine Learning Research*. PMLR.

Sahil Verma and Julia Rubin. 2018. Fairness definitions explained. In *2018 IEEE/ACM International Workshop on Software Fairness (FairWare)*.

Zhao Wang and A. Culotta. 2021. Robustness to spurious correlations in text classification via automatically generated counterfactuals. In *AAAI*.

Zhao Wang and Aron Culotta. 2020. Identifying spurious correlations for robust text classification. In *Findings of the Association for Computational Linguistics, EMNLP 2020*.

Christopher Winship and Stephen L Morgan. 1999. The estimation of causal effects from observational data. *Annual review of sociology*, 25(1):659–706.

Zach Wood-Doughty, Ilya Shpitser, and Mark Dredze. 2018. Challenges of using text classifiers for causal inference. *EMNLP*.

Tongshuang Wu, Marco Tulio Ribeiro, Jeffrey Heer, and Daniel S. Weld. 2021. Polyjuice: Generating counterfactuals for explaining, evaluating, and improving models. In *Proceedings of the 59th Annual Meeting of the Association for Computational Linguistics*. Association for Computational Linguistics.

Depeng Xu, Shuhan Yuan, L. Zhang, and Xintao Wu. 2018. Fairgan: Fairness-aware generative adversarial networks. *2018 IEEE International Conference on Big Data (Big Data)*, pages 570–575.

Shen Yan, H. Kao, and Emilio Ferrara. 2020. Fair class balancing: Enhancing model fairness without observing sensitive attributes. *Proceedings of the 29th ACM International Conference on Information & Knowledge Management*.

Adrienne Yapo and Joseph W. Weiss. 2018. Ethical implications of bias in machine learning. In *HICSS*.

Omar Zaidan, Jason Eisner, and Christine Piatko. 2007. Using "annotator rationales" to improve machine learning for text categorization. In *Human Language Technologies 2007*. ACL.

Cheng Zhang and Yingzhen Li. 2020. A causal view on robustness of neural networks.

Guanhua Zhang, Bing Bai, Junqi Zhang, Kun Bai, Conghui Zhu, and T. Zhao. 2020. Demographics should not be the reason of toxicity: Mitigating discrimination in text classifications with instance weighting. In *ACL*.

Jieyu Zhao, Tianlu Wang, Mark Yatskar, Vicente Ordonez, and Kai-Wei Chang. 2018. Gender bias in coreference resolution: Evaluation and debiasing methods. *ArXiv*.

Tianxiang Zhao, Enyan Dai, Kai Shu, and Suhang Wang. 2021. You can still achieve fairness without sensitive attributes: Exploring biases in nonsensitive features. *ArXiv*, abs/2104.14537.

What Makes a Scientific Paper be Accepted for Publication?

Panagiotis Fytas[1] **Georgios Rizos**[1] **Lucia Specia**[1, 2]
[1]Department of Computing, Imperial College London, UK
[2]Department of Computer Science, University of Sheffield
{pf2418, georgios.rizos12, l.specia}@imperial.ac.uk

Abstract

Despite peer-reviewing being an essential component of academia since the 1600s, it has repeatedly received criticisms for lack of transparency and consistency. We posit that recent work in machine learning and explainable AI provide tools that enable insights into the decisions from a given peer-review process. We start by simulating the peer-review process using an ML classifier and extracting global explanations in the form of linguistic features that affect the acceptance of a scientific paper for publication on an open peer-review dataset. Second, since such global explanations do not justify causal interpretations, we propose a methodology for detecting confounding effects in natural language and generating explanations, disentangled from textual confounders, in the form of lexicons. Our proposed linguistic explanation methodology indicates the following on a case dataset of ICLR submissions: a) the organising committee follows, for the most part, the recommendations of reviewers, and b) the paper's main characteristics that led to reviewers recommending acceptance for publication are originality, clarity and substance.

1 Introduction

The peer review process has been instrumental in academia for determining which papers meet the quality standards for publication in scientific journals and conferences. However, it has received several criticisms, including inconsistencies among review texts, review scores, and the final acceptance decision (Kravitz et al., 2010), arbitrariness between different reviewer groups (Langford and Guzdial, 2015) as well as reviewer bias in "single-blind" peer reviews (Tomkins et al., 2017).

Explainable AI (XAI) techniques have been shown to provide global understanding of the data behind a model.[1] Assume we build a classifier that predicts whether a paper is accepted for publication based on a peer review. Interpreting the decision of such a classifier can help comprehend what the reviewers value the most on a research paper. XAI allows us to elicit knowledge from the model about the data (Molnar, 2019). However, in order to determine what aspects of a paper lead to its acceptance, we need to interpret the peer review classifier explanations *causally*. Generally, XAI methods do not provide such guarantees since most Machine Learning models simply detect correlations (Molnar, 2019). Nevertheless, in recent years there has been a trend towards enabling Machine Learning to adjust for causal inference (Schölkopf, 2019).

Simply interpreting a non-causal classifier does not suffice when attempting to gain insight into human decision-making in the peer review process. For instance, words such as "gan", and "efficiency" appear to be important in such a classifier (Section 4). We argue that correlation between such words and paper acceptance is confounded on the subject of the paper: different subjects have different probabilities of acceptance, as well as different degrees to which algorithmic "efficiency" is an important factor. Since paper subject ground truth is not necessarily available, we can treat the abstract of a paper as a proxy for its subject, similar to Veitch et al. (2019).

Previous approaches that aim to reconcile NLP with causal inference are limited to either binary treatment variables (Veitch et al., 2019; Roberts et al., 2020; Saha et al., 2019) or nominal confounders (Pryzant et al., 2017, 2018a,b). This paper takes a first step towards using learnt natural language embeddings both as the treatment and the confounder. We achieve this by generating deconfounded lexicons (Pryzant et al., 2018a) through

[1]Among the several definitions for explainability and interpretability (Lipton, 2016; Rudin, 2018; Murdoch et al., 2019), we follow the definition of explainability as a *plausible* justification for the prediction of a model (Rudin, 2018), and use the terms interpretability and explainability interchangeably.

Proceedings of CI+NLP: First Workshop on Causal Inference and NLP, pages 44–60
November 10, 2021.

interpreting causal models that predict the acceptance of a scientific paper, based on their peer reviews and confounded on their abstract. Our **main contributions** are:

- We provide a methodology for developing text classifiers that are able to adjust for confounding effects expressed in natural language. Our evaluation is quantitative, reporting the Informativeness Coefficient measure (Pryzant et al., 2018a,b), and we also showcase the highest scoring words from the lexicons.
- We extend the classifier of Pryzant et al. (2018b) to use a black-box, instead of an interpretable classifier, which can be explained through model-agnostic tools, such as LIME (Ribeiro et al., 2016).
- We utilise our methodology to extract insights about the peer-review process of ICLR 2017, given that certain assumptions hold. Those insights validate our perceptions of how the peer-review process works, indicating that the method provides meaningful reasoning.
- We develop novel models for the task of peer review classification, which achieve a 15.79% absolute increase in accuracy over previous state-of-the-art (Ghosal et al., 2019).

In experiments with a dataset from ICLR 2017, we found that the organising committee mostly followed the recommendations of the reviewers, and that the reviewers focused on aspects such as originality, clarity, impact, and soundness of a paper, when suggesting whether or not the paper should be accepted for publication.

The paper is organised as follows: Section 2 presents related work regarding computational analyses of the peer-review process and explainability in NLP. Section 3 gives an overview of PeerRead, the peer review dataset we used in this paper. Section 4 presents our initial exploration on explanation of peer-reviewing, while Section 5 describes our methodology to account for causality by generating deconfounded lexicons.

2 Related Work

Peer Review Analysis. The PeerRead dataset (Kang et al., 2018) is the only openly available peer review dataset. It contains submission data for arXiv and the NeurIPS, ICLR, ACL, and CoNLL conferences, however, review data for both accepted and rejected submissions exist only for ICLR. The authors devised a series of NLP prediction baselines on the tasks of paper acceptance based on engineered features, as well as reviewer score prediction based on modelling abstract and review texts. Improvements on these baselines have been proposed by using better text representations as well as joint abstract/review modelling for predicting paper acceptance (Ghosal et al., 2019; Wang and Wan, 2018). Stappen et al. (2020) revisited the latter task on a dataset containing all the Interspeech 2019 conference abstracts and reviews (which unfortunately is not available) by utilising a review text fusion mechanism. The aforementioned studies model correlations between textual indices and the desired targets, without attempts towards explainability or identification of causal relationships. Hua et al. (2019), utilise argumentation mining on review texts from the ICLR and UAI conferences. Whereas their methodology focuses on proposition type statistics and transitions, it is a distinct approach to understanding peer-reviewing compared to ours, which is based on XAI.

Interpretability in NLP. Interpreting aspects of the input as conducive to the model prediction aims to: a) increase model trustworthiness, and b) allow for greater understanding of the data (Molnar, 2019). One way to do this is via **local explanations**, which explain the result of a single prediction, such as the view of high, learnt, class-agnostic attention weights (Bahdanau et al., 2015) applied to Recurrent Neural Network (RNN) hidden states, as proxies of word importance. However, the use of attention weights as explanations has been controversial, as Jain and Wallace (2019) have pointed out that for the same prediction, there can be counterfactual attentional explanations. Inversely, Wiegreffe and Pinter (2019) offer the justification that there may indeed exist multiple plausible explanations, out of which the attention mechanism captures one. An additional limitation of the attention mechanism is the inability to provide class-specific insights, due to the use of the softmax activation function. Alternatively, the predictions of black-box classifiers can be interpreted through model-agnostic frameworks, such as LIME (Ribeiro et al., 2016) and SHAP (Lundberg and Lee, 2017).

We are interested in **global explanations**, which explain either a set of predictions or provide insights about the general behaviour of the model.

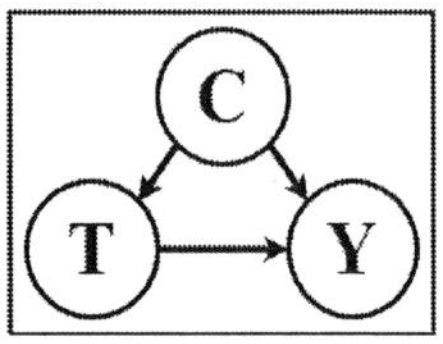

Figure 1: Graphical model depicting the confounding effect: C – Confounder, T – Treatment, Y – Outcome.

Current research is limited either to feature-based classifiers (Altmann et al., 2010), image classifiers (Kim et al., 2017) or combining local explanations to generate global explanations (Lundberg et al., 2019; Ibrahim et al., 2019).

Causal Inference in NLP. Let us assume two observed random variables: the treatment T and the outcome Y. Correlation between those two variables does not necessarily entail causation. Instead, this correlation could be the product of a confounding effect: a third random variable C causes both of the observed random variables (Peters, 2017). A depiction of the confounding effect can be observed in Figure 1. Recently, researchers have provided frameworks for treating text as a confounder, but their approaches are limited to binary treatment variables (Veitch et al., 2019; Roberts et al., 2020; Saha et al., 2019). Keith et al. (2020) have compiled a review of research that utilises text for adjusting for confounding. Fong and Grimmer (2016) explore extracting treatments from text corpora and estimating their causal effect on human decisions. However, they require human annotators for the constructions of training and test sets. Pryzant et al. (2017, 2018a,b) examine the problem of identifying a deconfounded lexicon (a set of linguistic features such as words or n-grams) from the text, which acts as a treatment variable. A deconfounded lexicon is "predictive of a target variable" but "uncorrelated to a set of confounding variables" (Pryzant et al., 2018b). However, their work is limited to using nominal confounders. In this paper, we explore the use of natural language both as the treatment variable and the confounder.

3 Dataset

The PeerRead dataset (Kang et al., 2018) consists of 14.7k papers and 10.7k peer reviews, including the meta-reviews by the editor. The papers are from different venues, having been collected with different methods, which leads to a non-uniform dataset. For instance, arXiv papers do not contain any reviews, and consequently, they are out of scope for our study. Furthermore, the NeurIPS section contains 2k reviews for only accepted papers. Therefore, using them will lead to a significant imbalance in our data. For those reasons, we decided to examine the 1.3k ICLR 2017 reviews of PeerRead. The ICLR 2017 section is divided into training, validation and test sets with an 80%-10%-10% split. In the Appendix, we can observe the proportion of the accepted to rejected paper in the various partitions of ICLR 2017.

PeerRead suffers from various data quality issues, which we have resolved. Firstly, we have removed several empty and duplicate reviews. More importantly, for ICLR 2017 the meta-reviews which contain the review and final decision of the conference chair are not marked as *meta-reviews* (the meta-review boolean field is marked as false) as they should have been (Kang et al., 2018). Instead, they are all marked as normal reviews with the title "ICLR Committee Final Decision". We explicitly treat them as meta-reviews, a differentiation that we believe is crucial in an XAI study like ours. Notably, subsequent studies that utilise PeerRead, like DeepSentiPeer (Ghosal et al., 2019), do not mention whether they have addressed this issue. This hinders a direct comparison with results from DeepSentiPeer as, expectedly, according to our experiments, the use of the meta-reviews significantly increases the performance of classifiers.

4 Data Exploration with Global XAI

We make an initial exploration into global explanations in the form of lexicons by mapping each word to an aggregate of scores corresponding to local explanations of PeerRead test sample predictions, as suggested both by the creators of SHAP (Lundberg et al., 2019) and by Pryzant et al. (2018b). We follow a train-test split setup in our modelling experiments, and only extract explanations from the test set, following Molnar et al. (2020).

We experimented with three different classification tasks: a) the *Final Decision Peer Review Classifier* fuses the multiple peer reviews to predict the final acceptance decision for a paper, b) the *Meta-Review Classifier* uses the singular meta-review to predict the final acceptance decision for a paper, and c) the *Individual Peer Review Classifier* predicts the recommendation of the reviewer for a single review, where we consider as accepted the papers with scores above 5, given a range of 1-10.

4.1 Interpreting Two Classifier Architectures

After preliminary experiments with Transformer Language Models (TLMs), we have opted to use the $\texttt{SciBERT}_{\texttt{SciVocab}}$ `uncased` model (Beltagy et al., 2019) trained on 1.7M papers from Semantic Scholar (Ammar et al., 2018) that contain a total of 3.17B tokens for text representation.

We experimented with two different text modelling approaches, each allowing for a different local explanation generation technique. In our **first approach**, we used the [CLS] token of our `SciBERT` model for *review text representation*. We truncate the end of reviews longer than 512 words. The effect of this truncation is not extremely adverse since only 10.5% of the reviews exceed the maximum length. More details about the length of peer reviews are included in the Appendix. We are not fine-tuning our model due to the risk of overfitting on our small dataset of $1.3k$ reviews. For the Meta Review and the Individual Review Classifiers, an additional feed forward neural layer is required, followed by a sigmoid activation function to predict the decisions. In the case of the Final Decision Peer Review Classifier, multiple reviews exist, leading to an equal number of `SciBERT` representations. In order to avoid introducing an arbitrary ordering among the reviews, we fused them into a single representation using an attention mechanism, following Stappen et al. (2020). We used two more attention layers to produce variant fused embeddings, and concatenated them into a single vector of fixed dimensionality in order to simulate multi-headed attention (Vaswani et al., 2017).

For the **second approach**, we only explore the Meta-Review and Individual Peer Review Classifiers. We treat each review as a sequence of word representations given by `SciBERT`, which we further process using an RNN layer with a Gated Recurrent Unit cell (GRU), followed by an attention mechanism, which is used to provide interpretability to our model. The output of the RNN layer is a vector produced through attention pooling. This vector is input to a feed-forward layer to produce the classification decision.

For the `SciBERT` [CLS] approach, we treat our model as a black-box and use **LIME** (Ribeiro et al., 2016) to produce explanations for each test set sample. More important words will have larger absolute scores. For the `GRU`-based approach, the attention mechanism is used to generate local explanations. More important words will have larger weights. Global explanation scores are then computed as the average of either the LIME score or the attention weights. The implementation details of our model are discussed in the Appendix.

4.2 Results

The validity of the explanations in drawing conclusions about peer reviewing is tied to the model predictive performance (Molnar et al., 2020). Table 1 summarises the performance on the PeerRead held-out test set for the task of predicting the final acceptance recommendation. Although not directly comparable, as explained in Section 3, we also report the baseline performances of PeerRead (Kang et al., 2018) and DeepSentiPeer (Ghosal et al., 2019), as well as that of the Majority Baseline, according to which the prediction is equal to the multiple reviewer recommendation majority vote. In the case of Individual Peer Review classification, this aggregate prediction is the same for all review samples pertaining to the same paper. We achieve superior performance over the baselines, both when using the meta-review and when fusing all the peer reviews for a specific paper. We note that the meta-review based model is the highest performer as the text is expected to correspond very well to the final recommendation. However, even our regular review fusion model outperforms DeepSentiPeer by a 15.79% absolute increase in accuracy. We hypothesise that this happens due to DeepSentiPeer treating each review (even along with the paper) as a different sample; we use fusion. Another reason for this improvement is presumably the use of the `SciBERT` model which was fine-tuned on biomedical and computer science papers.

Table 2 summarises the results for the Individual Peer Review Classification task. From the above experiments, we see that the `SciBERT` [CLS] approach is superior to sequential GRU.

In Table 3, we present the top 50 important words in the peer reviews for the Individual Peer Review Classification. In the Appendix, we include explanations for the other models. For both meta-reviews and peer reviews, we observe various technical terms ("lda", "gans", "variational", "generative", "adversarial", "convex", etc.). While this indicates a positive correlation between some subjects (such as GANs) and the acceptance to ICLR 2017, it is hard to argue about a causal relationship. For instance, a possible non-causal relationship could be the following confounding effect: top re-

Model Type	Model	Accuracy	Macro-F1	Weighted-F1
Baselines	Majority Baseline	59.52	0.3731	0.4442
	PeerRead (only paper)	65.30	N/A	N/A
	DeepSentiPeer (paper & review)	71.05	N/A	N/A
Meta-Review	SciBERT	**89.47**	**0.8899**	**0.8947**
	GRU	86.84	0.8661	0.8698
Final Decision Peer Review	SciBERT	86.84	0.8606	0.8676

Table 1: Performance of the classifiers that predict the final decision prediction (i.e., whether a paper is accepted for publication on ICLR 2017) for a paper on the test set of PeerRead. We see that using Meta-reviews in training yields an advantage, as does peer review fusion.

Model Type	Model	Accuracy	Macro-F1	Weighted-F1
Baselines	Majority Baseline	50.76	0.3367	0.3418
	Logistic Regression	58.33	0.5725	0.5756
Individual Peer Review	SciBERT	**80.30**	**0.8026**	**0.8028**
	GRU	70.45	0.7007	0.7012

Table 2: Performance on the Individual Peer Review Prediction (i.e., whether a reviewer suggests that a paper is accepted for publication), using on the test set of PeerRead.

searchers perform novel research, such as GANs, and top researchers have a higher probability of having their work published.

Furthermore, we observe plenty of terms that seem to directly criticise the quality of the work accomplished in a paper: "efficiently", "confusing", "unconvincing", "superficial", "comprehensive", "systematically", "carefully", "untrue" and more. Again, it is easy to make the mistake of assuming a causal relationship between the "efficiency" of an algorithm, suggested in a paper, and the acceptance for publication. For instance, depending on the subject of a paper, the efficiency may or may not increase the chances of a publication. To elaborate, for a paper about real-time language interpretation, the efficiency of the algorithm may directly influence the acceptance decision. On the contrary, the efficiency of training a GAN model may be inconsequential, as far as the ICLR reviewers are concerned.

5 Producing Causal Explanations

"Unjustified Causal Interpretation" is one of the pitfalls of global explanations (Molnar et al., 2020). Simply put, global explanations detect correlation and correlation does not entail causation. In order to learn what leads to a scientific paper being accepted for publication, we need causality. For instance, words such as "efficiency" and "novelty" appear to be important. However, there may not exist a causal relationship between them and the acceptance of a paper. Specifically, more theoretical subjects may demand "novelty", and the chances of a theoretical subject being accepted may be greater. Therefore, the correlation of the novelty and the acceptance of a paper may be an artefact of this confounding effect on the subject of the paper.

Adjusting for every possible confounding and mediating effect is not possible for most machine learning models, partially due to lack of ground truth data. Causality in machine learning is limited to taking several strong assumptions and providing a causal interpretation, for as long as those assumptions hold (Molnar et al., 2020). When text is involved, even more assumptions must be made, due to its high dimensionality (Veitch et al., 2019). We assume that: a) the subject of a paper is sufficient to identify the causal effect, b) the abstract can act as a proxy to the subject, and c) the embedding method extracts information relevant to the subject. In Section 5.4, we discuss the validity and limitations of those assumptions. Even when such assumptions are violated, our methodology is meaningful since it allows disentangling explanations of text classifiers from the natural language embedding of the text we want to control.

5.1 Background

In Figure 1, we depict the confounding effect. In this context, Y is the target variable (e.g. the acceptance of a paper for publication), T is the text (e.g. a peer review), and C are the confounding variables (e.g. the subject of a paper).

The task is to extract a deconfounded lexicon L such that $L(T)$ (the set of words of L that exist in the text T) is correlated to the target variable Y but not to the confounders C (Pryzant et al., 2018a). For our purposes, this means that the extracted lexicon can offer explanations about the acceptance of a paper for publication regardless of the subject of a paper. Pryzant et al. (2018a) have introduced the concept of *Informativeness Coefficient* $I(L)$:

$$I(L) = \mathbb{E}[\text{Var}[\mathbb{E}[Y|L(T), C]]|C]$$

where $\text{Var}[\mathbb{E}[Y|L(T), C]]$ is the amount of information in the target variable Y that can be explained both by $L(T)$ and C. In order to extract a deconfounded lexicon L, we must maximise the Informativeness Coefficient $I(L)$. The use of $I(L)$ as an evaluation of the quality of causal explanations is motivated by the ability of $I(L)$ to measure the causal effect of the text T on Y, under certain assumptions (Pryzant et al., 2018b).

To further understand this concept, let us consider a lexicon L of fixed length. $L(T)$ contains either words descriptive of $T \setminus C$ or words descriptive of $T \cap C$. Words related to the confounders (from $T \cap C$), in theory, do not increase the Informativeness Coefficient since the confounder C is treated as a fixed variable that directly affects Y. For instance, the word "gan" in a peer review may not be as important when the subject of the paper (the confounder) is already taken into consideration. On the contrary, words like "enjoyable", which are potentially unrelated to the subject of the paper, can contain more information. Therefore, the fewer the words in the lexicon that are related to the confounders C, the more deconfounded a lexicon will be, and $I(L)$ will take larger values.

An ANOVA decomposition is used to write the Informativeness Coefficient of a lexicon $I(L)$ (Pryzant et al., 2018a):

$$\begin{aligned} I(L) =& \mathbb{E}[(Y - \mathbb{E}[Y|C])^2] \\ &- \mathbb{E}[(Y - \mathbb{E}[Y|L(T), C])^2] \end{aligned} \quad (1)$$

In practice, $I(L)$ can be estimated by fitting a logistic regression on the confounders C to predict the outcome Y and a logistic regression on both C and $L(T)$ (a Bag-of-Word created from the lexicon and the text T). Then, for binary classification, the Binary Cross Entropy error is used to measure $I(L)$:

$$I(L) \simeq BCE_C - BCE_{L(T),C}$$

Deep Residualisation (DR) (Pryzant et al., 2018a) is a method for extracting a deconfounded lexicon. A visualisation of the DR model can be seen in Figure 2. The main idea is to utilise a neural model to predict the target variable $\hat{Y}'$ using only **nominal** confounders C, and an **interpretable** model that encodes the text T into an embedding vector e. Then, the intermediate prediction $\hat{Y}'$ is concatenated with the embedding vector e and forwarded through a feed-forward network to produce the final prediction $\hat{Y}$. In order to train this model, two loss functions are used. Firstly, the errors from the intermediate prediction $\hat{Y}'$ (i.e. BCE_C) are propagated through the Intermediate Prediction Neural Network. Secondly, the errors from the final prediction $\hat{Y}$ (i.e. $BCE_{T,C}$) are propagated through the complete neural network (Pryzant et al., 2018a).

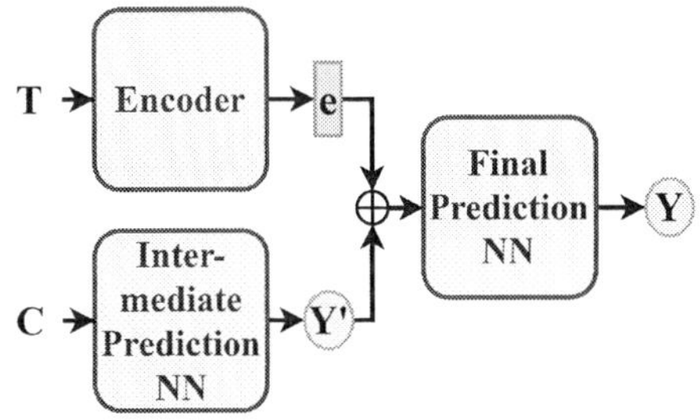

Figure 2: Deep Residualisation Architecture (Pryzant et al., 2018a). The confounders C are used for intermediate predictions Y'. The treatment T (i.e. the review of a paper) is encoded to a vector e, which is concatenated with Y' to produce the final prediction Y.

The DR architecture and the choice of loss functions are directly influenced by the Informativeness Coefficient. Specifically, Equation 1 provides additional intuition behind the Informativeness Coefficient: $I(L)$ "measures the ability of a lexicon $L(T)$ to enhance the predictions of the outcome Y made from the confounders C" (Pryzant et al., 2018b). The DR architecture utilises C to produce intermediate Y' predictions, while the text T is used to improve upon the intermediate predictions (Pryzant et al., 2018b). Intuitively, if the encoder learns to focus on aspects of the text, which are unrelated to the confounders but predictive of the outcome, the improvement of the intermediate predictions, and consequently $I(L)$, will be maximised.

5.2 Submission Subject as a Confounder

Although there may exist multiple confounders to the outcome (e.g., reviewer guidelines, or the paper content itself), we focus specifically on the subject of the paper as a confounder. Such annotation, however, is not part of the available data. Similar to the study performed in Veitch et al. (2019), we assume that the paper abstract is predictive of its subjects, and opt to utilise it for adjusting for confounding.

A limitation of the work of (Pryzant et al., 2018b) is that they only consider nominal confounders, which they forward through a Multi-layer Perceptron (MLP). We have extended the DR algorithm to extract deconfounded explanations from the reviews while using learnt natural language embeddings as the confounder. Specifically, we are forwarding our confounder (the abstract text) through a SciBERT Language Model to produce an embedding and then, forward that embedding through an MLP, with a sigmoid activation function at the end, to predict the intermediate classification outcome $\hat{Y}'$. For the task of meta-review classification, $\hat{Y}'$ aims to predict the final acceptance outcome, and for the task of individual peer review classification, $\hat{Y}'$ aims to predict the recommendation of the reviewer. Similarly with Veitch et al. (2019), we assume that the embedding method is able to extract information relevant to the subject of the paper.

Firstly, we have extended the **DR+ATTN** and **DR+BoW** models (Pryzant et al., 2018b) to allow for treating of natural language as the confounder, using the aforementioned methodology. The DR+ATTN model utilises an RNN-GRU layer with an attention mechanism to encode the text into the vector e. Therefore, interpretability is achieved through the attention mechanism. The DR+BoW model, forwards a Bag-of-Words (BoW) representation of the text through a single linear neural layer to produce an one-dimensional vector e. Each feature of our model is an n-gram that may appear on the text of the review. Therefore, we can globally interpret our model by using the weight of an n-gram in the single linear layer as the importance of that word (Pryzant et al., 2018b).

Secondly, instead of an interpretable model, we utilise a black-box that encodes the text into the vector e and then, use LIME to explain the predictions of our classifier. Therefore, we have developed the **DR+LIME** variant which can be used to extract a deconfounded lexicon from BERT-based models.

5.3 Quantitative Evaluation

In Table 4, we present metrics for benchmarking the performance of our various lexicons. In order to add more clarity, apart from the Informativeness Coefficient $I(L)$, we include the performance (F1-score) of the different logistic regression models. Furthermore, we report the Informativeness Coefficient of the lexicons generated by the Logistic Regression (LR) and the Logistic Regression with Confound features (LRC) (McNamee, 2005) baselines.

The Informativeness Coefficient is useful for measuring the degree to which the lexicons are deconfounded. However, the metric by itself is useful for comparing lexicons of **fixed size** and for **a specific task**. Therefore, comparing the $I(L)$ of the meta-review with the one from peer reviews is an uneven comparison. The reason for this is that, as we have observed, classifying meta-reviews is a much simpler problem. This leads to lexicons that perform much better and therefore, having higher $I(L)$ values even when words related to the confounders persist in the lexicon.

An important observation is that the deconfounded lexicons are less predictive of the final outcome compared to the non-causal lexicons, when not combined with the Confounder. For instance, in the case of Peer-Review GRU model, the F1-Score of $L(T)$ drops from 60% to 59% with Deep Residualisation. On the contrary, when the deconfounded lexicons are coupled with the confounders, the logistic regression performs better compared to the non-causal lexicon. For the Peer-Review GRU model, the F1-Score of $L(T), C$ increases from 60% to 64% with Deep Residualisation. The intuition behind this is that the initial lexicon had some words related to the confounders that were important for the final prediction. The DR method does not attend to those words because they are related to the confounders. Instead, they are replaced with words, which may be less predictive of the final outcome, yet uncorrelated to the confounders.

Ultimately, DR+LIME and DR+BoW are less successful than DR+ATTN in generating a deconfounded lexicon for the peer reviews since the lexicon generated from DR+ATTN achieves a superior Informativeness Coefficient. Still, our DR+LIME technique manages to produce a more informative lexicon than the DR+BoW model and the LRC baseline.

5.4 Discussion on our Assumptions

Causal inference is limited to making several assumptions and providing causal guarantees for as long as those assumptions hold (Molnar et al., 2020; Pryzant et al., 2018a; Veitch et al., 2019). We assume that:

1. The subject of a paper is sufficient to identify the causal effect, i.e., there is no unobserved

GRU (Non-Causal)	GRU (DR+ATTN)	SciBERT (Non-Causal)	SciBERT(DR+LIME)
not, attempt, comprehensive, interfere, variational, entirely, systematically, perfect, sure, lda, formalize, tolerant, valid, belief, gan, imposible, adagrad, semantically, aware, clear, carefully, j., and/or, arguably, fully, offer, vs., confident, message, object, receive, probably, multimodality, strictly, directly, twitter, join, e.g., observe, complete, explain, novelty, dualnets, convince, handle, nintendo, theorem, satisfy, ready, demand	identical, sure, premise, carefully, heavy, specify, tease, interfere, necessarily, adagrad, attempt, novelty, fully, repeat, systematically, not, gray, theoretically, anymore, role, belief, recommendation, almost, consistently, primary, subtraction, good, satisfactory, background, write, compute, easy, teach, enough, convince, except, ready, explain, usage, sell, unfortunately, arguably, yet, especially, elegantly, sufficiently, handle, cdl, setup, reception	interspeech, zhang, prons, dismissed, third, p6, confusing, resulting, geometry, unconvincing, honestly, not, community, cannot, superficial, readership, big, suggestion, dialogue, revisit, bag, analysed, icml, taken, typo, submitted, energy, nice, spirit, competitive, per, highlighted, multimodality, far, 04562, lack, preprint, dcgan, conduct, word2vec, wen, gan, rejected, start, towards, multiplication, generalisation, auxiliary, parametric, enjoyed	interspeech, dismissed, prons, geometry, p6, submitted, unfair, unconvincing, readership, honestly, not, spirit, confusing, analysed, bag, unable, cannot, rejected, insightful, multiplication, highlighted, enjoyed, misleading, disagree, dialogue,mu_, wen, lack, nice, multimodality, welcome, conduct, recommender, encourage, dualnets, thanks, cdl, preprint, 04562, enjoy, revisit, community, appreciate, principled, medical, coding, drnn, accompanying, factorization, jmlr

Table 3: Top 50 salient words for Individual Peer Review Classification. We present class-agnostic explanations both for some of the non-causal models (Section 4) and for some DR models (Section 5).

Model Type	Model	$I(L)$	Logistic Regression Macro F1-Score		
			Only Text $L(T)$	Only Conf. C	Text and Conf. $L(T), C$
Meta Reviews	LR Baseline	0.1547	0.68	0.50	0.71
	LRC Baseline	0.1906	0.69	0.50	0.74
	GRU	0.1862	0.71	0.50	0.74
	DR+ATTN (GRU)	**0.2113**	0.65	0.50	**0.75**
Individual Peer Reviews	LR Baseline	0.0058	0.45	0.55	0.56
	LRC Baseline	0.0163	0.46	0.55	0.58
	GRU	0.0252	0.60	0.55	0.60
	DR+ATTN (GRU)	**0.0907**	0.59	0.55	**0.64**
	SciBERT	0.0115	0.58	0.55	0.58
	DR+LIME (SciBERT)	**0.0301**	0.56	0.55	**0.60**
	BoW	0.0039	0.43	0.55	0.55
	DR+BoW	**0.0128**	0.43	0.55	**0.56**

Table 4: Performance of the Deconfounded lexicons. All lexicons have a size of 50 words. For each type of classifier, we present the Informativeness Coefficient both of the non-causal lexicon and of the deconfounded lexicon, generated through Deep Residualisation (DR).

confounding. This is a standard causality assumption, albeit a strong one (Veitch et al., 2019). This assumption essentially means that there should not be other external confounders. The first way to attack this assumption is to argue that a reviewer could have biases that affect their decisions. Those biases can act as external confounders. For instance, a famous author may receive preferential treatment from some reviewers. Indeed, in "single-blind" peer reviews, as was the case for ICLR 2017, it has been observed that reviewers tend to accept more papers from top universities and companies (Tomkins et al., 2017), compared to "double-blind" peer reviews, where the author is anonymous during the review process. However, it is practically impossible to adjust for every potential source of reviewer bias. Another way to attack this assumption is by arguing that the writing quality, for instance, could be another confounder. Nevertheless, when a paper lacks clarity, we can assume that the reviewer will point out the poor writing quality in the review. In that case, the review text accounts for the writing quality and therefore, it is not an external confounder.

2. The abstract of the paper can act as a proxy to its subject. Indeed, an abstract should reflect the main topic of the paper. In that setting, the abstract can be thought of as a "noisy realisation" of the subject (Veitch et al., 2019).

3. The embedding method is able to extract information relevant to the subject of the paper. The use of state-of-the-art language models justifies this assumption (Veitch et al., 2019). In this case, we are using SciBERT embeddings, which achieve state-of-the-art performance on scientific NLP tasks (Beltagy et al., 2019). We could further bolster this assumption by fine-tuning our SciBERT model. However, this would require a larger dataset of peer

reviews to avoid overfitting.

4. The outcome $Y(t)$ is generated from the following data generated process: $Y(t) = f_c(t) + \epsilon$, where t is the text and c the fixed observed confounders. This is a standard assumption in observational studies, and along with the assumption that there is no unobserved confounding, they guarantee that the Informativeness Coefficient measures the causal effect of the full text T on the outcome Y (Pryzant et al., 2018b).

5.5 Lexicons Inspection

As long as our assumptions hold, we can causally interpret the explanations of our models. Since we value the degree with which DR has managed to deconfound our lexicon, the explanations for the peer reviews should be extracted from DR+ATTN, which achieves the greater $I(L)$ values.

In Table 3, we can observe a comparison of the top 50 salient words between the causal and non-causal models for the peer reviews. In the first place, we can observe that in the top 50 explanations of DR+ATTN, technical words, like "generative", "variational" and "lda" disappear in the explanations of the causal model. This occurrence fits our expectations: the technical words are generally related to the confounder (the subject of a paper) and should not appear in the explanation. As far as the BERT-based causal model is concerned, its lexicon still has plenty of technical terms. This is because the DR+LIME method is less successful in removing the confounding effect.

For the meta-reviews, we notice the prevalence of words like "enjoyed", "accepted", "mixed", "positively" and "recommend". Those words are, for the most part, related with to the opinions of the peer reviewers (e.g. "The reviewers all **enjoyed** reading this paper"). Furthermore, a logistic regressor fitted on the average recommendation score of the reviewers is able to predict the final outcome of the submission with an accuracy of 95%. All this evidence suggests that the ICLR 2017 committee chair for the vast majority of papers followed the recommendation of the reviewers.

In the case of peer reviews, highly ranked in our explanations, we can observe the word "novelty". We can deduce that the Originality of a paper is indeed essential for ICLR 2017. In the top 50 words we observe words such as "explain", "carefully", "systematically", "consistently", "convince" and "sufficiently". Those words indicate the importance of the Soundness of the scientific approach and how convincingly the claims are presented. Moreover, in the top 100 words, there words that reflect the Clarity and the quality of writing: "elegantly", "polish", "readable", "clear". We can, also, detect words like "comprehensive" and "extensive", which reflect the Substance (and completeness) of a paper. Lastly, various words exist that potentially reflect other aspects of a paper, such as Meaningful Comparison ("compare"), Impact ("contribute") and Appropriateness ("appropriate").

Therefore, if our assumptions hold, we can claim that certain characteristics of a paper, such as Originality, Soundness and Clarity, lead the reviewers to recommend that a scientific paper is accepted for publication.

6 Conclusions

With peer-reviewing as a use case, we have proposed a framework for interpreting the decisions of text classifiers causally, by using natural language to adjust for confounding effects. Our methodology succeeds in extracting deconfounded lexicons that exclude terms related to the paper subject (i.e., the confounders), a task where established, non-causal global explanation approaches fail. Prior work was limited to either nominal confounders (Pryzant et al., 2017, 2018a,b) or binary treatment variables (Veitch et al., 2019). Furthermore, we have extended the Deep Residualisation (Pryzant et al., 2018a) to allow for black-box models.

As is standard in causal inference (Molnar et al., 2020), the causal guarantees of the deconfounded lexicon we generate is limited by certain assumptions. Future work could explore strengthening our assumptions through fine-tuning of the Transformer Language Model representation of the confounder text. Furthermore, fine-tuning the Encoder of DR+LIME may lead to producing more informative lexicons. To avoid overfitting in this fine-tuning process, we intend to apply our methodology on larger datasets that the one used in this paper for peer reviews.

References

André Altmann, Laura Toloşi, Oliver Sander, and Thomas Lengauer. 2010. Permutation importance: a corrected feature importance measure. *Bioinformatics*, 26(10):1340–1347.

Waleed Ammar, Dirk Groeneveld, Chandra Bhagavatula, Iz Beltagy, Miles Crawford, Doug Downey, Jason Dunkelberger, Ahmed Elgohary, Sergey Feldman, Vu Ha, Rodney Kinney, Sebastian Kohlmeier, Kyle Lo, Tyler Murray, Hsu-Han Ooi, Matthew E. Peters, Joanna Power, Sam Skjonsberg, Lucy Lu Wang, Chris Wilhelm, Zheng Yuan, Madeleine van Zuylen, and Oren Etzioni. 2018. Construction of the literature graph in semantic scholar. *CoRR*, abs/1805.02262.

Dzmitry Bahdanau, Kyunghyun Cho, and Yoshua Bengio. 2015. Neural machine translation by jointly learning to align and translate. *CoRR*, abs/1409.0473.

Iz Beltagy, Arman Cohan, and Kyle Lo. 2019. Scibert: Pretrained contextualized embeddings for scientific text. *CoRR*, abs/1903.10676.

Jacob Devlin, Ming-Wei Chang, Kenton Lee, and Kristina Toutanova. 2018. BERT: pre-training of deep bidirectional transformers for language understanding. *CoRR*, abs/1810.04805.

Christian Fong and Justin Grimmer. 2016. Discovery of treatments from text corpora. In *Proceedings of the 54th Annual Meeting of the Association for Computational Linguistics (Volume 1: Long Papers)*, pages 1600–1609, Berlin, Germany. Association for Computational Linguistics.

Tirthankar Ghosal, Rajeev Verma, Asif Ekbal, and Pushpak Bhattacharyya. 2019. DeepSentiPeer: Harnessing sentiment in review texts to recommend peer review decisions. In *Proceedings of the 57th Annual Meeting of the Association for Computational Linguistics*, pages 1120–1130, Florence, Italy. Association for Computational Linguistics.

Xinyu Hua, Mitko Nikolov, Nikhil Badugu, and Lu Wang. 2019. Argument mining for understanding peer reviews. *CoRR*, abs/1903.10104.

Mark Ibrahim, Melissa Louie, Ceena Modarres, and John W. Paisley. 2019. Global explanations of neural networks: Mapping the landscape of predictions. *CoRR*, abs/1902.02384.

Sarthak Jain and Byron C. Wallace. 2019. Attention is not explanation.

Dongyeop Kang, Waleed Ammar, Bhavana Dalvi, Madeleine van Zuylen, Sebastian Kohlmeier, Eduard H. Hovy, and Roy Schwartz. 2018. A dataset of peer reviews (peerread): Collection, insights and NLP applications. *CoRR*, abs/1804.09635.

Katherine A. Keith, David Jensen, and Brendan O'Connor. 2020. Text and causal inference: A review of using text to remove confounding from causal estimates. *CoRR*, abs/2005.00649.

Been Kim, Martin Wattenberg, Justin Gilmer, Carrie Cai, James Wexler, Fernanda Viegas, and Rory Sayres. 2017. Interpretability beyond feature attribution: Quantitative testing with concept activation vectors (tcav).

Diederik P. Kingma and Jimmy Ba. 2014. Adam: A method for stochastic optimization.

Richard L Kravitz, Peter Franks, Mitchell D Feldman, Martha Gerrity, Cindy Byrne, and William M Tierney. 2010. Editorial peer reviewers' recommendations at a general medical journal: are they reliable and do editors care? *PLoS One*, 5(4):e10072.

John Langford and Mark Guzdial. 2015. The arbitrariness of reviews, and advice for school administrators. *Commun. ACM*, 58(4):12–13.

Zachary C. Lipton. 2016. The mythos of model interpretability.

Scott M. Lundberg, Gabriel G. Erion, Hugh Chen, Alex DeGrave, Jordan M. Prutkin, Bala Nair, Ronit Katz, Jonathan Himmelfarb, Nisha Bansal, and Su-In Lee. 2019. Explainable AI for trees: From local explanations to global understanding. *CoRR*, abs/1905.04610.

Scott M Lundberg and Su-In Lee. 2017. A unified approach to interpreting model predictions. In I. Guyon, U. V. Luxburg, S. Bengio, H. Wallach, R. Fergus, S. Vishwanathan, and R. Garnett, editors, *Advances in Neural Information Processing Systems 30*, pages 4765–4774. Curran Associates, Inc.

R McNamee. 2005. Regression modelling and other methods to control confounding. *Occupational and Environmental Medicine*, 62(7):500–506.

Christoph Molnar. 2019. *Interpretable Machine Learning*. `https://christophm.github.io/interpretable-ml-book/`.

Christoph Molnar, Gunnar König, Julia Herbinger, Timo Freiesleben, Susanne Dandl, Christian A. Scholbeck, Giuseppe Casalicchio, Moritz Grosse-Wentrup, and Bernd Bischl. 2020. Pitfalls to avoid when interpreting machine learning models.

W. James Murdoch, Chandan Singh, Karl Kumbier, Reza Abbasi-Asl, and Bin Yu. 2019. Definitions, methods, and applications in interpretable machine learning. *Proceedings of the National Academy of Sciences*, 116(44):22071–22080.

Jonas Peters. 2017. Elements of causal inference.

Reid Pryzant, Sugato Basu, and Kazoo Sone. 2018a. Interpretable neural architectures for attributing an ad's performance to its writing style. In *Proceedings of the 2018 EMNLP Workshop BlackboxNLP: Analyzing and Interpreting Neural Networks for NLP*, pages 125–135, Brussels, Belgium. Association for Computational Linguistics.

Reid Pryzant, Youngjoo Chung, and Dan Jurafsky. 2017. Predicting sales from the language of product descriptions. In *eCOM@SIGIR*.

Reid Pryzant, Kelly Shen, Dan Jurafsky, and Stefan Wagner. 2018b. Deconfounded lexicon induction for interpretable social science. In *Proceedings of the 2018 Conference of the North American Chapter of the Association for Computational Linguistics: Human Language Technologies, Volume 1 (Long Papers)*, pages 1615–1625, New Orleans, Louisiana. Association for Computational Linguistics.

Marco Tulio Ribeiro, Sameer Singh, and Carlos Guestrin. 2016. "why should i trust you?": Explaining the predictions of any classifier. In *Proceedings of the 22nd ACM SIGKDD International Conference on Knowledge Discovery and Data Mining*, KDD '16, page 1135–1144, New York, NY, USA. Association for Computing Machinery.

Margaret E. Roberts, Brandon M. Stewart, and Richard A. Nielsen. 2020. Adjusting for confounding with text matching. *American Journal of Political Science*, 64(4):887–903.

Cynthia Rudin. 2018. Stop explaining black box machine learning models for high stakes decisions and use interpretable models instead.

Koustuv Saha, Benjamin Sugar, John Torous, Bruno Abrahao, Emre Kıcıman, and Munmun De Choudhury. 2019. A social media study on the effects of psychiatric medication use. *Proceedings of the International AAAI Conference on Web and Social Media*, 13(01):440–451.

Bernhard Schölkopf. 2019. Causality for machine learning.

Lukas Stappen, Georgios Rizos, Madina Hasan, Thomas Hain, and Björn W. Schuller. 2020. Uncertainty-Aware Machine Support for Paper Reviewing on the Interspeech 2019 Submission Corpus. In *Proc. Interspeech 2020*, pages 1808–1812.

Andrew Tomkins, Min Zhang, and William D. Heavlin. 2017. Reviewer bias in single- versus double-blind peer review. *Proceedings of the National Academy of Sciences*, 114(48):12708–12713.

Ashish Vaswani, Noam Shazeer, Niki Parmar, Jakob Uszkoreit, Llion Jones, Aidan N. Gomez, Lukasz Kaiser, and Illia Polosukhin. 2017. Attention is all you need. *CoRR*, abs/1706.03762.

Victor Veitch, Dhanya Sridhar, and David M. Blei. 2019. Using text embeddings for causal inference. *CoRR*, abs/1905.12741.

Ke Wang and Xiaojun Wan. 2018. Sentiment analysis of peer review texts for scholarly papers. In *The 41st International ACM SIGIR Conference on Research & Development in Information Retrieval*, SIGIR '18, page 175–184, New York, NY, USA. Association for Computing Machinery.

Sarah Wiegreffe and Yuval Pinter. 2019. Attention is not not explanation.

Partition	#Papers	Accepted / Rejected
Training Set	349	139 / 210
Validation Set	40	18 / 22
Test Set	38	15 / 23
Total	427	172 / 255

Table 5: Description of ICLR 2017 section of PeerRead.

A Dataset statistics

Dataset statistics are summarised in Table 5.

B Implementation Details

In the section, we provide implementation details such as the number of neurons in our networks and the training hyperparameters. All hidden layers of our neural networks have a ReLU activation function, and the output layers have a Sigmoid activation function.

Let us first focus on the non-causal `SciBERT` [CLS] approach. For the Final Decision Peer Review Classifier, we are using two attention layers and therefore the concatenated fused embeddings $768 * 2 = 1536$ dimensions. The first layer of the MLP has 1536 input neurons and 128 output neurons. The second layer has 128 input neurons and 64 output neurons. The third (and last) layer has 64 input neurons and 1 output neuron. The probability of the Dropout for each layer is 20%. The Individual Decision Peer Review Classifier and the Meta-Review Classifier have essentially the same MLP as the Final Decision Peer Review Classifier but with 768 input neurons. For all `SciBERT` [CLS] classifiers, we are using Binary Cross Entropy as the loss function and an Adam optimiser (Kingma and Ba, 2014) with a learning rate of 1×10^{-4}. However, we are training our classifiers for a different amount of epochs and with different batch sizes. For the Final Decision Peer Review Classifier, we are training for 500 epochs with a batch size of 100. The Meta-Review Classifier is trained for the 100 epochs, with a batch size of 100. Finally, the Individual Peer Review Classifier has 220 training epochs and a batch size of 300 samples.

Focusing on the parameters of the non-causal GRU classifiers, the GRU cell has 768 input neurons (the size of the BERT embedding) and 30 output neurons. The first layer of the MLP has 30 input neurons and 16 output neurons. The last layer has 16 input neurons and 1 output neuron. The probability of the Dropout for each layer is

20%. Similarly with before, we are using a Binary Cross Entropy loss function with an Adam optimiser. The Individual Peer Review classifier has a learning rate of 5×10^{-4} and is trained for 80 training epochs with a batch size of 500 samples. The Meta-Review classifier has a learning rate of 8×10^{-5}, is trained for 70 epochs and has a batch size of 30 samples.

Focusing on the causal DR models, all models have the same architecture for the MLP that produces the intermediate predictions $\hat{Y}'$. The first layer has 768 input neurons, 10 output neurons. The second layer has 10 input neurons, 5 output neurons. The last layer is going to have 5 input neurons, 1 output neuron.

In the case of the DR+LIME causal model, the MLP that produces the embedding e has 2 layers. The first one has 768 input neurons and 300 output neurons. The second layer has 300 input neurons and 100 output neurons. The embedding e is constructed as a 100 dimensional vector. The MLP that predicts the final acceptance decision has 3 layers. The first layer has 101 input neuron, 64 output neurons. The second one has 64 input neurons and 16 output neuron. The last layer has 16 input neurons and 1 output neuron. An Adam optimiser is used, with a learning rate of 1×10^{-4}. The model is trained for 125 epochs, with a batch size of 300.

As far the DR+LIME models are concerned, in the case of Individual Peer Review Classification, the embedding e is a 30 dimensional vector. The MLP that predicts the final acceptance decision has 2 layers. The first layer has 31 input neurons, 16 output neurons. The last layer has 16 input neurons and 1 output neuron. An Adam optimiser is used, with a learning rate of 5×10^{-4}. The model is trained for 70 epochs, with a batch size of 250. In the case of meta-review classification, the embedding e is a 64 dimensional vector. Similarly with before, The MLP that predicts the final acceptance decision has 2 layers. The first layer has 65 input neurons, 32 output neurons. The last layer has 12 input neurons and 1 output neuron. Lastly, an Adam optimiser is used, with a learning rate of 1×10^{-4}. The model is trained for 80 epochs, with a batch size of 30.

For the DR+BoW model, the MLP that predicts the final acceptance decision has a single layer with 2 input neurons and 1 output neuron. An Adam optimiser is used, with a learning rate of 8×10^{-4}. The model is trained for 200 epochs, with a batch size of 500.

B.1 Preprocessing

B.1.1 SciBERT Model Preprocessing

For the SciBERT models (Beltagy et al., 2019), we perform standard BERT preprocessing, which includes tokenisation and lowercasing. Additionally, we truncate the end of the reviews that exceed 512 input tokens, which is the maximum supported by BERT (Devlin et al., 2018). The mean length of an ICLR 2017 peer review is 346 input tokens, with a standard deviation of 213 (Kang et al., 2018). For meta-reviews, the mean length drops to 93 and the standard deviation to 77.

Truncating reviews will affect the performance of our models. However, that effect is limited to an extent. Namely, only 10.5% of the peer reviews have a length of more than 512 tokens. From that 10.5%, around half of those reviews have less than 15% of their tokens truncated. Therefore, for those reviews, the effect of the truncation is not extremely adverse. Lastly, 0.5% of all peer reviews have more than half of their tokens truncated which could have a substantial impact in the classification of those few reviews. A histogram with the lengths of peer reviews can be seen in Figure 3.

For meta-reviews, the effect of truncation is negligible since only 0.05% have more than 512 input tokens. The histogram with the lengths of meta-reviews can be seen in Figure 4.

B.1.2 GRU Model Preprocessing

For GRU models, apart from tokenisation, we perform punctuation removal, lemmatisation and lowercasing.

C Confusion Matrix

A summary of the confusion matrices can be seen in Figure 6.

D Explanations

In this Appendix, we present tables with the explanations we generate with our various models. In Table 7, we provide the top 50 important words for every non-causal model. In Table 8, we present the top 50 non-causal and causal words from meta-reviews. Table 9 contains the top 50 words for causal and non-causal Individual Peer Review Classifiers. Lastly, Table 10 provides the top salient n-grams for causal and non-causal Bag-of-Words models.

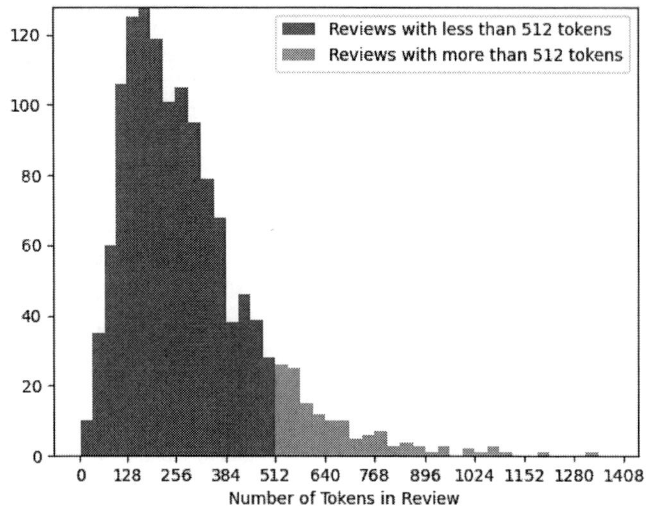

Figure 3: Histogram of the number of input tokens per peer review.

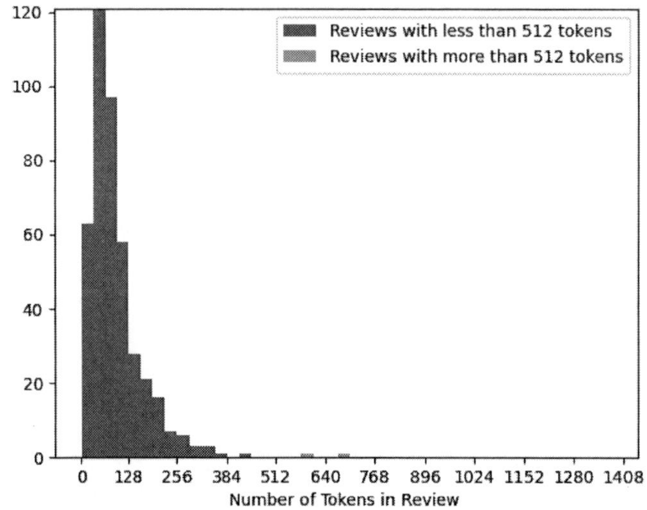

Figure 4: Histogram of the number of input tokens per meta-review.

		Predicted					
		Meta-Review SciBERT		Meta-Review GRU		Peer Review SciBERT	
		Accepted	Rejected	Accepted	Rejected	Accepted	Rejected
Actual	Accepted	13	2	14	1	12	3
	Rejected	2	21	4	19	2	21

Table 6: Final Decision Classifier Confusion Matrices on the test set of PeerRead (Kang et al., 2018)

BERT - Meta-Review	GRU - Meta-Review	BERT - Individual Peer Review	GRU - Individual Peer Review	BERT - Final Decision Peer Review
enjoyed	positively	interspeech	not	kolter
cnns	accept	zhang	attempt	aaai
resubmit	suspiciously	prons	comprehensive	not
community	wrong	dismissed	interfere	third
limited	yet	third	variational	efficiently
experimentation	perhaps	p6	entirely	untrue
3	mix	confusing	systematically	cifar10
workshop	limit	resulting	perfect	venue
poster	guidance	geometry	sure	recovered
topic	read	unconvincing	lda	huffman
variational	impressive	honestly	formalize	riemannian
limit	surprise	not	tolerant	cifar
although	enough	community	valid	arxiv
not	incremental	cannot	belief	accompanying
sound	sufficiently	superficial	gan	extended
none	timely	readership	imposible	convex
accepted	journal	big	adagrad	github
dropout	post	suggestion	semantically	trace
imagenet	contribute	dialogue	aware	eigenspectra
agent	ready	revisit	clear	encourage
justify	not	bag	carefully	code
generative	variational	analysed	j.	asynchronous
advantage	nicely	icml	and/or	crucial
unfortunately	receive	taken	arguably	auxiliary
video	submit	typo	fully	investigated
review	relevant	submitted	offer	iclrw2016
solver	much	energy	vs.	hyperparameters
three	high	nice	confident	discus
task	weak	spirit	message	dcgan
use	good	competitive	object	interesting
confident	write	per	receive	nice
generalisation	whilst	highlighted	probably	game
supervised	into	multimodality	multimodality	demonstration
promise	below	far	strictly	lample
raised	benefit	04562	directly	the
understanding	rebuttal	lack	twitter	significance
timely	generative	preprint	join	seq2seq
reject	strengthen	dcgan	e.g.	community
unsatisfactory	meet	conduct	observe	perspective
yet	variety	word2vec	complete	paper
mixed	give	wen	explain	thanks
shot	hide	gan	novelty	investigates
propose	recommend	rejected	dualnets	insightful
how	badly	start	convince	uploaded
rejection	long	towards	handle	narrow
thus	clear	multiplication	nintendo	match
salimans	convince	generalisation	theorem	seed
provided	gain	auxiliary	satisfy	tsp
goal	serious	parametric	ready	adversarial
reservation	maintain	enjoyed	demand	isn

Table 7: Top 50 salient words for non-causal models.

GRU (Non-Causal)	GRU (DR+ATTN)
positively	nicely
accept	overcomplicated
suspiciously	positively
wrong	yet
yet	rebuttal
perhaps	ready
mix	sufficiently
limit	properly
guidance	acceptance
read	surprise
impressive	usual
surprise	into
enough	describe
incremental	finding
sufficiently	organize
timely	execution
journal	insight
post	receive
contribute	criterion
ready	overall
not	good
variational	closely
nicely	wise
receive	suspiciously
submit	well
relevant	badly
much	write
high	pair
weak	explain
good	not
write	simple
whilst	weak
into	asset
below	great
benefit	out
rebuttal	execute
generative	helpful
strengthen	enjoy
meet	conditional
variety	mix
give	entirely
hide	contribution
recommend	world
badly	demonstrate
long	accept
clear	assume
convince	post
gain	publication
serious	effective
maintain	clearly

Table 8: Top 50 salient words for meta-reviews. The first column contains the explanations of the non-causal models. The second column contains the deconfounded lexicon.

BERT (Non-Causal)	BERT (DR+LIME)	GRU (Non-Causal)	GRU (DR+ATTN)
interspeech	interspeech	not	identical
zhang	dismissed	attempt	sure
prons	prons	comprehensive	premise
dismissed	geometry	interfere	carefully
third	p6	variational	heavy
p6	submitted	entirely	specify
confusing	unfair	systematically	tease
resulting	unconvincing	perfect	interfere
geometry	readership	sure	necessarily
unconvincing	honestly	lda	adagrad
honestly	not	formalize	attempt
not	spirit	tolerant	novelty
community	confusing	valid	fully
cannot	analysed	belief	repeat
superficial	bag	gan	systematically
readership	unable	imposible	not
big	cannot	adagrad	gray
suggestion	rejected	semantically	theoretically
dialogue	insightful	aware	anymore
revisit	multiplication	clear	role
bag	highlighted	carefully	belief
analysed	enjoyed	j.	recommendation
icml	misleading	and/or	almost
taken	disagree	arguably	consistently
typo	dialogue	fully	primary
submitted	mu_	offer	subtraction
energy	wen	vs.	good
nice	lack	confident	satisfactory
spirit	nice	message	background
competitive	multimodality	object	write
per	welcome	receive	compute
highlighted	conduct	probably	easy
multimodality	recommender	multimodality	teach
far	encourage	strictly	enough
04562	dualnets	directly	convince
lack	thanks	twitter	except
preprint	cdl	join	ready
dcgan	preprint	e.g.	explain
conduct	04562	observe	usage
word2vec	enjoy	complete	sell
wen	revisit	explain	unfortunately
gan	community	novelty	arguably
rejected	appreciate	dualnets	yet
start	principled	convince	especially
towards	medical	handle	elegantly
multiplication	coding	nintendo	sufficiently
generalisation	drnn	theorem	handle
auxiliary	accompanying	satisfy	cdl
parametric	factorization	ready	setup
enjoyed	jmlr	demand	resception

Table 9: Top 50 salient words for the task of Individual Peer Classification. In order to make comparisons, we present both causal and non-causal models.

BoW (Non-Causal)	BoW (DR+BoW)
(not, enough)	(not, enough)
(much, be)	(much, be)
(literature, and)	(not, compare)
(need, a)	(evidence, to)
(evidence, to)	(be, insufficient)
(be, not, enough)	(comparison, with, other)
(not, compare)	(be, mention)
(on, use)	(literature, and)
(comparison, with, other)	(need, a)
(doe, not, provide)	complementary
(claim, that, this)	(be, not, enough)
(network, weight)	(method, need)
(do, not, compare)	(would, require)
(work, need)	(doe, not, provide)
gans	(on, use)
(layer, this)	(to, compare, the)
(be, insufficient)	(have, see)
(it, look, like)	(comparison, with, the)
(push, the)	(network, weight)
(work, so)	(do, not, compare)
(to, compare, the)	(sure, if, the)
(not, compare, to)	(no, quantitative)
(not, surprise)	(no, new)
(and, compare, to)	(experiment, there, be)
(have, see)	(on, the, previous)
(very, hard)	(improve, version)
(of, the, dataset)	(not, compare, to)
(be, mention)	(adversarial, train, to)
(should, be, mention)	(dataset, which, be)
(not, find, the)	(limit, in)
(not, ready)	(experiment, there)
(novelty, and)	(layer, this)
(no, quantitative)	(work, so)
(the, theoretical, analysis)	(be, write)
(experiment, there)	(the, basis)
(no, new)	(claim, that, this)
(to, control)	(not, ready)
complementary	(work, need)
(would, require)	(the, theoretical, analysis)
(enough, detail)	incomplete
(train, neural, network)	(reasonably, good)
(of, video)	(it, hard, to)
(the, combination, of)	(a, system)
incomplete	(and, compare, to)
(the, claim, about)	gans
(they, introduce)	(they, introduce)
(comparison, on)	(result, be, provide)
(limit, in)	(not, find, the)
push	(should, be, mention)
(cover, a)	(push, the)

Table 10: Top 50 salient n-grams for peer reviews and top 50 deconfounded n-grams.

Sensitivity Analysis for Causal Mediation through Text: an Application to Political Polarization

Graham Tierney and **Alexander Volfovsky**
Department of Statistical Science
Polarization Lab
Duke University
{graham.tierney,alexander.volfovsky}@duke.edu

Abstract

We introduce a procedure to examine a text-as-mediator problem from a novel randomized experiment that studied the effect of conversations on political polarization. In this randomized experiment, Americans from the Democratic and Republican parties were either randomly paired with one-another to have an anonymous conversation about politics or alternatively not assigned to a conversation — change in political polarization over time was measured for all participants. This paper analyzes the text of the conversations to identify potential mediators of depolarization and is faced with a unique challenge, necessitated by the primary research hypothesis, that individuals in the control condition do not have conversations and so lack observed text data. We highlight the importance of using domain knowledge to perform dimension reduction on the text data, and describe a procedure to characterize indirect effects via text when the text is only observed in one arm of the experiment.

1 Introduction

Increasing large and varied text corpora are becoming available to researchers. Especially in the field of computational social science, text data are yielding new insights and opening new areas of study (Grimmer and Stewart, 2013; Gentzkow et al., 2019a; Salganik, 2019). Text are being used to study who sets the political agenda (Barberá et al., 2019), measure partisanship in congressional speeches (Gentzkow et al., 2019b), and legislator attitudes expressed on Twitter (Spell et al., 2020).

An understudied area of this rapidly expanding field is how to perform causal inference with text data, especially when text is the treatment or outcome (Keith et al., 2020). Text data pose unique challenges due to the complex and high-dimensional structure that they impose on the already complex task of causal inference. For instance, concerns that social media might be causing political polarization by increasing ideological segregation (Bakshy et al., 2015; Barberá, 2015) or spreading disinformation (Lazer et al., 2018) must disentangle the effect of exposure to social media text on polarization and the propensity of highly polarized individuals to be active on social media.

The contributions of this paper are two-fold: (1) We introduce a sensitivity analysis for mediation when the information on the mediator is observed for only one group in an experiment. (2) We demonstrate the difficulty of using unsupervised text models for performing a causal analysis.

To illustrate these contributions, we analyze data from a novel randomized experiment studying the dynamics of political polarization (Bail, 2021; Combs et al., 2021). American voters were randomly paired across party lines to have meaningful, political conversations. Of particular interest is the text of the conversations. We want to characterize the kind of conversations that cause depolarization. This is inherently a question of *causal mediation*: we are interested in both the direct effect of simply having a conversation and the indirect effect of the conversation content.

The study we analyze follows a common design where information must be observed asymetrically for the different treatment arms. Specifically, text data are only available for the units who had conversations and are not available for control individuals, making explicit causal mediation impossible. This asymmetry is required by the research question. The original study sought to estimate the effect of *having a conversation with an out-partisan about politics*, which necessitates the control group having no conversation. Contrasting treatment with a control that had a non-political conversation, for example, would only estimate the effect of having a conversation with an out-partisan *about politics*.

This asymmetry is also a common feature of peer encouragement or counseling studies where treated units have a conversation with a peer or

Proceedings of CI+NLP: First Workshop on Causal Inference and NLP, pages 61–73
November 10, 2021.

professional and control units have no interactions (Anderson et al., 2005; Carandang et al., 2020; Malchodi et al., 2003). The natural followup to such studies is to identify what kind of conversations produce the best results. However, the experimental data cannot answer such questions because those mediators are missing for the control group. To accommodate such designs, we develop a procedure for a *mediation sensitivity analysis* designed to benchmark the observed correlation with the causal mediation effects that could be observed if control units had produced text data.

Our work also highlights the difficulty of using unsupervised models of text in the context of causal inference. In our application, we have expert knowledge of likely causal pathways, but, because these models do not leverage this expert knowledge, they are unable to identify semantically meaningful conversation features. Moreover, the features they do identify appear to not play a significant role in the causal story of the experimental data.

The outline of the paper is as follows: First, we introduce our illustration data and describe the causal and text complications. Section 3 describes the causal inference framework, concentrating on effect mediation and on how to incorporate text data into causal inference pipelines, and prior work on these issues. Section 4 demonstrates our finding that partner politeness is correlated with depolarization. Section 5 develops the mediation sensitivity procedure for this result. Section 6 demonstrates the failure of unsupervised text models to capture causal mechanisms. Section 7 concludes.

2 Polarization and Insights from Text

A growing body of research raises concerns that social media are increasing ideological segregation and incivility between political parties in the United States (Bakshy et al., 2015; Barberá, 2015). A particular concern, is that increasing exposure to elites from the other side may produce a backlash effect that increases polarization (Bail et al., 2018). In this paper we revisit data from a study that experimentally tested whether prolonged out-group contact could decrease polarization in the U.S. by having Democrats and Republicans engage on an anonymous chat platform (Bail, 2021; Combs et al., 2021).

In February 2020, approximately 1,500 Republicans and Democrats were recruited by a prominent survey firm and given a survey to measure their political views. The questions covered both issue-based polarization (how close one is to each party on policy views) and affect-based polarization (one's sentiment toward the other party). Individuals randomized to treatment were sent a seemingly-unrelated invitation to download a mobile chat application within 48 hours of completing the survey. Each person who logged into the app was randomly assigned a partner from the other party and prompted to discuss either gun control or immigration. Politics were not mentioned in the recruitment dialog or prior to logging into the app. After the conversations were finished, another seemingly unrelated survey was sent to all study participants that contained the same questions as the first survey. Within-person depolarization was measured by averaging the difference in post- and pre-survey responses to all polarization questions. The original study reveals that individuals assigned to treatment became significantly more depolarized (Combs et al., 2021; Bail, 2021, Appendix).

This paper focuses on analyzing the text of the conversations. We want to identify what conversation features caused the depolarization. However, we cannot rely on the randomization to identify causal effects for two reasons. The first and primary reason is that the control group did not have conversations, so we cannot compare treatment and control text. The original experiment was designed to estimate the effect of *having a conversation about politics* with an out-partisan, and as such, individuals in the control group had no conversations.

The second reason we cannot rely on the randomization to identify causal effects is that the conversation text is properly thought of as a mediator variable, something causally affected by treatment that also affects the outcome. Randomized treatment does not guarantee that there is no unobserved confounding of the mediator-outcome relationship. The conversation itself is both an outcome and exposure of interest. Use of text in both of those contexts is challenging, and the subject of much of our literature review.

We address these challenges by first, relying on prior work that identifies politeness or civility as a key feature in producing persuasive text, measuring politeness of messages received by individuals in treatment, then linking that measure to the outcome of interest, depolarization. Next, we impute politeness measures for control individuals in a way that preserves the observed relationship between politeness and depolarization among the treated and test how large the difference in politeness between treatment and control must be to observe significant mediation.

3 Causal Inference and Prior Work

The general goal behind causal inference is to understand "what if?" questions — what happens to an outcome of interest Y if one intervenes to set variable T. Information is frequently collected alongside the intervention and outcome; modern causal inference is often concerned with how this additional information interacts with the causal effects of interest. In this paper we are concerned with one such mechanism — that of causal mediation — and how text acts as part of that mechanism.

3.1 Mediation Analysis

Causal mediation analysis attempts to understand the mechanisms through which exposures affect an outcome (Pearl, 2014; VanderWeele, 2015). A mediator M is a variable that is causally affected by treatment T and also affects the outcome of interest Y. The directed acyclic graph (DAG) of such a process is depicted in Figure 1.

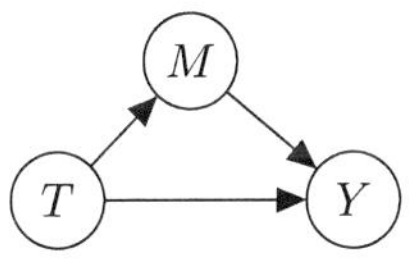

Figure 1: Causal DAG for treatment T, mediator M, and outcome Y.

This can be clearly represented in terms of potential outcomes, let $Y_i(T_i)$ note the potential outcome for unit i if treatment were T_i (Rubin, 1974). The total effect (TE) or average treatment effect is defined as $E[Y_i(1)] - E[Y_i(0)]$ (where the expectation is taken over the finite experimental population or over some global population distribution). This effect can be *identified* from simple observable quantities if the following three assumptions are satisfied: the potential outcome for unit i depends only on T_i (SUTVA), treatment is assigned independent of the potential outcome $Y_i(0), Y_i(1) \perp T_i|X_i$ (conditional independence or unconfoundedness), and for all i, $P(T_i = t) > 0$ for all t (positivity). A randomized experiment guarantees that conditional independence and positivity hold.

For mediation, we consider the decomposition of this total effect into *the natural direct effect* and the *natural indirect effect*, hereafter referred to as simply direct and indirect effects (Pearl, 2001). The direct effect measures the difference in expected outcome when changing treatment but holding the mediator at its natural level were treatment fixed, and the indirect effect measures the difference in expected outcome when holding treatment fixed and allowing the mediator change as it would naturally were treatment changed. These introduce a second level of potential outcome notation, let $M_i(T_i)$ note the potential outcomes for the mediator value for unit i when treatment is set to T_i. Additionally, let $Y_i(T_i, M_i(T_i))$ be the potential outcome Y_i as a function of both treatment and mediator for unit i. Note $Y_i(T_i) = Y_i(T_i, M_i(T_i))$. The total effect can be decomposed into:

$$TE = E[Y(1, M(1))] - E[Y(0, M(1))] + \quad (1)$$
$$E[Y(0, M(1))] - E[Y(0, M(0))] \quad (2)$$

The first line is the direct effect, the second is the indirect effect.[1] The direct effect corresponds to the effect measured along the direct $T \rightarrow Y$ path in the DAG in Figure 1, while the indirect effect is measured along the $T \rightarrow M \rightarrow Y$ path.

Additional assumptions are required to estimate the direct and indirect effects as functions of observed data. For details, see VanderWeele and Vansteelandt (2009); Nguyen et al. (2020). Essentially, the same assumptions regarding T_i and $Y_i(T_i)$ for estimating the TE are required for the mediator-outcome and treatment-mediator relationships with an additional assumption regarding cross-world quantities $M_i(1)$ and $Y_i(0, M_i(1))$. Importantly, randomizing T_i does not guarantee the $M \rightarrow Y$ relation from Figure 1 is unconfounded.

A variety of estimation methods exist for mediation analysis, which depend on the target estimands and modeling assumptions. For a full overview see Nguyen et al. (2021). Imai et al. (2010) provide a commonly used general method and framework for estimating both parametric and non-parametric models for mediation analysis. To facilitate inference in this paper we will consider a set of structural equation models (Eq. 3 and 4, which are discussed in detail in Section 5).

[1]The decomposition can also be performed by adding and subtracting $E[Y(1, M(0))]$, resulting in slightly different expressions of the direct and indirect effects. Under commonly used linear structural equation models that we apply in Section 5.2, these expressions are equivalent (VanderWeele, 2016).

3.2 Causal Inference with Text Data

Text data are extremely rich and can play important and complex roles in a causal pipeline. However, this richness makes satisfying the necessary assumptions that much harder. In large part, the difficulty arises from the fact that we want the actual text to play the role of outcome Y, treatment T, confounder X, or mediator M, but during analysis we must rely on summary measures of the text. These summaries might be parameters in an unsupervised text model, word counts, sentiment measures or other objects, but this requires replacing the existing assumptions with ones that include the summarization procedure.

Much of the prior work on text in causal settings has focused on text as a confounder, e.g. Saha et al. (2019) and Roberts et al. (2020). See Keith et al. (2020) for a full overview of the text-as-confounder literature. In general, these methods attempt to compare treated and control units with *similar* text or features inferred from text. In our work, we are interested in comparing polarization for participants who saw *different* text from their partner.

Methods directly related to our question of interest, linking the conversation features to depolarization, come from viewing text-as-treatment. These procedures generally transforming the high-dimensional text data into some low-dimensional representation, interpretable as treatments, and model outcome Y as a function of those treatments.

Wood-Doughty et al. (2018) studies the use of text classifiers to infer binary treatment when treatment is affected by measurement error or partial missingness. Fong and Grimmer (2016) discover latent binary treatments from text, which are then used to estimate causal effects using a supervised Indian Buffet Process (sIBP). Egami et al. (2018) develop a framework for causal inference with text as either treatment or outcome. They recommend using a train-test split where a low-dimensional representation of the text is learned on the training set, then causal quantities are estimated on the test set. We explore this procedure in Section 6.

To our knowledge, the only paper specifically about text-as-mediator is Veitch et al. (2020).[2] They develop a method for causal text embeddings by fine-tuning a pre-trained BERT network to estimate propensity scores and conditional outcomes. In our experiment, if control units had produced text, this method could decompose the treatment effect into the direct effect and total text-based mediation. However, the method would not produce interpretable measures of which text features are driving the depolarization. At the core of many mediation analyses is a desire to understand the causal pathways through which treatment operates.

3.3 Measuring Politeness in Conversations

The importance of politeness in conversations has been studied in the computational linguistics literature: Danescu-Niculescu-Mizil et al. (2013) identify politeness as a signifier of social power, Niu and Bansal (2018) and Firdaus et al. (2020) focus on generating polite dialogues, Kang and Hovy (2019) show that politeness can be delineated from the context, and Madaan et al. (2020) use style transfer techniques to translate polite and impolite messages while preserving the underlying context.

Politeness and incivility have also been studied in political contexts. Jaidka et al. (2019) find Twitter's increase of the character limit significantly improved the politeness of replies to politicians, Mutz and Reeves (2005) find that incivility in televised political disagreement harms citizens' political trust, and Papacharissi (2004) and Theocharis et al. (2016) highlight the role of civility in online political discourse in both citizen-citizen and citizen-politician interactions. All of the above emphasise the importance of civility and politness as necessary components of democratic deliberation.

4 Preliminary analysis of text data

The work on politeness and incivility lead us to focus on politeness as a potential mediator of depolarization. Individuals exposed to more polite partners may change their prior beliefs about the other side more than those exposed to less polite partners. We use the R package `politeness` to identify linguistic features of politeness with sentence parsing and dictionary methods (Yeomans et al., 2018). This package extends the work of Danescu-Niculescu-Mizil et al. (2013) and Voigt et al. (2017) by combing the indicators of politeness in both works.[3]

[2]Vig et al. (2020) apply causal mediation analysis to large, neural network-based language models to identify gender bias in the network itself. While this paper uses mediation tools, it is not focused on estimating causal effects with text as a mediator.

[3]When using the `convokit` Python library to identify politeness features, our results are unchanged (Chang et al., 2020). We use `politeness` in our main results because it identifies a broader set of features. The original application of these tools was not to political discussions of gun control and

To measure exposure to politeness, we extract all of the politeness features for each message sent by participants. Then, we standardize each feature to be mean zero variance one, and sum the results across all messages received by each user. *We focus on messages received rather than sent because we want to measure how one's conversation partner affects one's own depolarization.* We sum rather than average across politeness features because we want to measure total experienced politeness rather than a per-message measure. We wish to characterize a short and polite conversation as less exposure than a long and polite conversation. We refer to this constructed measure as the *politeness index*. Note that the random assignment of partners makes the no unmeasured confounding assumption plausible.

First, we examine the relationship between the politeness index and depolarization among the treated units who finished their conversations (completed at least 10 exchanges). We regress depolarization on politeness both in the full sample and split by party, controlling for demographic features. The results are shown in Table 1. We observe that participants with more polite partners depolarized significantly more; a 1 standard deviation increase in partner politeness is associated with a 0.069 standard deviation increase in depolarization. This relationship is stronger among Democrats with polite Republican partners.

We also look at how politeness and the relationship between depolarization and politeness differ by conversation topic. While participants assigned to talk about immigration were significantly more polite, there was no significant difference in the relationship between depolarization and politeness by topic. Figure 2 shows scatter-plots of politeness and the depolarization index by topic. Adding conversation topic to the regressions in Table 1 does not change any of results. Nevertheless, because control individuals do not have conversation topics assigned to them, we do not adjust for topic in the remaining analysis in the paper.

Crucially, we cannot conclude that the above are causal relationships based on these regressions. While partners were randomly assigned, partner *politeness* was not. If partner politeness is affected by one's own messages, as is likely the case, then there could be unmeasured confounding whereby certain participant features cause both polite replies by the conversation partner and depolarization. We believe our demographic controls cover many of the potential confounders but must rely on the untestable assumption that there are no other confounders. In the next section we develop a framework for understanding the causal nature of the relationship between conversations, the text and depolarization.

immigration. As such, we only use the context-independent politeness features, e.g. whether a participant expresses gratitude, not the specific projection of those features learned in a different, non-political context.

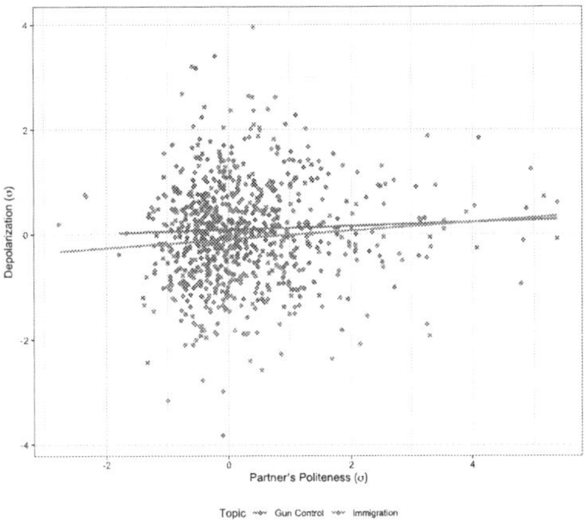

Figure 2: Depolarization and partner politeness. All units are in standard deviations. While those assigned to talk about immigration were 0.23 standard deviations more polite than those assigned to talk about gun control ($p < 0.01$), the relationship between politeness and depolarization was not significantly different across conversation topics (difference in slopes 0.04, $p \approx 0.50$).

5 Mediation Sensitivity

We would like to use politeness as a mediator and estimate the direct and indirect effects (introduced in Section 3) using the structural equation model:

$$Y_i = \tau T_i + \alpha M_i + \gamma X_i + \epsilon_i \quad (3)$$

$$M_i = \beta T_i + \theta X_i + \nu_i \quad (4)$$

where Y is the outcome (depolarization), M is the mediator (politeness), T is a binary treatment indicator, X is measured covariates, and ϵ and ν are error terms. The natural direct effect is τ, the difference in expected outcome while changing treatment and holding M fixed, the natural indirect effect is $\alpha\beta$, the difference in expected outcome while holding treatment fixed and allowing politeness to change as it would if treatment was changed. The total effect, identified by regressing Y on T *without* M, is $\tau + \alpha\beta$.

	All	Dem	Rep
	(1)	(2)	(3)
Politeness	0.069*	0.119*	0.002
	(0.035)	(0.046)	(0.052)
Constant	0.160	0.565	−0.294
	(0.215)	(0.288)	(0.312)
Observations	819	408	411

Table 1: Partner Politeness and Depolarization. Columns show results from regressing depolarization on partner politeness and demographic control variables. Column 1 uses all participants, column 2 only Democrats, and column 3 only Republicans. Participants with more polite partners significantly depolarized, especially Democrats. All regressions control for demographic factors: gender, age, education, race, and geographic region. Stars indicate statistical significance at the 5% level.

While control individuals clearly have a perceived level of politeness for the opposite party, because they did not participate in a conversation, there is no politeness to measure for them. This means β cannot be estimated. What we can do is benchmark the strength of the relationship identified in Table 1 by simulating politeness values for control units that preserve the relationships encoded in $p(Y, M|T = 1, X)$. The remainder of this section describes how the simulation and estimation should be conducted. Section 5.2 applies the procedure to the experimental data. We refer to simulated mediator values for control units as $\widetilde{M}$.

5.1 Procedure Description

The total effect $E[Y_i(1)] - E[Y_i(0)] = \tau + \alpha\beta$ will remain the same regardless of what values are imputed for the control mediator values $\widetilde{M}$ because it is estimated using Y and T alone. Similarly, α is a structural parameter that captures the relationship between politeness and depolarization—if simulated $\widetilde{M}$ changed structural parameter α, the estimated indirect effect, $\alpha\beta$, will not measure indirect effects as they would occur in real data. As such, we study the sensitivity of the decomposition of direct and indirect effects to the size of β, how much does treatment affect the mediator, while keeping $\tau + \alpha\beta$ and α fixed.

A naive approach of simulating $\widetilde{M}$ as random draws from observed M_i among treated units will not reflect information learned about α. With this simulation, Y and M are independent among control units, and α will shrink towards zero in the full sample. In this case, $p(M|T = 0)$ and $p(M|T = 1)$ will match, but the conditional outcome distributions will not, $p(Y|T = 0, M) = p(Y|T = 0)$ whereas among treatment M does provide information about Y.

In principle, one can use any model to learn the joint distribution $p(Y, M|T = 1, X)$, then using observed X and Y among control, impute or simulate $\widetilde{M}$ and continue. Using the outcome is often important to ensure that the mediator-outcome relationship is preserved. However, depending on the estimation method, it is not always necessary.

If one sets $\widetilde{M}$ to the linear projection of M on X learned among treated units ($\widetilde{M} = X_c(X_t^T X_t)^{-1} X_t^T M_t$) and uses OLS to estimate 3 and 4, then (a) the estimated $\widehat{\alpha}$ on the full sample will be exactly equal to the $\widehat{\alpha}$ estimated among treatment only, (b) the estimated $\widehat{\tau}$ will be exactly equal to the total effect, and (c) the estimated $\widehat{\beta}$ will be exactly 0. For proof see Appendix A. The intuition is that OLS estimates $\widehat{\alpha}$ and $\widehat{\tau}$ are learned from the residual variability in Y and M after removing the linear effects of X (Frisch and Waugh, 1933; Lovell, 1963). Because of the imputation, control units have no variability in M after removing the effects of X, so $\widehat{\alpha}$ is learned only from variability in treatment, preserving the structural parameter. $\widehat{\tau}$ and $\widehat{\beta}$ results follow because residual variability in M across T is zero.[4]

Implicit in this construction is the assumption that $p(Y|M)$ is the same for $T = 1$ and $T = 0$. In Equation 3, this assumption is encoded in the parameter α and the fact that there is no treatment-mediator interaction term. Note that α is not a parameter directly related to an intervention; it is the relationship between how polite an out-partisan is to someone and the change in that someone's feelings towards the other party. Simulations that change α among control units, i.e. do not assume that $p(Y|M)$ is the same for $T = 1$ and $T = 0$, would be simulating data that are inconsistent with observed relationships between variables among

[4]When linear projection is not desirable for imputing $\widetilde{M}$, matching methods can be used. Each control unit should be matched with treated unit(s) based on covariates X and Y, and $\widetilde{M}$ imputed from the matched treatment units where M is observed. This will not exactly preserve the relationships. As such, we recommend practitioners look at results such as Table 2 to ensure that the estimated relationship between Y and M is not too different between the full sample and treatment units.

treated units. In our application, $p(Y|M, T=0)$ is not observable because the mediator cannot be measured for $T=0$, so a direct assessment of the assumption is impossible. This assumption becomes testable only by changing the underlying research questions. For example, imagine if control participants were matched with an out-partisan to have a conversation about a non-political topic on which they disagreed. The assumption in question would imply that partner politeness affects depolarization the same whether the partner is talking about politics or not.

Once $\widetilde{M}$ has been generated, the remaining task is to test different β values to observe when significant mediation effects are detected. The implementation will depend on the particular mediation model specified. In Equation 4, we can set $\beta=c$ by subtracting constant c from all $\widetilde{M}$ values. Given our specification, c could be subtracted from control or added to treatment with identical results. However, for more complex models, this equivalency may not hold. We recommend changing the imputed values $\widetilde{M}$ rather than observed M among treatment to avoid changing any observed data. The range of values for β should be from 0 to the value such that the direct effect τ is zero. For the structural equation set up here, that is when $\beta = TE/\alpha$ where TE is the total effect, also estimable as the direct effect when $\beta=0$.

5.2 Procedure Application

We set $\widetilde{M}$ equal to the linear projection described above. We show the empirical validation of the imputation properties in Table 2. Column 1 reports coefficients from regressing Y on M and X for only treated units, column 2 coefficients from regressing Y on T and X for all units, and column 3 the results for regressing Y on T, X, and M with the imputation as described above.

Next, we set β values between 0 and $\widehat{\tau}/\widehat{\alpha}$ from column 3 of Table 2, and compute direct and indirect effects (Tingley et al., 2014). We note that once α and β are fixed, point estimates of mediation effects are immediate. However, uncertainty quantification is not. We can construct $1-\phi\%$ confidence intervals using a non-parametric bootstrap and identify the smallest β such that the null hypothesis that the indirect effect $\alpha\beta=0$ is rejected with confidence level ϕ.

Figure 3 shows the results of our procedure with 95% confidence intervals. The total effect, as expected, remained constant, and the direct and indirect effects each range from 0 to the total effect. The smallest β where we reject the null hypothesis that the indirect effect is zero is 0.09 standard deviations. *This means that having a conversation with someone from the other political party only needs to move beliefs about politeness by about 0.09 standard deviations for politeness to be a significant mediator.* The imputation sets $\widetilde{M}$ to the best guess as to how a typical member of the other party interacts with each control participant using a linear projection from their demographic variables. If the baseline level of politeness was 0.09 or more standard deviations lower among control units, then we would have observed a statistically significant indirect effect from partner politeness, representing mediation of about 4% of the total effect. If treatment moved politeness by the same amount that switching the topic from gun control to immigration does (0.23 standard deviations), we would still have observed a statistically significant indirect effect, representing mediation of about 10% of the total effect.

	Treatment Only	Total Effect	Imputed Politeness
	(1)	(2)	(3)
Treatment		0.156*	0.156*
		(0.076)	(0.076)
Politeness	0.069*		0.069*
	(0.035)		(0.035)
Constant	0.159	0.119	0.134
	(0.214)	(0.202)	(0.202)
N	819	1,037	1,037

Table 2: Politeness Imputation Results. Results from regressing depolarization on (1) partner politeness among treatment only, (2) treatment indicator among all units, and (3) treatment indicator and partner politeness (imputed for control) among all units. All regressions control for demographic factors: gender, age, education, race, and geographic region. The imputation is computed using the linear projection learned among treatment units. Stars indicate statistical significance at the 5% level.

6 Raw Text Methods

In this section, we adapt two text-as-treatment models that perform dimension reduction on the con-

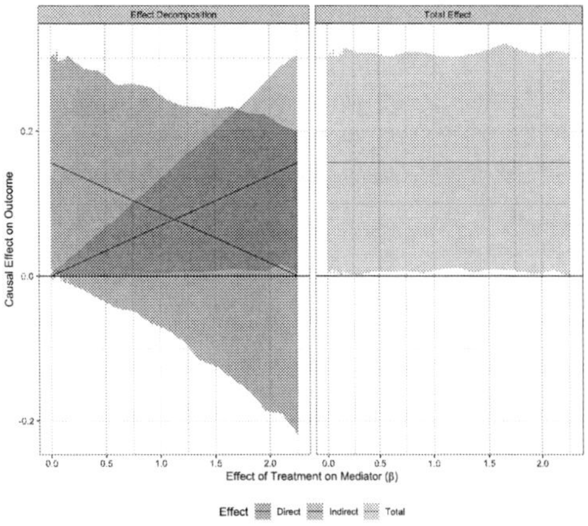

Figure 3: Decomposition of treatment effects by simulated effect on mediator. Figures shows point estimates and 95% confidence intervals for the direct (τ), indirect ($\alpha\beta$), and total ($\tau + \alpha\beta$) effects. Significant indirect effects are first detected at $\beta = 0.09$.

versation data to study if unsupervised methods can identify alternatives or improvements to "politeness." We refer to these methods as "unsupervised" because they take as an input, the raw text of the conversations, rather than using an analyst-specified dimension reduction as in the previous section. *These methods do not perform well and highlight the need for domain knowledge and prior work to select conversation features to explore as potential mediators*. It is possible that the small size of the data plays a role in this poor performance: randomized experiments are expensive and lead to datasets that might be too small for such unsupervised models. However, high-quality experiential data are extremely useful for learning causal effects as treatment-related unconfoundedness assumptions are guaranteed by randomization.

We apply standard LDA (Blei et al., 2003) topic modeling without using any outcome information to learn topics and the supervised Indian Buffet process (sIBP) of Fong and Grimmer (2016), which does use the outcome when learning treatments in the documents. We do not claim these methods are exhaustive, but they are representative of common practice, see e.g. Roberts et al. (2020) and Egami et al. (2018).[5]

For both methods, we combine all messages received and treat those as the documents for analysis. To create a document-word matrix as required by both methods, we pre-process the data by making all words lower case, removing standard stopwords, and dropping words that appear in fewer than 1% documents. The result is 819 documents covering a vocabulary of 3,715 words. For both methods, we need only explore the effect of the output of the text model on depolarization. Because no meaningful relationship is identified, the mediation sensitivity procedure is not needed.

LDA. We estimate the LDA model using 4 through 12 topics without considering the outcome data. Then, we extract posterior estimates of topic prevalence for each set of received messages, and use those in a regression analysis along with the same demographic control variables.

The top panel of Figure 4 shows point and interval estimates for the effect of each topic on depolarization for each model.[6] The only significant results across all models are three topics from the 10 topic model. Under the global null hypothesis that all true topic coefficients are 0, we'd expect about 2 coefficients to be significant due to random chance. The top 10 words for these topics are shown in Table 3. While these topics might suggest mediation is occurring, Topic 7 really only identifies immigration words, one of the two assigned discussion issues, and the other two do not have any clear interpretation. Discussion of immigration is really a measure of compliance, adhering to the researcher-assigned topic, rather than mediation.

Topic 7 ($K = 10$): immigration, people, country, illegal, immigrants, border, legal, wall, agree, law
Topic 8 ($K = 10$): people, agree, feel, good, make, issue, country, issues, change, things
Topic 9 ($K = 10$): people, pay, country, money, work, good, $, jobs, things, president

Table 3: Top Words for Significant Topics. The 10 highest probability words are shown for the three topics with $p < 0.05$. All are from the LDA, 10 topic model.

sIBP. Fong and Grimmer (2016) note that interpreting marginal effects of topic prevalence in the LDA model is difficult. LDA topic prevalence in a document is a point on the simplex, so it must

[5]The LDA model is estimated with default parameter settings using the `topicmodels` package (Grün and Hornik, 2011). The sIBP model has hyperparameters optimized over a search grid using provided functionality in the `texteffect` package (Fong, 2019).

[6]Note that because topic prevalence must sum to one, for a model with K topics, only $K - 1$ coefficients are estimable.

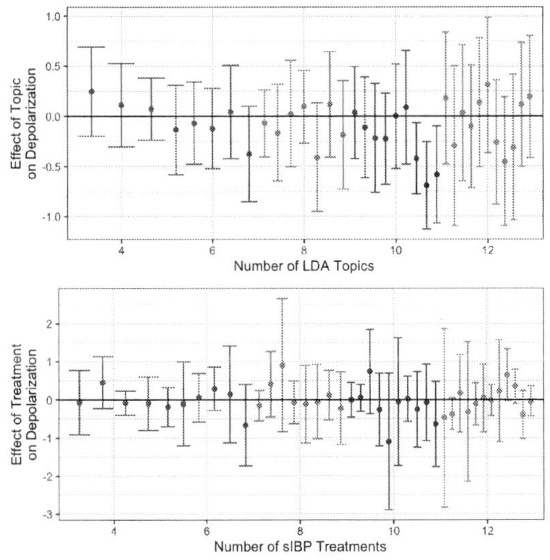

Figure 4: Point and 95% confidence intervals are shown for the effects of topics and treatments on depolarization. No effects are significant at the 5% level. Each regression controls for the following variables: conversation topic, political party, age, gender, race, and education.

sum to one. An increase in one topic must be offset with a decrease in another. Thus, they propose defining a K dimensional binary vector for each document that captures whether each of the topics is present in that document. Per their implementation, the data are split into a 50/50 training and test set. Topics are learned jointly with the document text and the outcome variable in the training set. Then, topics are inferred from the text in the test set, and effects corresponding to each topic are learned using only the test set. We augment their procedure by also including control variables in the test-set estimation of treatment effects.

The bottom panel of Figure 4 shows the results. None of the effects are statistically significant. In part, this is because the procedure requires splitting the data, with effects being estimated using only half of the data that the other models are learned on. Manual review of the top words from the topics shows some have semantic coherence, successfully splitting gun control and immigration issues, but their lack of meaningful correlation with the outcome limits their usefulness in understanding how the conversations cause depolarization.

7 Conclusion

This paper contributes to the methodological literature on text in causal inference by considering text as a mediator, i.e. considering text simultaneously as both a treatment and outcome, and the substantive literature on political polarization and exposure to members of opposing parties.

We develop a sensitivity procedure for mediation analysis when the mediator is only observed for one arm of the experiment. Our procedure allows researchers to assess the strength of correlations between the outcome and mediators by determining how much treatment would have to affect the mediator to observe a significant indirect effect. When applied to text data, domain knowledge is especially important to both guide selection of potential mediators and assess practical significance of the required treatment effect on the mediator.

Beyond the experiment analyzed here, this procedure is useful in marketing applications when one wants to assess the alignment of digital advertisements with surrounding web-page context in reference to control units shown no ads (Zanjani et al., 2011). Observational studies sometimes collect data on treated and control units from different sources with different sets of covariates, as in observational analysis of the Lallonde data (Dehejia and Wahba, 1999). This procedure can also be used in a power analysis to guide sample size selection for future studies with similar treatments that will collect mediator data for all participants.

References

Alex K Anderson, Grace Damio, Sara Young, Donna J Chapman, and Rafael Pérez-Escamilla. 2005. A randomized trial assessing the efficacy of peer counseling on exclusive breastfeeding in a predominantly latina low-income community. *Archives of Pediatrics & Adolescent Medicine*, 159(9):836–841.

Chris Bail. 2021. *Breaking the Social Media Prism: How to Make Our Platforms Less Polarizing*. Princeton University Press.

Christopher A. Bail, Lisa P. Argyle, Taylor W. Brown, John P. Bumpus, Haohan Chen, M. B. Fallin Hunzaker, Jaemin Lee, Marcus Mann, Friedolin Merhout, and Alexander Volfovsky. 2018. Exposure to opposing views on social media can increase political polarization. *Proceedings of the National Academy of Sciences of the United States of America*, 115(37):9216–9221.

Eytan Bakshy, Solomon Messing, and Lada A. Adamic. 2015. Exposure to ideologically diverse news and opinion on Facebook. *Science*, 348(6239):1130–1132.

Pablo Barberá. 2015. Birds of the same feather tweet together: Bayesian ideal point estimation using twitter data. *Political Analysis*, 23(1):76–91.

Pablo Barberá, Andreu Casas, Jonathan Nagler, Patrick J. Egan, Richard Bonneau, John T. Jost, and Joshua A. Tucker. 2019. Who Leads? Who Follows? Measuring Issue Attention and Agenda Setting by Legislators and the Mass Public Using Social Media Data. *American Political Science Review*, 113(4):883–901.

David M Blei, Andrew Y Ng, and Michael I Jordan. 2003. Latent dirichlet allocation. *The Journal of Machine Learning Research*, 3:993–1022.

Rogie Royce Carandang, Akira Shibanuma, Junko Kiriya, Karen Rose Vardeleon, Edward Asis, Hiroshi Murayama, and Masamine Jimba. 2020. Effectiveness of peer counseling, social engagement, and combination interventions in improving depressive symptoms of community-dwelling filipino senior citizens. *PloS one*, 15(4):e0230770.

Jonathan P. Chang, Caleb Chiam, Liye Fu, Andrew Wang, Justine Zhang, and Cristian Danescu-Niculescu-Mizil. 2020. ConvoKit: A toolkit for the analysis of conversations. In *Proceedings of the 21th Annual Meeting of the Special Interest Group on Discourse and Dialogue*, pages 57–60, 1st virtual meeting. Association for Computational Linguistics.

Aidan Combs, Graham Tierney, Brian Guay, Friedolin Merhout, Christopher Bail, D. Sunshine Hillygus, and Alexander Volfovsky. 2021. Anonymous cross-party conversations can decrease political polarization: A field experiment on a mobile chat platform. *Unpublished Manuscript*.

Cristian Danescu-Niculescu-Mizil, Moritz Sudhof, Dan Jurafsky, Jure Leskovec, and Christopher Potts. 2013. A computational approach to politeness with application to social factors. In *Proceedings of the 51st Annual Meeting of the Association for Computational Linguistics (Volume 1: Long Papers)*, pages 250–259, Sofia, Bulgaria. Association for Computational Linguistics.

Rajeev H Dehejia and Sadek Wahba. 1999. Causal effects in nonexperimental studies: Reevaluating the evaluation of training programs. *Journal of the American statistical Association*, 94(448):1053–1062.

Naoki Egami, Christian J. Fong, Justin Grimmer, Margaret E. Roberts, and Brandon M. Stewart. 2018. How to make causal inferences using texts. *arXiv*, pages 1–47.

Mauajama Firdaus, Asif Ekbal, and Pushpak Bhattacharyya. 2020. Incorporating politeness across languages in customer care responses: Towards building a multi-lingual empathetic dialogue agent. In *Proceedings of the 12th Language Resources and Evaluation Conference*, pages 4172–4182, Marseille, France. European Language Resources Association.

Christian Fong. 2019. *texteffect: Discovering Latent Treatments in Text Corpora and Estimating Their Causal Effects*. R package version 0.3.

Christian Fong and Justin Grimmer. 2016. Discovery of treatments from text corpora. In *Proceedings of the 54th Annual Meeting of the Association for Computational Linguistics (Volume 1: Long Papers)*, pages 1600–1609, Berlin, Germany. Association for Computational Linguistics.

Ragnar Frisch and Frederick V. Waugh. 1933. Partial time regressions as compared with individual trends. *Econometrica*, 1(4):387–401.

Matthew Gentzkow, Bryan Kelly, and Matt Taddy. 2019a. Text as data. *Journal of Economic Literature*, 57(3):535–74.

Matthew Gentzkow, Jesse M. Shapiro, and Matt Taddy. 2019b. Measuring group differences in high-dimensional choices: Method and application to congressional speech. *Econometrica*, 87(4):1307–1340.

Justin Grimmer and Brandon M Stewart. 2013. Text as data: The promise and pitfalls of automatic content analysis methods for political texts. *Political analysis*, 21(3):267–297.

Bettina Grün and Kurt Hornik. 2011. topicmodels: An R package for fitting topic models. *Journal of Statistical Software*, 40(13):1–30.

Kosuke Imai, Luke Keele, and Dustin Tingley. 2010. A General Approach to Causal Mediation Analysis. *Psychological Methods*, 15(4):309–334.

Kokil Jaidka, Alvin Zhou, and Yphtach Lelkes. 2019. Brevity is the soul of twitter: The constraint affordance and political discussion. *Journal of Communication*, 69(4):345–372.

Dongyeop Kang and Eduard H. Hovy. 2019. xslue: A benchmark and analysis platform for cross-style language understanding and evaluation. *CoRR*, abs/1911.03663.

Katherine Keith, David Jensen, and Brendan O'Connor. 2020. Text and causal inference: A review of using text to remove confounding from causal estimates. In *Proceedings of the 58th Annual Meeting of the Association for Computational Linguistics*, pages 5332–5344, Online. Association for Computational Linguistics.

David M. J. Lazer, Matthew A. Baum, Yochai Benkler, Adam J. Berinsky, Kelly M. Greenhill, Filippo Menczer, Miriam J. Metzger, Brendan Nyhan, Gordon Pennycook, David Rothschild, Michael Schudson, Steven A. Sloman, Cass R. Sunstein, Emily A.

Thorson, Duncan J. Watts, and Jonathan L. Zittrain. 2018. The science of fake news. *Science*, 359(6380):1094–1096.

Michael C. Lovell. 1963. Seasonal adjustment of economic time series and multiple regression analysis. *Journal of the American Statistical Association*, 58(304):993–1010.

Aman Madaan, Amrith Setlur, Tanmay Parekh, Barnabas Poczos, Graham Neubig, Yiming Yang, Ruslan Salakhutdinov, Alan W Black, and Shrimai Prabhumoye. 2020. Politeness transfer: A tag and generate approach. In *Proceedings of the 58th Annual Meeting of the Association for Computational Linguistics*, pages 1869–1881, Online. Association for Computational Linguistics.

Carolyn S Malchodi, Cheryl Oncken, Ellen A Dornelas, Laura Caramanica, Elizabeth Gregonis, and Stephen L Curry. 2003. The effects of peer counseling on smoking cessation and reduction. *Obstetrics & Gynecology*, 101(3):504–510.

Diana C. Mutz and Byron Reeves. 2005. The new videomalaise: Effects of televised incivility on political trust. *American Political Science Review*, 99(1):1–15.

Trang Quynh Nguyen, Elizabeth B. Sarker, Ian Schmid, Noah Greifer, Elizabeth L. Ogburn, Ina M. Koning, and Elizabeth A. Stuart. 2021. Clarifying causal mediation analysis: From simple to more robust strategies for estimation of marginal natural (in)direct effects.

Trang Quynh Nguyen, Ian Schmid, Elizabeth L. Ogburn, and Elizabeth A. Stuart. 2020. Clarifying causal mediation analysis for the applied researcher: Effect identification via three assumptions and five potential outcomes.

Tong Niu and Mohit Bansal. 2018. Polite dialogue generation without parallel data. *Transactions of the Association for Computational Linguistics*, 6:373–389.

Zizi Papacharissi. 2004. Democracy online: Civility, politeness, and the democratic potential of online political discussion groups. *New Media and Society*, 6(2):259–283.

Judea Pearl. 2001. Direct and indirect effects. In *Proceedings of the Seventeenth conference on Uncertainty in artificial intelligence*, pages 411–420.

Judea Pearl. 2014. Interpretation and identification of causal mediation. *Psychological methods*, 19(4):459.

Margaret E Roberts, Brandon M Stewart, and Richard A Nielsen. 2020. Adjusting for confounding with text matching. *American Journal of Political Science*, 64(4):887–903.

Donald B Rubin. 1974. Estimating causal effects of treatments in randomized and nonrandomized studies. *Journal of educational Psychology*, 66(5):688.

Amrita Saha, Ghulam Ahmed Ansari, Abhishek Laddha, Karthik Sankaranarayanan, and Soumen Chakrabarti. 2019. Complex program induction for querying knowledge bases in the absence of gold programs. *Transactions of the Association for Computational Linguistics*, 7:185–200.

Matthew J Salganik. 2019. *Bit by bit: Social research in the digital age*. Princeton University Press.

Gregory Spell, Brian Guay, Sunshine Hillygus, and Lawrence Carin. 2020. An Embedding Model for Estimating Legislative Preferences from the Frequency and Sentiment of Tweets. In *Proceedings of the 2020 Conference on Empirical Methods in Natural Language Processing (EMNLP)*, pages 627–641, Online. Association for Computational Linguistics.

Yannis Theocharis, Pablo Barberá, Zoltán Fazekas, Sebastian Adrian Popa, and Olivier Parnet. 2016. A bad workman blames his tweets: the consequences of citizens' uncivil twitter use when interacting with party candidates. *Journal of communication*, 66(6):1007–1031.

Dustin Tingley, Teppei Yamamoto, Kentaro Hirose, Luke Keele, and Kosuke Imai. 2014. mediation: R package for causal mediation analysis. *Journal of Statistical Software*, 59(5):1–38.

Tyler VanderWeele. 2015. *Explanation in causal inference: methods for mediation and interaction*. Oxford University Press.

Tyler J. VanderWeele. 2016. Mediation Analysis: A Practitioner's Guide. *Annual Review of Public Health*, 37:17–32.

Tyler J VanderWeele and Stijn Vansteelandt. 2009. Conceptual issues concerning mediation, interventions and composition. *Statistics and its Interface*, 2(4):457–468.

Victor Veitch, Dhanya Sridhar, and David Blei. 2020. Adapting text embeddings for causal inference. In *Proceedings of the 36th Conference on Uncertainty in Artificial Intelligence (UAI)*, volume 124 of *Proceedings of Machine Learning Research*, pages 919–928. PMLR.

Jesse Vig, Sebastian Gehrmann, Yonatan Belinkov, Sharon Qian, Daniel Nevo, Yaron Singer, and Stuart Shieber. 2020. Investigating gender bias in language models using causal mediation analysis. In *Advances in Neural Information Processing Systems*, volume 33, pages 12388–12401. Curran Associates, Inc.

Rob Voigt, Nicholas P. Camp, Vinodkumar Prabhakaran, William L. Hamilton, Rebecca C. Hetey, Camilla M. Griffiths, David Jurgens, Dan Jurafsky, and Jennifer L. Eberhardt. 2017. Language from police body camera footage shows racial disparities in officer respect. *Proceedings of the National Academy of Sciences*, 114(25):6521–6526.

Zach Wood-Doughty, Ilya Shpitser, and Mark Dredze. 2018. Challenges of using text classifiers for causal inference. In *Proceedings of the 2018 Conference on Empirical Methods in Natural Language Processing*, pages 4586–4598, Brussels, Belgium. Association for Computational Linguistics.

Michael Yeomans, Alejandro Kantor, and Dustin Tingley. 2018. The politeness Package: Detecting Politeness in Natural Language. *The R Journal*, 10(2):489–502.

Shabnam H. A. Zanjani, William D. Diamond, and Kwong Chan. 2011. Does ad-context congruity help surfers and information seekers remember ads in cluttered e-magazines? *Journal of Advertising*, 40(4):67–84.

A Proof of Linear Projection Imputation Properties

Let $\mathbf{Y}_t$, $\mathbf{Y}_c$ be the outcome among treatment and control respectively. Let $\mathbf{X}_t$ and $\mathbf{X}_c$ be $n_t \times p$ and $n_c \times p$ matrices of covariates for treatment and control, including an intercept term. Let $\mathbf{M}_t$ be observed mediator values for treatment. $\mathbf{M}_c$ is not observed. Let $\mathbf{T}$ be the vector of binary treatment indicators. The above variables without a subscript refer to column-stacked (treatment on top of control) versions, e.g. $\mathbf{Y} = \begin{pmatrix}\mathbf{Y}_t \\ \mathbf{Y}_c\end{pmatrix}$.

If $\mathbf{M}_c$ is imputed using the linear regression learned among treatment, $\mathbf{M}_c = \mathbf{X}_c(\mathbf{X}_t^T\mathbf{X}_t)^{-1}\mathbf{X}_t^T\mathbf{M}_t = \mathbf{X}_c\widehat{\beta}_M$, then the OLS regression of $\mathbf{Y}$ on $\mathbf{T}$, $\mathbf{X}$ and $\mathbf{M}$, will (a) estimate coefficient $\widehat{\alpha}$ on the mediator that is exactly equal to the coefficient when regressing $\mathbf{Y}_t$ on $\mathbf{M}_t$ and $\mathbf{X}_t$ and (b) estimate coefficient $\widehat{\tau}$ on the treatment indicator that is exactly equal to the coefficient when regressing $\mathbf{Y}$ on $\mathbf{X}$ without $\mathbf{M}$. And (c), the OLS regression of $\mathbf{M}$ on $\mathbf{X}$ and $\mathbf{T}$ will estimate a coefficient on $\mathbf{T}$ of 0.

Proof. This proof makes extensive use of the Frisch–Waugh–Lovell theorem (FWL) (Frisch and Waugh, 1933; Lovell, 1963). The theorem states that the multivariate OLS regression coefficient for any predictor is exactly equal to the coefficient from a univariate regression of the residualised outcome on the residualised predictor, where the residuals are computed from regressions of the outcome and predictor on all other predictors in the multivariate regression. Specifically, the OLS coefficient β_1 estimated from regression equation $Y = X_1\beta_1 + X_2\beta_2 + e$ is exactly equal to the OLS coefficient estimated from $A_{X_2}Y = A_{X_2}X_1 + A_{X_2}e$ where A_{X_2} is the annihilator matrix for X_2, $A_{X_2} = I - P_{X_2}$, $P_{X_2} = X_2(X_2^TX_2)^{-1}X_2^T$. P_{X_2} is the projection matrix onto the column space of X_2, A_{X_2} is the projection matrix onto the complement of the column space of X_2.

$\mathbf{Y}$ can be expressed as:

$$\mathbf{Y} = \mathbf{X}\widehat{\beta}_Y + \mathbf{T}\widehat{\tau} + \mathbf{M}\widehat{\alpha} + \mathbf{e},$$

where $\mathbf{e}$ is linearly independent from all other predictors, e.g. $\mathbf{e}^T\mathbf{M} = \mathbf{0}$. OLS on the full sample will estimate coefficients of $\widehat{\beta}_Y$, $\widehat{\tau}$, and $\widehat{\alpha}$ with residuals $\mathbf{e}$.

$\mathbf{M}_t$ can be expressed as:

$$\mathbf{M}_t = \mathbf{X}_t\widehat{\beta}_M + \mathbf{r}_t$$

where $\mathbf{r}_t^T\mathbf{X}_t = 0$. Thus, by the assumed construction of $\mathbf{M}_c = \mathbf{X}_c\widehat{\beta}_M$, $\mathbf{M}$ can be expressed as:

$$\mathbf{M} = \mathbf{X}\widehat{\beta}_M + \begin{pmatrix}\mathbf{r}_t \\ \mathbf{0}\end{pmatrix}$$

Proof of (a). Now, consider the regression among just treated units. By FWL, we can consider just the regression of $\mathbf{A}_{X_t}\mathbf{Y}_t$ on $\mathbf{A}_{X_t}\mathbf{M}_t$. Call the estimated coefficient $\widetilde{\alpha}$. We show that $\widetilde{\alpha} = \widehat{\alpha}$. Note that among treatment, $T_i = 1$, so $\mathbf{T}_t$ is in the column space of $\mathbf{X}_t$ because it contains an intercept term. Thus, $\mathbf{A}_{X_t}T_t = 0$.

$$\begin{aligned}\widetilde{\alpha} &= \left(\mathbf{M}_t^T\mathbf{A}_{X_t}\mathbf{A}_{X_t}\mathbf{M}_t\right)^{-1}\mathbf{M}_t^T\mathbf{A}_{X_t}\mathbf{A}_{X_t}\mathbf{Y}_t \\ &= \left(\mathbf{M}_t^T\mathbf{A}_{X_t}\mathbf{M}_t\right)^{-1}\mathbf{M}_t^T\mathbf{A}_{X_t}\mathbf{Y}_t \\ &= \left(\mathbf{M}_t^T\mathbf{A}_{X_t}\mathbf{M}_t\right)^{-1}(\mathbf{M}_t^T\mathbf{A}_{X_t}\mathbf{M}_t\widehat{\alpha} + \\ &\quad \mathbf{M}_t^T\mathbf{A}_{X_t}\mathbf{e}_t) \\ &= \left(\mathbf{M}_t^T\mathbf{A}_{X_t}\mathbf{M}_t\right)^{-1}\mathbf{M}_t^T\mathbf{A}_{X_t}\mathbf{M}_t\widehat{\alpha} \\ &= \widehat{\alpha}\end{aligned}$$

The second to last line is because $\mathbf{M}_t^T\mathbf{A}_{X_t}\mathbf{e}_t = 0$. By construction, $0 = \mathbf{M}^T\mathbf{e} = \left(\mathbf{X}\widehat{\beta}_M + \begin{pmatrix}\mathbf{r}_t \\ \mathbf{0}\end{pmatrix}\right)^T\mathbf{e} = \mathbf{r}_t^T\mathbf{e}_t = \mathbf{M}_t^T\mathbf{A}_{X_t}\mathbf{e}_t$. Thus, $0 = \mathbf{M}_t^T\mathbf{A}_{X_t}\mathbf{e}_t$.

Proof of (b). Here we consider the regression of $\mathbf{A}_X\mathbf{Y}$ on $\mathbf{A}_X\mathbf{T}$, which estimates the multivariate regression coefficient from regressing $\mathbf{Y}$ on $\mathbf{X}$ and $\mathbf{T}$ without $\mathbf{M}$. We show that $\widetilde{\tau}$ estimated from this regression is exactly equal to $\widehat{\tau}$.

$$
\begin{aligned}
\widetilde{\tau} &= (\mathbf{T}^T\mathbf{A}_X\mathbf{T})^{-1}\mathbf{T}^T\mathbf{A}_X\mathbf{Y} \\
&= (\mathbf{T}^T\mathbf{A}_X\mathbf{T})^{-1}\mathbf{T}^T(\mathbf{A}_X\mathbf{M}\widehat{\alpha} + \mathbf{A}_X\mathbf{T}\widehat{\tau} + \mathbf{e}) \\
&= \widehat{\tau} + (\mathbf{T}^T\mathbf{A}_X\mathbf{T})^{-1}\mathbf{T}^T\mathbf{A}_X\mathbf{M}\widehat{\alpha}, \\
&\quad \text{because } \mathbf{T}^T\mathbf{e} = 0 \\
&= \widehat{\tau}
\end{aligned}
$$

Again, the above uses $\mathbf{T}^T\mathbf{A}_X\mathbf{M} = 0$. $\mathbf{T}^T\mathbf{A}_X\mathbf{M} = \mathbf{T}^T\begin{pmatrix}\mathbf{r}_t \\ \mathbf{0}\end{pmatrix} = \mathbf{1}^T\mathbf{r}_t = 0$, with the final equality because $\mathbf{r}_t$ are the residuals from the regression of $\mathbf{M}_t$ on $\mathbf{X}_t$, so must sum to zero.

Proof of (c). Consider the regression of $\mathbf{M}$ on $\mathbf{T}$ and $\mathbf{X}$. Using FWL, the coefficient on $\mathbf{T}$ will be a the regression of $\mathbf{A}_X\mathbf{M}$ on $\mathbf{A}_X T$. From the above decomposition of $\mathbf{M}$, $\mathbf{A}_X\mathbf{M} = \begin{pmatrix}\mathbf{r}_t \\ \mathbf{0}\end{pmatrix}$.

$$
\begin{aligned}
\widehat{\tau}_M &= (\mathbf{T}^T\mathbf{A}_X\mathbf{T})^{-1}\mathbf{T}^T\mathbf{A}_X\mathbf{M} \\
&= (\mathbf{T}^T\mathbf{A}_X\mathbf{T})^{-1}\mathbf{T}^T\begin{pmatrix}\mathbf{r}_t \\ \mathbf{0}\end{pmatrix} \\
&= (\mathbf{T}^T\mathbf{A}_X\mathbf{T})^{-1}(\mathbf{1}^T\mathbf{r}_t) \\
&= 0
\end{aligned}
$$

$\mathbf{1}^T\mathbf{r}_t = 0$ because $\mathbf{X}_t$ contains an intercept term and $\mathbf{r}_t^T\mathbf{X}_t = \mathbf{0}$.

B Ethical Considerations

This study makes extensive use of data collected from the experiment described in detail in Combs et al. (2021), Bail (2021) and Section 2. This study was conducted with approval from an Institutional Review Board. The target population is registered voters in the United States that have a smartphone and lean towards either the Democratic or Republican political party. Participants were given informed consent dialogues regarding compensation, expected time to complete the tasks, and that their data would be used for research purposes before each survey and when invited to download the mobile application. After completing the final post-survey, participants were debriefed on the study purpose. Participants were told that at any time, they may request the study authors destroy any data collected from them.

Participants were compensated \$12.50 for the pre- and post-surveys and \$17.50 for using the conversation application. These values were set to be approximately 2-3 times the minimum wage in the United States given estimates of survey and conversation completion time. While participants were told they would only be compensated if they completed a conversation with a partner, all app-users were given full compensation so that no one would be denied compensation due to a partner who failed to respond promptly.

Participants shared personally identifying information, such as names and social media profiles, as well as sensitive personal information regarding their experiences with gun violence and immigration. For these reasons, the conversation data and identifying demographic data cannot be shared per the IRB protocol. We do share the code for all analyses and residualized versions of the outcome, mediator, and treatment variables that permit exact replication of the regression results in Section 5 without the identifying demographics.

A Survey of Online Hate Speech through the Causal Lens

Antigoni-Maria Founta and **Lucia Specia**
Department of Computing
Imperial College London
United Kingdom
{a.founta20,l.specia}@imperial.ac.uk

Abstract

The societal issue of digital hostility has previously attracted a lot of attention. The topic counts an ample body of literature, yet remains prominent and challenging as ever due to its subjective nature. We posit that a better understanding of this problem will require the use of causal inference frameworks. This survey summarises the relevant research that revolves around estimations of causal effects related to online hate speech. Initially, we provide an argumentation as to why re-establishing the exploration of hate speech in causal terms is of the essence. Following that, we give an overview of the leading studies classified with respect to the direction of their outcomes, as well as an outline of all related research, and a summary of open research problems that can influence future work on the topic.

1 Introduction

User-generated content has flourished with the evolution of social media platforms, and with it there has been an emergence of several social phenomena. Some of them can have a positive impact on mental health and eventually prove beneficial for societies; for example, it has been shown that the use of social networks from individuals of advanced age can lead to social benefits as well as have promising cognitive effects (Quinn, 2018). There is, however, a plethora of societal issues on the digital world which are proliferating in these platforms; such are several types of online misbehaviours.

Despite the clear interest of the research community to prevent, detect and filter harmful content (Schmidt and Wiegand, 2017; Fortuna and Nunes, 2018; MacAvaney et al., 2019; Mishra et al., 2019; Tontodimamma et al., 2021; Vidgen et al., 2019), the problem is very complex and still far from addressed. For instance, its multifactorial character poses already a large obstacle with manifold parameters to consider: diversity of platforms, abundance of languages, various facets it can manifest on, and different forms of language, to name a few. Even at a higher level, there are some deeply philosophical issues to contemplate, such as the thin line between awry, unwelcome content and freedom of speech. Nonetheless, the impact of online communications on society is considered more beneficial than harmful, hence it is important to advance the current scientific work to address its limitations.

The matter of unhealthy discourse is widely context-dependent (Saleem et al., 2017) and subjective (Salminen et al., 2018; Aroyo et al., 2019). A racial slur, for instance, will be interpreted differently from individuals with separate ethnic or racial backgrounds. Conversely, however, most existing approaches operate on the individual post/comment level or aggregate isolated pieces of information – usually of textual nature – and seek simplistic, ostensibly universal, decisions. Even though this was a necessary course of action at the beginning, such nuanced task requires higher sophistication. To combat the issue to the core, it is of utmost importance to deeply understand the factors that drive it and determine them in a definite way.

An increasingly popular scientific approach to ensure certainty is via the application of causal methods. Causality suggests an area of study that is ubiquitous in many parts of modern science (Russo and Williamson, 2011; Young, 2016; Landes et al., 2018; Hicks et al., 1980), among which social sciences (Marini and Singer, 1988; Reiss, 2009). Especially with the development of methodologies to extract causation from observational, instead of experimental, studies, it is now possible to utilise the profusion of web content for the extraction of causal knowledge (De Choudhury and Kiciman, 2017; Saha et al., 2019b; Doan et al., 2019).

Driven from the necessity of contemplating hate speech from a causal prism, there exists a relevant, yet still narrow, body of literature. In this survey, we attempt to summarise the existing research

Proceedings of CI+NLP: First Workshop on Causal Inference and NLP, pages 74–82
November 10, 2021.

which analyse phenomena of digital misbehaviours from a causal perspective, quantifying the influence on fundamental sociological outcomes related to harmful language online. In addition, we highlight the important research gaps and make suggestions for future directions. The goal of the present paper is to call attention to the importance of causation in the context of the discussed issue. In addition, it is intended to act as a point of reference for aspiring practitioners in the topic.

The rest of the paper revolves around the compilation of relevant publications, first classified based on their focus of sociological impact (§2) and, subsequently, arranged according to their approach towards salient methodological settings. The latter section (§3) is organised into several prominent hurdles, which include information regarding how they are treated from the reviewed work and points of discussion about the research gaps.

2 Sociological Causal Impact

Digital profanity is, first and foremost, a sociological phenomenon that affects many aspects of the virtual world. There are some pronounced directions which require thorough examination, such as the consequences of such actions on the affected communities as well as their targets, or the impact of banning policies aiming at fighting against it. Moreover, there are several other underlying effects that could get in the spotlight, including the ramifications of interventions or the reasons that drive toxic actors. As a result, it is of paramount importance to examine hate speech in a holistic way and concretely quantify the drivers of these outcomes. However, it is impossible to achieve this task without considering causality, because non-causal inferences can never be conclusive. Surprisingly, despite the broad interest of the research community in this topic, very little work has been done on attempting causal links, even on the most prominent tasks related to online hate speech (OHS).

In the present survey, we classify fundamental sociological outcomes related to OHS and outline the most distinguished body of literature. The classification results into three major pillars, with respect to the following:

- **Digital misbehaviours versus the physical world**: we summarise studies concerning the propagation of online hate speech to real life (Müller and Schwarz, 2018, 2020) as well as the influence of offline events to the dissemination of the issue online (Olteanu et al., 2018; Thomas et al., 2021)[1].

- **Harmful content versus the individuals**: we outline research concerning the impact of toxic behaviours on the targets or passive readers (Saha et al., 2019a) as well as the by-products of web characteristics (such as anonymity) on hate speech producers (von Essen and Jansson, 2020).

- **Effect of interventions**: finally, we review works that revolve around quantifying the effect of combating strategies which various platforms adopt. Existing research has focused on limiting policies, censoring and counter-speaking (Álvarez-Benjumea and Winter, 2018), social sanctioning (Munger, 2017), quarantining (Chandrasekharan et al., 2020) and banning hateful communities (Chandrasekharan et al., 2017; Thomas et al., 2021).

In all the of the cases, we can consider the role of hate speech both from the position of a phenomenon which is the result of (potentially) multiple causes, but also from the position of the causal root and study its effects. Therefore, in the following sections we review both directions.

2.1 Digital and Physical World

The first and most apparent pillar concerns the interrelation of online hate speech with the physical world, in a range of simple dissemination to absolute influence. Towards this direction, Müller and Schwarz (2018, 2020) have conducted research on the causal effect of social media on the propagation of hate sentiments offline, whether anti refugee (Müller and Schwarz, 2018) or more specifically anti-Muslim (Müller and Schwarz, 2020). In (Müller and Schwarz, 2018), the authors provide evidence that there is significant association between negative content against refugees existing on Facebook and offline hate crimes in Germany on a municipal level, while controlling for multiple potentially confounding factors such as German municipalities' characteristics and overall social media usage. To reach to this conclusion

[1]This direction has also been studied by (Scharwächter and Müller, 2020), however they merely calculate correlations and do not control for potential confounders, hence are not included in the present survey.

they combine a variety of data sources; online anti-refugee sentiment is represented by content from a widespread Facebook page of a German right-wing party, which hosts plenty of far-right content; controlling for the network's popularity in Germany, the authors measure Facebook outages and internet disruptions; finally, to further measure user activity on the network and create controls based on a neutral subject, they explore another broadly popular page of a famous commercial product. The causal framework they implement is a fixed-effects regression model (inspired by Bartik (1991)), which considers the aforementioned panel data combined with a range of controls. They discover that the effect is stronger in areas with higher Facebook usage and demonstrate a robustly strong connection between the activity of the right-wing group and severe hate crimes.

Similarly, in (Müller and Schwarz, 2020), they study the causal impact of Islamophobic social media content on registered crimes and overall negative sentiment against Muslims, and whether former US president Donald Trump's Twitter campaign has contributed to the propagation of Islamophobia. To ensure validity and robustness of their findings, they fuse a number of different data sources and employ a difference-in-differences approach. The data originate mainly from Twitter for the social media information, a survey by FBI to discover hate crimes, data from mass media, demographic information about US counties etc. Their findings provide evidence to associate a 38% larger increase in hate crimes, between 2010 and 2017, with higher exposure to social media. Moreover, consistently with previous research, they also provide evidence which shows a connection amid the start of Trump's presidential campaign with an increase of anti-Muslim sentiments in USA. Both projects illustrate there is strong evidence linking OHS with offline occurrences of hate-related crimes, with the former having a causal effect on the latter. [2]

Looking at the opposite direction, online hate speech is frequently affected by events taking place in the offline world. For example, following the September 11th, 2001 attack to the twin towers of New York City, there seems to be an increase in Islamic terrorist attacks as much as an increase in Islamophobia. It is very well expected that this will affect the online world and the way Muslims are perceived, which seems to actually be the case according to Olteanu et al. (2018). In (Olteanu et al., 2018) they analyse the influence of offline events on online hate speech. More specifically, they study the impact of several attacks related to the Islamic State – both Islamic terrorist attacks and Islamophobic ones – in terms of online hate speech and counter-hate speech. Their findings indicate that terrorist attacks show an increase in OHS, especially towards Muslims and Arabs.

To calculate the causal effect, they construct time series from Reddit and Twitter – representing the number of posts and unique users involved with the event – and then synthesize counterfactual time series for the same period of time, such as they would be produced had the attacks not happened. The counterfactual data are created by composing timelines of the same event, while adjusting for a temporal shift prior to the event, so that the time series will reflect a similar period of time but in different time windows. The produced timelines, put together with other external data sources, are then fit into a state space model (Brodersen et al., 2015) using maximum likelihood estimation, to predict the synthesized control time series. Comparing the treatment and control series, they calculate relative effects for a number of manually curated terms, which are also annotated across four hate speech dimensions (stance, targets, severity, and framing).

2.2 Actors and Targets

Beyond broadly looking at the overall impact of OHS, the next step would be to concentrate on the individuals and speculate how OHS affects and is affected by the participating members, whether these are at the producing or receiving end of such content. For example, in the aforementioned works, Olteanu et al. (2018) and Müller and Schwarz (2020) have made some general remarks regarding OHS, but in order to effectively focus on the task they narrow the type of hate speech to be racism and, more specifically, Islamophobism. Emphasis, however, is given on understanding the dynamics of diffusion and not on studying the impact on individuals who support Islam.

On the these grounds, Saha et al. (2019a) study the effect of hate prevalence on the stress levels of

[2] It goes without saying that results from papers that employ causality need to be interpreted with great care. As Müller and Schwarz (2018) emphasise, for instance, their findings do not indicate that social media can cause crimes against minorities, but rather "*social media can act as a propagating mechanism [...]*" so that "*shifts in exposure to anti-refugee sentiment on social media can increase the number of anti-refugee attacks*".

US college students, within Reddit college communities. To measure the levels of toxicity, they employ hate lexicons, with the help of which they compute the College Hate Index (CHX), as fractions of hateful keywords in each community compared to other subreddits banned for violating the hate-limiting policies of Reddit. Similarly, they quantify the exposure of users to hateful content based on the threads they have participated and to account for their stress levels they use a binary classifier based on existing models. They examine numerous observable confounders – such as the subreddit and user activity – and apply propensity score matching to calculate the causal effect whilst controlling for the covariates. Their results demonstrate an increase in stress expression caused by exposure to hateful speech.

Additionally, inherent characteristics of online environments, such as anonymity, ease of access, and size of audience (Brown, 2018) are highly likely to affect the behaviour of online social networks' users and sometimes make it easier for them to misbehave. von Essen and Jansson (2020) discuss the outcomes of the by-products of online world characteristics – in this case anonymity – on hate speech actors. In particular, they compare the degree of hatefulness before and after the identities of a large set of users from Flashback, an anonymous Swedish discussion platform similar to Reddit, have been publicly exposed. Their hypothesis suggests that once running the risk of exposure, users decrease the volume of hateful content they post. To detect hate, they implement a machine learning model and make predictions on the data, which will afterwards be used with a difference-in-differences approach to make causal claims. According to their estimates, the reduction of anonymity, as in risk of exposure, leads to a decline in general hate and overall activity, and even more on xenophobic content. Surprisingly, levels of misogyny increase. These empirical findings mostly support the author's original hypothesis.

2.3 Interventions

Last but not least, perhaps the most extensively studied of all three pillars is the effect of interventions, possibly due to its relatively close connection to causality. Interventions here refer to actions that are taken towards the elimination of the phenomenon; such strategies include quarantining (Chandrasekharan et al., 2020), banning (Chandrasekharan et al., 2017; Thomas et al., 2021), censoring (Álvarez-Benjumea and Winter, 2018), sanctioning (Munger, 2017), and counter speaking (Álvarez-Benjumea and Winter, 2018). Reverberations of each policy vary, depending on the platform and the methodology followed.

Chandrasekharan et al. (2017) first studied the effect of banning an entire hateful community using causal inference methods. More specifically, they investigate through a quasi-experiment how banning targeted communities influenced hate speech levels on Reddit. Initially, they investigate the activity of the participants, post-banning the examined subreddits, with respect to activity level and hateful content volume. To control for potential confounders related to user characteristics – such as the activity, popularity, or age of user accounts – they employ Mahalanobis Distance Matching (Rubin et al., 2006) between treatment and control users, which is then further enhanced with a difference-in-differences analysis (Abadie, 2005) of the two groups over time. Subsequently, they inspect the level of hate propagation to other *invaded* (as they call them) subreddits. In this case, matching needs to be applied on a subreddit level, rather than user level, so instead they employ the Interrupted Time Series approach (Bernal et al., 2017). Their results show that the ban worked *for Reddit*, meaning that having targeted a particular area of the platform, they have successfully eliminated hateful content without conveying the problem elsewhere within Reddit.

In addition to this work, the authors also studied the causal effect of *quarantining* Reddit communities, in a similar experimental framework (Chandrasekharan et al., 2020). Quarantining is a form of intervention that Reddit applies, where communities are indicated as potentially problematic and users have to deliberately choose to enter them, after being warned about toxicity levels within. This approach is less stern than banning, however according to the findings of this study, it is still effective to restrict the influx of users in hostile communities, while preserving the freedom of speech. In this case, the causal inference strategy used is the Interrupted Time Series regression (Bernal et al., 2017), which models interruptions caused by the treatment variable.

Paper	Domain	Treatment	Outcome	Controls	Causal Method
Chandrasekharan et al. (2017)	Reddit	Banning subreddits	Former members' activity, language & migration trends	Subreddits that could potentially have been banned	MDM, DiD & ITS Regression Analysis
Munger (2017)	Twitter	Social sanctioning, varying by influence & identity	Race-based harassment	Gender & race of harassers, and anonymity	Randomized Control Experiment
Olteanu et al. (2018)	Twitter & Reddit	Islamophobic & Islamist terrorist attacks in Western countries	Hateful content	Synthetic counterfactual time series	Comparison of observed vs counterfactual time series
Álvarez-Benjumea and Winter (2018)	Custom forum	Censoring & counter-speaking	Hate speech score	Number of comments	Experimental approach
Müller and Schwarz (2018)	Facebook	Anti-refugee Facebook group	Hate crimes against refugees in Germany	Characteristics of German municipalities	Fixed effects panel regressions
Saha et al. (2019a)	Reddit	Hateful speech in college subreddits	Online stress levels	Subreddit & User activity	Propensity score matching & DiD Regression Analysis
Müller and Schwarz (2020)	Twitter	High Twitter usage	Anti-Muslim hate crimes	Characteristics of US counties	DiD approach
von Essen and Jansson (2020)	Flashback	Web anonymity	Hateful posts	Risk of web exposure	DiD approach
Chandrasekharan et al. (2020)	Reddit	Quarantining subreddits	Member participation & language, and new member influx	Subreddits that could potentially have been quarantined	ITS & Bootstrapping tests
Thomas et al. (2021)	Reddit	External events & regulatory actions (ie. bans)	Member activity & attrition	User participation	MDM & DiD analysis & Multivariate Bayesian changepoint analysis
Ananthakrishnan and Tucker (2021)	YouTube	Presence of hate speech	Propagation (or "virality") of hate speech	Popularity, quality and posting time of videos	Instrumental Variables

Table 1: Following the format of (Keith et al., 2020), this table summarises research papers related to causal effects of web hostility. The abbreviations used stand for the following; Difference-in-Differences (DiD) (Abadie, 2005); Interrupted Time Series (ITS) (Bernal et al., 2017); Mahalanobis Distance Matching (MDM) (Rubin et al., 2006).

3 Difficulties and Causal Methods

Experimentation for the sole purpose of causality is fairly costly and, in this case, can be largely unethical, considering that it would mean deliberate exposure of people to toxic material. As a result, it is crucial to exploit the available methodologies of observational causality, in combination with its intersection with natural language processing. There are, however, several open research problems which lie at the heart of textual causality and thus are inherited by this task. A prominent hurdle, for instance, exists in the conception of the causal diagram, contemplating all the possible covariates and determining their roles. Such graphs are domain-specific and can greatly deviate, due to differences introduced by the platforms or niche types of speech. Furthermore, there are challenges such as the discovery of effective linguistic representations for the various parts where text can act as a surrogate.

In this section we discuss some prevailing difficulties, summarise the route of relevant literature, and finally, provide some suggested directions based on previous studies.

3.1 Confounding Bias

To establish true causation among a target variable X and an outcome Y, there should not be any indirect connections influencing the effect of X on Y. In reality it is rarely the case that this will hold organically true, hence being aware of any confounding factors is fundamental in order to intervene accordingly and eliminate their impact. Many confounders can be detected after careful exploration of the domain and quantified through unadjusted versus adjusted estimates. These are called *observable* confounders and are largely discovered based on domain expertise or previous research. It is well possible, however, that not all such factors can be anticipated; there are cases where they might not be discoverable or their computations might not be feasible.

One very relevant work on treating *latent* confounders is the one of Cheng et al. (2019), who attempt to create a somewhat causally-aware cyberbullying detection model for observed data, making it robust on confounding bias by controlling for latent (or plausible, as they call them) confounders. To achieve that, they look for pairs of variables that demonstrate Simpson's paradox and then employ a clustering algorithm to group the data based on the discovered p-confounders. They afterwards perform classification within the clusters. Their proposed framework of detecting latent confounding factors is potentially generalisable outside the scope of this topic. Nevertheless, to the best of our knowledge, this is the only research project considering cyberbullying detection from a causal prism.

Suggestions While controlling for confounders, and in case they are categorical or numerical variables, it is possible to follow well established techniques such as matching (De Graaf et al., 2011). In simple terms, matching is a method to create pairs of samples from the same category and of different outcomes, to approximate randomised conditions and obliterate confounding bias so that any effect that remains must be realistic. For example, Zhang et al. (2018) perform their task while controlling for topical confounding, by creating pairs of "good" and "bad" conversations from the same Wikipedia page. This way, they ensure that any differences caused by the nature of the Wikipage topic are removed. However, it is not always possible to know the confounding factors. In that case, it is more useful to consider ways of eradicating confounding in a holistic way, such as the clustering approach of (Cheng et al., 2019).

Additionally, it is highly likely for features of this language-dominated topic to be textual. In that case, treating the covariates can be fairly challenging. Drawing inspiration from the textual causality literature (Keith et al., 2020), there are a number of approaches both for observable and latent textual confounders. For the former, it is possible to follow the strategies that will be described in Section 3.2 and extract features that best represent each specific factor. The case of latent confounders, though, is more elaborate. One suggestion proposed by Landeiro et al. (2019) is the use of adversarial learning as a combating method to confounding shift, although it has yet to be examined within the context of OHS.

3.2 Linguistic Representations

Most of the body of literature described in Section 2 base their research on numerical features, regression, and time series analysis and do not look at the actual content of the social media platforms or question the validity of hatefulness. Contrary to traditional approaches to hate speech detection, which mostly work with text, these causal analyses largely overlook language. One possible explanation for this could be the inherent difficulty of constructing representative vectors that will capture the verbal essence. Language as a means of communication is intrinsically high-dimensional and reducing it in lower dimensions to allow for processing requires strenuous effort.

Saha et al. (2019a) and Cheng et al. (2019) are the only previous papers, to the best of our knowledge, to exploit the texts and attempt to represent them with some feature vectors, to produce causal representations of OHS: frequency of hate keywords in the first case, and Linguistic Inquiry and Word Count (LIWC –Tausczik and Pennebaker (2010)) in the second. There is great need for experimentation and improvement to attempt more holistic approaches to the problem.

Suggestions Since this task is significantly understudied in the context of online hate speech, there are a lot of possible directions to follow. For example, it might prove meaningful to extract high-level representations like sentiment features or toxicity scores. The latter is supported by von Essen and Jansson (2020), who claim that "hate begets hate", meaning that hateful content triggers replies of the same style. Furthermore, one could use the framework implemented by Pryzant et al. (2018), which automatically induces representative lexicons for social science tasks, while controlling for potential confounding factors. Having previously established some factors as such, it is possible to employ this framework and observe the performance of the lexicon. Lastly, it could prove fruitful to explore pre-trained language representation models that are focused on capturing profanity (e.g. HateBERT (Caselli et al., 2020)) or causality (e.g. Causal-BERT (Khetan et al., 2020; Veitch et al., 2020)), or even attempt to fine-tune a hate- and causal-specific version of the original BERT model (Devlin et al., 2018), for a combination of the two. The latter would probably be very demanding with respect to the need for training data, albeit promising.

3.3 Causal Transportability

Finally, a big benefit of true causal knowledge is the ability to transfer this knowledge across domains and achieve comparably optimal performance (Pearl and Bareinboim, 2011). Such an achievement can then work as an evaluation method, showing that the exhibited causal attributions are, in fact, correct and sufficient. For example, consider racist material, which is possibly similar across social networks. A detection model that takes into account any previously attributed causal factors, and controls for all discovered confounders, should be able to train with data from one network and exhibit satisfactory performance on a different network. (Cheng et al., 2019) is the only existing study that is attempting to address causal transferability in the context of this topic, by experimenting on one domain and testing on a different, switching between Twitter and Formspring. Despite the challenging task, it would be of great interest to apply this evaluation method across alternate platforms, various labels, or even multiple languages.

4 Conclusions

The task of hate speech mitigation can never be conclusively accomplished unless the research community seriously speculates about its roots. This would mean a methodological experimentation with the phenomenon, from a causal prism. Simply put, it would mean taking a step back from its detection and focusing on scientifically breaking it into its causes. If the causes are known, then any further steps can make meaningful change. Practitioners should then be able to take crucial actions towards either its efficient and interpretable detection or, even further, its *a priori* prevention. By understanding the most prominent and fundamental factors leading to the phenomenon, it is possible to conclusively build on its holistic solution.

The present survey is intended to initiate discussions towards this direction. By introducing some of the most relevant studies while simultaneously highlighting several points of interest, we aspire for this paper to work as a point of reference, as much as an inspiration and an open call for further research. To make any definite causal claims it is necessary to have a well defined system, where all influential factors are understood or known. All the existing research, including this survey, can only serve as a prelude to future discussions regarding this ubiquitous issue, which will consequently lead to more sophisticated and generalisable models.

References

Alberto Abadie. 2005. Semiparametric difference-in-differences estimators. *The Review of Economic Studies*, 72(1):1–19.

Amalia Álvarez-Benjumea and Fabian Winter. 2018. Normative change and culture of hate: An experiment in online environments. *European Sociological Review*, 34(3):223–237.

Uttara M Ananthakrishnan and Catherine E Tucker. 2021. The drivers and virality of hate speech online. *Available at SSRN 3793801*.

Lora Aroyo, Lucas Dixon, Nithum Thain, Olivia Redfield, and Rachel Rosen. 2019. Crowdsourcing subjective tasks: the case study of understanding toxicity in online discussions. In *Companion proceedings of the 2019 world wide web conference*, pages 1100–1105.

Timothy J Bartik. 1991. Boon or boondoggle? the debate over state and local economic development policies.

James Lopez Bernal, Steven Cummins, and Antonio Gasparrini. 2017. Interrupted time series regression for the evaluation of public health interventions: a tutorial. *International journal of epidemiology*, 46(1):348–355.

Kay H Brodersen, Fabian Gallusser, Jim Koehler, Nicolas Remy, and Steven L Scott. 2015. Inferring causal impact using bayesian structural time-series models. *The Annals of Applied Statistics*, 9(1):247–274.

Alexander Brown. 2018. What is so special about online (as compared to offline) hate speech? *Ethnicities*, 18(3):297–326.

Tommaso Caselli, Valerio Basile, Jelena Mitrović, and Michael Granitzer. 2020. Hatebert: Retraining bert for abusive language detection in english. *arXiv preprint arXiv:2010.12472*.

Eshwar Chandrasekharan, Shagun Jhaver, Amy Bruckman, and Eric Gilbert. 2020. Quarantined! examining the effects of a community-wide moderation intervention on reddit. *arXiv preprint arXiv:2009.11483*.

Eshwar Chandrasekharan, Umashanthi Pavalanathan, Anirudh Srinivasan, Adam Glynn, Jacob Eisenstein, and Eric Gilbert. 2017. You can't stay here: The efficacy of reddit's 2015 ban examined through hate speech. *Proceedings of the ACM on Human-Computer Interaction*, 1(CSCW):1–22.

Lu Cheng, Ruocheng Guo, and Huan Liu. 2019. Robust cyberbullying detection with causal interpretation. In *Companion Proceedings of The 2019 World Wide Web Conference*, pages 169–175.

Munmun De Choudhury and Emre Kiciman. 2017. The language of social support in social media and its effect on suicidal ideation risk. In *Proceedings of the International AAAI Conference on Web and Social Media*, volume 11.

Michiel A De Graaf, Kitty J Jager, Carmine Zoccali, and Friedo W Dekker. 2011. Matching, an appealing method to avoid confounding? *Nephron Clinical Practice*, 118(4):c315–c318.

Jacob Devlin, Ming-Wei Chang, Kenton Lee, and Kristina Toutanova. 2018. Bert: Pre-training of deep bidirectional transformers for language understanding. *arXiv preprint arXiv:1810.04805*.

Son Doan, Elly W Yang, Sameer S Tilak, Peter W Li, Daniel S Zisook, and Manabu Torii. 2019. Extracting health-related causality from twitter messages using natural language processing. *BMC medical informatics and decision making*, 19(3):71–77.

Paula Fortuna and Sérgio Nunes. 2018. A survey on automatic detection of hate speech in text. *ACM Computing Surveys (CSUR)*, 51(4):1–30.

John Hicks et al. 1980. *Causality in economics*. Australian National University Press.

Katherine A Keith, David Jensen, and Brendan O'Connor. 2020. Text and causal inference: A review of using text to remove confounding from causal estimates. *arXiv preprint arXiv:2005.00649*.

Vivek Khetan, Roshni Ramnani, Mayuresh Anand, Shubhashis Sengupta, and Andrew E Fano. 2020. Causal bert: Language models for causality detection between events expressed in text. *arXiv preprint arXiv:2012.05453*.

Virgile Landeiro, Tuan Tran, and Aron Culotta. 2019. Discovering and controlling for latent confounds in text classification using adversarial domain adaptation. In *Proceedings of the 2019 SIAM International Conference on Data Mining*, pages 298–305. SIAM.

Jürgen Landes, Barbara Osimani, and Roland Poellinger. 2018. Epistemology of causal inference in pharmacology. *European Journal for Philosophy of Science*, 8(1):3–49.

Sean MacAvaney, Hao-Ren Yao, Eugene Yang, Katina Russell, Nazli Goharian, and Ophir Frieder. 2019. Hate speech detection: Challenges and solutions. *PloS one*, 14(8):e0221152.

Margaret Mooney Marini and Burton Singer. 1988. Causality in the social sciences. *Sociological methodology*, 18:347–409.

Pushkar Mishra, Helen Yannakoudakis, and Ekaterina Shutova. 2019. Tackling online abuse: A survey of automated abuse detection methods. *arXiv preprint arXiv:1908.06024*.

Karsten Müller and Carlo Schwarz. 2018. Fanning the flames of hate: Social media and hate crime. *Journal of the European Economic Association*.

Karsten Müller and Carlo Schwarz. 2020. From hashtag to hate crime: Twitter and anti-minority sentiment. *Available at SSRN 3149103*.

Kevin Munger. 2017. Tweetment effects on the tweeted: Experimentally reducing racist harassment. *Political Behavior*, 39(3):629–649.

Alexandra Olteanu, Carlos Castillo, Jeremy Boy, and Kush Varshney. 2018. The effect of extremist violence on hateful speech online. In *Proceedings of the International AAAI Conference on Web and Social Media*, volume 12.

Judea Pearl and Elias Bareinboim. 2011. Transportability of causal and statistical relations: A formal approach. In *Twenty-fifth AAAI conference on artificial intelligence*.

Reid Pryzant, Kelly Shen, Dan Jurafsky, and Stefan Wagner. 2018. Deconfounded lexicon induction for interpretable social science. In *Proceedings of the 2018 Conference of the North American Chapter of the Association for Computational Linguistics: Human Language Technologies, Volume 1 (Long Papers)*, pages 1615–1625.

Kelly Quinn. 2018. Cognitive effects of social media use: A case of older adults. *Social Media+ Society*, 4(3):2056305118787203.

Julian Reiss. 2009. Causation in the social sciences: Evidence, inference, and purpose. *Philosophy of the Social Sciences*, 39(1):20–40.

Donald B Rubin, Elizabeth A Stuart, et al. 2006. Affinely invariant matching methods with discriminant mixtures of proportional ellipsoidally symmetric distributions. *The Annals of Statistics*, 34(4):1814–1826.

Federica Russo and Jon Williamson. 2011. Epistemic causality and evidence-based medicine. *History and philosophy of the life sciences*, pages 563–581.

Koustuv Saha, Eshwar Chandrasekharan, and Munmun De Choudhury. 2019a. Prevalence and psychological effects of hateful speech in online college communities. In *Proceedings of the 10th ACM Conference on Web Science*, pages 255–264.

Koustuv Saha, Benjamin Sugar, John Torous, Bruno Abrahao, Emre Kıcıman, and Munmun De Choudhury. 2019b. A social media study on the effects of psychiatric medication use. In *Proceedings of the International AAAI Conference on Web and Social Media*, volume 13, pages 440–451.

Haji Mohammad Saleem, Kelly P Dillon, Susan Benesch, and Derek Ruths. 2017. A web of hate: Tackling hateful speech in online social spaces. *arXiv preprint arXiv:1709.10159*.

Joni Salminen, Fabio Veronesi, Hind Almerekhi, Soon-Gvo Jung, and Bernard J Jansen. 2018. Online hate interpretation varies by country, but more by individual: A statistical analysis using crowdsourced ratings. In *2018 Fifth International Conference on Social Networks Analysis, Management and Security (SNAMS)*, pages 88–94. IEEE.

Erik Scharwächter and Emmanuel Müller. 2020. Does terrorism trigger online hate speech? on the association of events and time series. *The Annals of Applied Statistics*, 14(3):1285–1303.

Anna Schmidt and Michael Wiegand. 2017. A survey on hate speech detection using natural language processing. In *Proceedings of the fifth international workshop on natural language processing for social media*, pages 1–10.

Yla R Tausczik and James W Pennebaker. 2010. The psychological meaning of words: Liwc and computerized text analysis methods. *Journal of language and social psychology*, 29(1):24–54.

Pamela Bilo Thomas, Daniel Riehm, Maria Glenski, and Tim Weninger. 2021. Behavior change in response to subreddit bans and external events. *arXiv preprint arXiv:2101.01793*.

Alice Tontodimamma, Eugenia Nissi, Annalina Sarra, and Lara Fontanella. 2021. Thirty years of research into hate speech: topics of interest and their evolution. *Scientometrics*, 126(1):157–179.

Victor Veitch, Dhanya Sridhar, and David Blei. 2020. Adapting text embeddings for causal inference. In *Conference on Uncertainty in Artificial Intelligence*, pages 919–928. PMLR.

Bertie Vidgen, Alex Harris, Dong Nguyen, Rebekah Tromble, Scott Hale, and Helen Margetts. 2019. Challenges and frontiers in abusive content detection. Association for Computational Linguistics.

Emma von Essen and Joakim Jansson. 2020. Misogynistic and xenophobic hate language online: a matter of anonymity.

Gerald Young. 2016. Unifying causality and psychology. *Cham: Springer*.

Justine Zhang, Jonathan P Chang, Cristian Danescu-Niculescu-Mizil, Lucas Dixon, Yiqing Hua, Nithum Thain, and Dario Taraborelli. 2018. Conversations gone awry: Detecting early signs of conversational failure. *arXiv preprint arXiv:1805.05345*.

Identifying Causal Influences on Publication Trends and Behavior: A Case Study of the Computational Linguistics Community

Maria Glenski and **Svitlana Volkova**

National Security Directorate

Pacific Northwest National Laboratory

{Maria.Glenski@pnnl.gov, Svitlana.Volkova@pnnl.gov}

Abstract

Drawing causal conclusions from observational real-world data is a very much desired but challenging task. In this paper we present mixed-method analyses to investigate causal influences of publication trends and behavior on the adoption, persistence, and retirement of certain research foci – methodologies, materials, and tasks that are of interest to the computational linguistics (CL) community. Our key findings highlight evidence of the transition to rapidly emerging methodologies in the research community (*e.g.,* adoption of bidirectional LSTMs influencing the retirement of LSTMs), the persistent engagement with trending tasks and techniques (*e.g.,* deep learning, embeddings, generative, and language models), the effect of scientist location from outside the US, *e.g.,* China on propensity of researching languages beyond English, and the potential impact of funding for large-scale research programs. We anticipate this work to provide useful insights about publication trends and behavior and raise the awareness about the potential for causal inference in the computational linguistics and a broader scientific community.

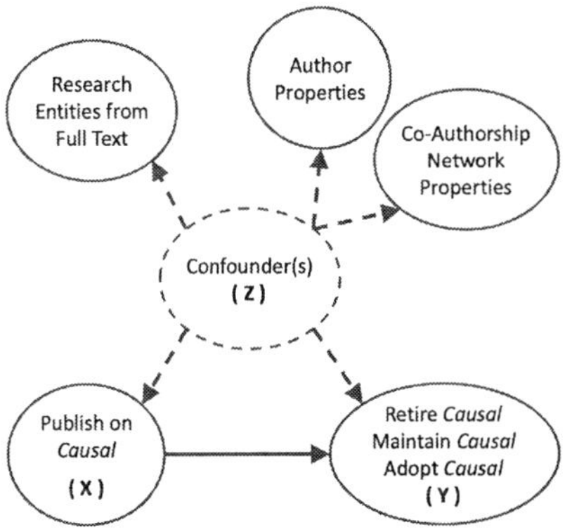

Figure 1: Causal diagram for scientific publications, where full text, author, and co-citation network properties encode causal confounders (e.g., author influence, research tasks and methodology) used as covariates. Our analyses rely on the assumption that latent confounders can be measured and adjusted for based on proxies in our covariates.

Causal understanding is essential for informed decision making (Pearl and Mackenzie, 2018; Pearl, 2019; Varian, 2016) to go beyond correlations and overcome the predictability limit of real-world partially observed systems including complex systems of human social behavior (Abeliuk et al., 2020; Hofman et al., 2017).

Unlike earlier work that focused on analysing publication trends, diversity and innovation in science relying on descriptive exploratory analysis primarily driven by correlations (Fortunato et al., 2018; Hofstra et al., 2020; Ramage et al., 2020), this work aims to provide empirical evidence of causal mechanisms driving publication trends and behavior in the computational linguistics community. Our key contributions are two-fold. First, we experiment and evaluate the potential of using complementary causal inference approaches, specifically causal structure learning models and several treatment effect estimation techniques to measure causal influences in high-dimensional observational data. Second, we analyze the temporal dynamics of causal influences of publication trends on the adoption, persistence and retirement of certain research foci in the CL community.

For our analyses we leverage public ACL anthology data and encode publication and scientist characteristics, as well as collaboration behavior as confounders, to measure the effect of previous research foci on the adoption, maintenance and retirement of future research foci focusing on most recent six years between 2014 and 2019. Figure 1 presents a causal diagram which illustrates our core assumption: that latent confounders (*e.g.,* author reputation, productivity, and collaborations, the strength and length of authors' research careers, novelty of research, papers' contributions to the

Proceedings of CI+NLP: First Workshop on Causal Inference and NLP, pages 83–94
November 10, 2021. ©2021 Association for Computational Linguistics

field, etc.) can be measured and adjusted for based on proxies in our covariates (*e.g.,* research entities extracted from publications, author properties including time since first paper, volume of papers, centrality within co-authorship networks etc.).

1 Related Work

There are two complementary causal inference frameworks – structural causal models (Pearl et al., 2009) and treatment effect estimation approaches (Rosenbaum and Rubin, 1983). Existing approaches to learn the causal structure (aka causal discovery) broadly fall into two categories: constraint-based (Spirtes et al., 2000; Yu et al., 2016) and score-based (Chickering, 2002).

Recently, there have been an increased interest in causal inference on observational data (Guo et al., 2020), including text data, in the computational linguistics and computational social science communities (Lazer et al., 2009). For example, recent work by (Roberts et al., 2020) estimated the effect of perceived author gender on the number of citations of the scientific articles and (Veitch et al., 2020) measured the effect that presence of a theorem in a paper had on the rate of the paper's acceptance.

Additional examples in the computational social science domain include: measuring the effect of alcohol mentions on Twitter on college success (Kiciman et al., 2018); estimating the effect of the "positivity" of the product reviews and recommendations on sales on Amazon (Pryzant et al., 2020; Sharma et al., 2015); understanding factors effecting user performance on StackExhange, Khan Academy, and Duolingo (Alipourfard et al., 2018; Fennell et al., 2019); estimating the effect of censorship on subsequent censorship and posting rate on Weibo (Roberts et al., 2020) and word use in the mental health community on users' transition to post in the suicide community on Reddit (De Choudhury et al., 2016; De Choudhury and Kiciman, 2017); or the effect of exercise on shifts of topical interest on Twitter (Falavarjani et al., 2017). Moreover, Keith et al. (2020) presented the overview of causal approaches for computational social science problems focusing on the use of text to remove confounders from causal estimates, which was also used by (Weld et al., 2020). Earlier work utilized matching methods to learn causal association between word features and class labels in document classification (Paul, 2017; Wood-Doughty et al., 2018), and use text as treatments (Fong and Grimmer, 2016; Dorie et al., 2019) or covariates e.g., causal embeddings (Veitch et al., 2020; Schölkopf et al., 2021).

Several studies have leveraged the ACL Anthology dataset to analyze diversity in computer science research (Vogel and Jurafsky, 2012), and perform exploratory data analysis such as knowledge extraction and mining (Singh et al., 2018b; Radev and Abu-Jbara, 2012; Gábor et al., 2016). However, unlike any other work, our approach focuses on leveraging complementary methods for causal inference – structural causal models and treatment effect estimation to discover and measure the effect of scientists' research focus on their productivity and publication behavior, specifically the emergence, retirement and persistence of computational linguistics methodologies, approaches and topics.

2 Data Preprocessing

Our causal analysis relies on the publication records from the Association of Computational Linguistic (ACL) research community from 1986 through 2020. We collect the ACL Anthology dataset[1] (Gildea et al., 2018) with the bibtex provided with the accompanying abstracts. Excluding all records that do not contain authors (*e.g.,* bibtex entries for the workshop proceedings), we convert the bibtex representation into a data representation where each row represents each paper-author combination (*i.e.,* for a paper (paperX) with three authors, there are three representative rows: paperX-author1, paperX-author2, and paperX-author3).

Then, we extract features that encode **paper** properties: the year it was published, whether the paper was published in a conference or journal, the number of authors, the number of pages, and word count in paper. We also compute Gunning fog index (Gunning et al., 1952) – influenced by the number of words, sentences, and complex words.

We then annotate each row with properties related to the **author** during the year the paper was published. As a proxy of the length of the author's research career in the computational linguistics community, we calculate the number of years since the author's first publication in the anthology. Each author's location is represented as the location (country) of the institution the author is associated with in the metadata or full text. To measure productivity at varying granularities, we calculate the number of one's papers published in

[1] `https://aclanthology.org/`

total, in the last year, and in the last five years.

We then construct a dynamic network representation of the anthology using author-to-paper relationships for each calendar year, as encoded in the metadata. After projecting those relationships into the dynamic co-authorship network that reflects author to co-author connections by year, we calculate centrality and page rank network statistics over time to measure the influence of the author. These **collaboration behavior** features complement previously described author properties. We also added three features to encode the diversity in co-authorship. First, the number of all co-authors who published the papers with the author. Second, the average number of papers co-authored per co-author, which is computed as the total number of papers co-authored per co-author divided by the number of co-authors. The last is a likelihood that a co-author is an author on a paper, which is the second feature divided by the total number of the author's papers. This enables us to measure the diversity, or lack thereof, of collaborative relationships of each author, and encodes how collaboration behavior evolves over time.

2.1 Encoding Research Focus

After extracting the full text of each paper from the PDF using GROBID (GRO, 2008–2021), we use the SpERT model trained to extract key research entities from scientific publications. The SpERT model (Luan et al., 2018) was trained to extract scientific entities of different types such as tasks, methods, and materials and the relationships between them such as "Feature-Of" and "Used-for", using the SciERC dataset[2]. After applying the model to the ACL data, we consolidate noisy references of research entities into representative clusters manually, resulting in 50 entities that encode research tasks, methods, and materials[3].

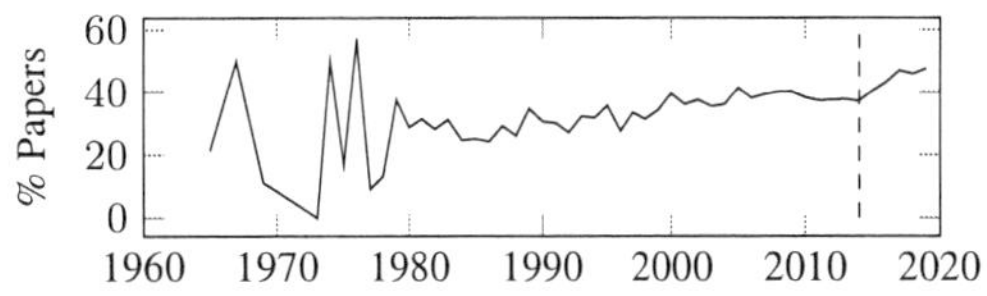

Figure 2: Relative coverage of consolidated research entity representations in the ACL data. Percentage of papers with at least one entity associated by publication year. Dashed line indicates the start of our causal analysis period (2014).

These consolidated entities are representative of the top 300 entities extracted from all ACL anthology publications for which we were able to extract the full text (121,134 out of 127,041 which is 95.3% of all records for which there was an ACL anthology bibtex entry), after removing trivial or general terms such as "system", 'approach", "it", "task", and "method". We present the coverage across papers (% of papers with at least one associated entity) over time in Figure 2, illustrating the coverage approximates the overall coverage (around 41%) for the bulk of the dataset (1980-2019), with coverage trending upwards over time.

3 Methodology

We investigate the causal relationships between characteristics of individual publications for each researcher who authored at least two publications hosted in the ACL Anthology. We identify causal influences of publication outcomes related to the adoption, retirement, and maintenance of computational linguistic methodologies, approaches, or topics, as well as the productivity of authors using both causal discovery and pairwise causal effect estimation.

3.1 Treatments and Outcomes

We consider the inclusion of our consolidated research entities to be treatments in our analyses — *e.g.,* does the inclusion of *biLSTM* architectures in the publication have a causal relationship with future research outcomes? — and the basis of several research outcomes related to the *adoption*, *retirement*, and *maintenance* of CL methodologies, tasks and approaches.

That is, the association of the identified research entities with authors' publications allows us to identify when authors adopt new emerging technologies (*e.g.,* the first use of *transformers*), retire previously used methods or research applications (*e.g.,* if au-

[2] `http://nlp.cs.washington.edu/sciIE/`

[3] Research entities trending in the CL community used for our causal analyses: "artificial intelligence", "adversarial", "annotation", "arabic", "attention", "baselines", "bidirectional lstm", "causal", "chinese", "classification", "coreference", "crowdsourcing", "deep learning", "dialog", "embeddings", "ethics", "explanation", "fairness", "french", "generative", "german", "grammars", "graph models", "heuristics", "interpretability", "language models", "lstm", "machine learning", "monolingual", "multilingual", "multiple languages", "NER", "node2vec", "non-English language", "pos/dependency/parsing", "QA", "reinforcement learning", "robustness", "russian", "sentiment", "statistical/probabilistic models", "summarization", "topic model", "transfer learning", "transformers", "translation", "transparency", "unsupervised methods", "word2vec", "benchmark".

thors stop publishing on *LSTM* architectures after *biLSTM* architectures are introduced), continue to use – or maintain publications in – methods (*e.g.,* when authors continue to publish on *NER*). We associate these behaviors as future outcomes for each author's publications in previous years.

For each year in which an author published in an ACL venue, we calculate adoption and retirement outcomes for each consolidated research element the following year, maintenance outcomes for each research element considering the following two years. Alongside these fine-grained research outcomes, we also examine coarse-grained, or general outcomes for authors:

- overall pauses in publishing within ACL venues (no publications in any ACL community for two years),
- persistent publication records (continuing to publish in consecutive years),
- publication volume increases (the increase or decrease in number of publications in ACL venues relative to the previous year).

In our analyses, we focus on recent six years (2014-2019) for which we have complete treatment and outcome annotations and consider each year independently. We leverage two types of publication record granularities – publication records and yearly research portfolios – to analyze the temporal dynamics of the causal system underpinning CL publication venues at multiple resolutions. Note, we present a detailed description of the treatments, covariates and outcomes we used in Appendix A.

3.2 Causal Structure Learning

Structural causal models are a way of describing relevant features of the world and how they interact with each other. Essentially, causal models represent the mechanisms by which data is generated. The causal model formally consists of two sets of variables U (exogenous variables that are external to the model) and V (endogenous variables that are descendants of exogenous variables), and a set of functions f that assign each variable in V a value based on the values of the other variables in the model. To expand this definition: a variable X is a direct cause of a variable Y if X appears in the function that assigns Y value. Graphical models or Directed Acyclic Graphs (DAGs) have been widely used as causal model representations.

The causal effect rule is defined as: given a causal graph G in which a set of variables $PA(X)$ are designated as a parents of X, the causal effect of X on Y is given by:

$$P(Y = y|do(X = x)) = \sum_z P(Y = y|X = x, PA = z)P(PA = z), \quad (1)$$

where z ranges over all the combinations of values that the variables in PA can take.

The first approach for our causal analysis aims to examine the causal relationships that are identified using an ensemble of causal discovery algorithms (Saldanha et al., 2020). Our ensemble considers the relationships identified by CCDR (Aragam and Zhou, 2015), MMPC (Max-Min Parents-Children) (Tsamardinos et al., 2003), GES (Greedy Equivalence Search) (Chickering, 2002), and PC (Peter-Clark) (Colombo and Maathuis, 2014). We use the implementations provided by the pcalg R package (Hauser and Bühlmann, 2012; Kalisch et al., 2012) and causal discovery toolbox (CDT) (Kalainathan and Goudet, 2019)[4]. The outcomes of our ensemble approach to causal discovery is a causal graph reflecting the relationships within the causal system, weighting edges by the agreement among the individual algorithms on whether the causal relationship exists.

After applying this causal discovery approach to each year individually, we are able to construct a dynamic causal graph and investigate trends in causal relationships – *e.g.,* as they are introduced, persist over time, or are eliminated.

3.3 Treatment Effect Estimation

We further investigate the magnitude and effect of causal relationships using average treatment effect (ATE) estimates. We compare pair-wise estimates using several causal inference models: *Causal Forest* (Tibshirani et al., 2018) and *Propensity Score Matching* (Ho et al., 2007) using the "MatchIt" R package[5], and a cluster-based conditional treatment effect estimation tool – *Visualization and Artificial Intelligence for Natural Experiments (VAINE)*[6] (Guo et al., 2021).

VAINE is designed to discover natural experiments and estimate causal effects using observational data and address challenges traditional approaches have with continuous treatments and high-

[4] https://fentechsolutions.github.io/CausalDiscoveryToolbox/html/index.html

[5] https://cran.r-project.org/web/packages/MatchIt/vignettes/MatchIt.html

[6] https://github.com/pnnl/vaine-widget

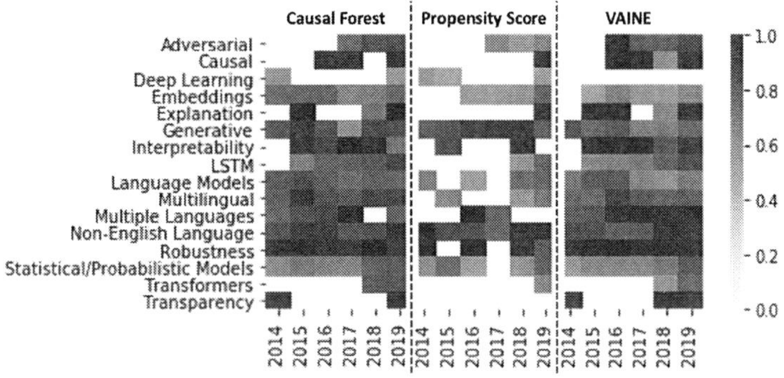

Figure 3: Treatment effect estimates obtained using three causal inference methods – Causal Forest, Propensity Score Matching and VAINE, for publish on $x \rightarrow$ retire x over time, across TEE methods.

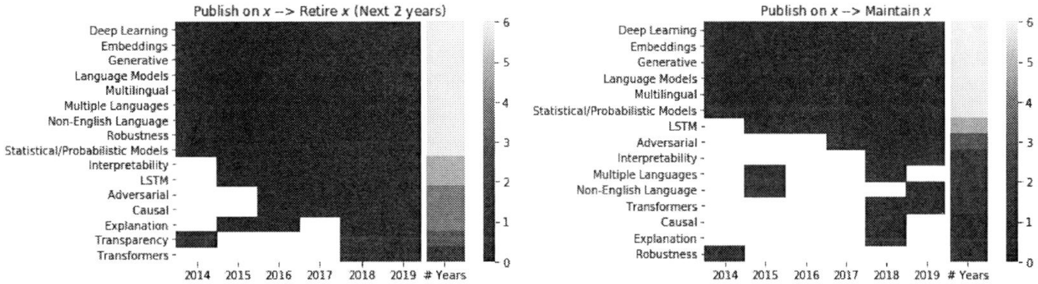

Figure 4: Summary of causal structure learning using our ensemble model discovered from Publish on x to Retire x (above) or Maintain x in the next 2 years (below), by year. Shaded cells indicate that an edge was discovered, white cells indicate that no edge was discovered for that year. At right is a summary of the number of years for which an edge was discovered.

dimensional feature spaces. First, VAINE allows users to automatically detect sets of observations controlling for various covariates in the latent space. Then, using linear modeling, VAINE allows to estimate the treatment effect within each group and then average these local treatment effects to estimate the overall average effect between a given treatment and outcome variable. VAINE's novel approach for causal effect estimation allows it to handle continuous treatment variables without arbitrary discretization and produces results that are intuitive, interpretable, and verifiable by a human. VAINE is an interactive capability that allows the user to explore different parameter settings such as the number of groups, the alpha threshold to identify significant effects, etc.

Below we define what we mean by learning a causal effect from observational data. Given n instances $[(x_1, t_1), \ldots, (x_n, t_n)]$ learning causal effects quantifies how the outcome y is expected to change if we modify the treatment from c to t, which can be defined as $\mathbb{E}(y \mid t) - \mathbb{E}(y \mid c)$, where t and c denote a treatment as a control.

Similarly to our causal discovery based analyses, we examine the growth and decay of causal influence for a series of treatments (research focus represented by materials, methodology, or application-based keywords) on our outcomes of interest.

3.4 Evaluation

Evaluating causal analysis methods is challenging (Saldanha et al., 2020; Weld et al., 2020; Gentzel et al., 2019; Shimoni et al., 2018; Mooij et al., 2016; Dorie et al., 2019; Singh et al., 2018a; Raghu et al., 2018). Broadly, evaluation techniques include structural, observational, interventional and qualitative techniques e.g., visual inspection. Observational evaluation by nature are non-causal and do not have the ability to measure the errors under interventions. Structural measures are limited due to the requirements of known structure, are oblivious to magnitude and type and dependence, as well as treatments and outcomes, and constrain research directions. Unlike structural and observational measures, interventional measures allow to evaluate model estimates of interventional effects e.g., "what-if counterfactual evaluation".

In this work we rely on both qualitative and quantitative evaluation. Methods that we use for causal inference were independently validated using structural and observational measures on synthetic datasets – causal forest (Wager and Athey, 2018), propensity score matching (Cottam et al., 2021), causal ensemble (Saldanha et al., 2020), and VAINE (Guo et al., 2021). Since we rely on four complementary causal inference techniques, we draw our conclusions based on their agreement. In addition, to perform qualitative evaluation with the human in the loop we rely on recently release visual analytics tools to evaluate causal discovery and inference (Cottam et al., 2021).

4 Results

In this section, we present a series of key findings surfaced within the causal mechanisms discovered and treatment effects estimated focusing on contrastive analysis over time: whether publishing on a given research entity (methodology, task, material) influences continuing to publish in that area or with that methodology, how authors shift from existing to novel methodology over time, and evidence of external events (*i.e.,* funding or large research programs) potentially impacts the adoption and maintenance of publication trends.

4.1 Continuing Existing Avenues of Research

One of the first trends we noticed, in both the causal structures and treatment effects, was a causal relationship between publishing on a given research entity (*e.g.,* robustness, LSTMs, transformers, NER, etc.) and whether an author would *continue* to publish on the same topic, task, or methodology in the following year(s). Does publishing once influence whether you will publish again? In short, no. We see a consistent trend in *positive* treatment effects, as illustrated in Figure 3, from publishing in the current year to not publishing (pausing or retiring research entities) in the future – publishing on x leads to *not publishing* on x in the future.

In Figure 4, we summarize the temporal dynamics of causal relationships from publishing on x in a current year's publication to retiring x (no publications associated with research entity x) in the next 2 years (above) or maintaining x (at least one publication associated) in the next 2 years (below) indicated by our causal structural learning analyses which aligns with our TEE results. We show the consistency in which research entities are included

Method	2014	2015	2016	2017	2018	2019
CF	0	0.71	-0.01	0.07	0.09	-0.03
VAINE	0	0.88	0.46	0.68	0.68	0.77
Mean	0	0.80	0.22	0.32	0.39	0.37

Table 1: Treatment effect estimates for the treatment *Publish on bidirectional LSTM* on outcome *Retire LSTM* by year, illustrating a decaying influence.

Method	2014	2015	2016	2017	2018	2019
CF	0	0.76	-0.03	0.36	-0.2	0.00
VAINE	0	0	0	0.39	-0.23	0
Mean	0	0.38	-0.02	0.38	-0.22	0.00

Table 2: Treatment effect estimates for the treatment *Publish on bidirectional LSTM* on outcome *Increase Publications next year*, illustrating a strong initial influence shift to negative (2018) then neutral (2019).

in these trends using Figure 5. We see that many of the elements where causal relationships were identified in all 6 years are present in both the retirement and maintenance relationships. Of all the elements, research on *Transparency* is the only case where there is only a retirement relationship. All elements with identified maintenance relationships in at least one year were also present in the set of retirement relationships.

4.2 Emerging Research Foci, and the Impacts on Retirement of Old Research Foci

The introduction or popularization of new model architectures (especially in deep learning) has an initial strong impact on retirement of previous SOTA architectures, but this is often focused on the initial adoption. We investigate several examples of such phenomena. Table 2 illustrates the decaying causal influence that using bidirectional LSTM-based architectures in current publications has on the retirement of (no longer using) LSTM in future publications. At first, there is a strong causal effect (approx. 0.8), where the use of biLSTM layers lead to no longer using LSTM layers. However, this reduces over time, with CF estimating close to no effect past 2015. We see a complementary trend on the relative publication volume increase outcome (*Increase # publications next year*), where there is an initial strong effect (0.76) that decays until it shifts to a negative effect (in 2018) then neutral (in 2019), as shown in Table 2.

In addition, we see a consistent divergence from the trend described above (publishing on x influ-

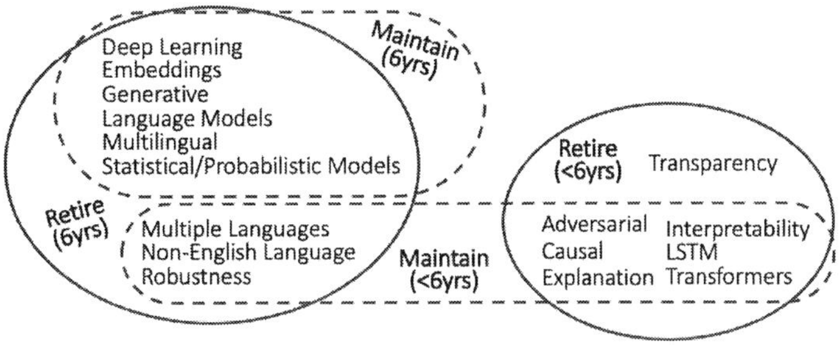

Figure 5: Venn diagram illustrating shared research focus among causal relationships discovered by multiple causal inference methods in Figure 4. This plot demonstrates long-lasting vs. short-lasting research trends in the CL community.

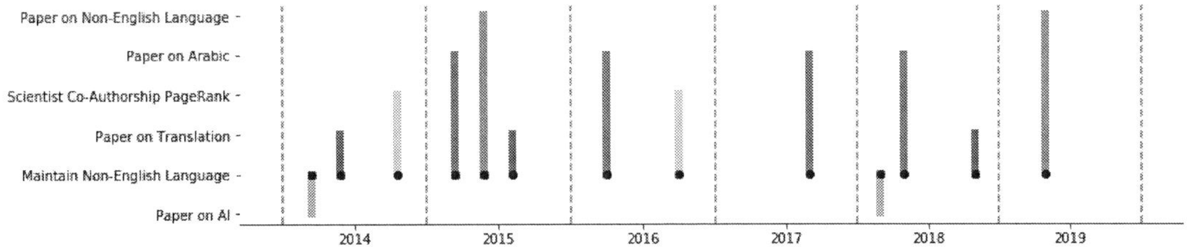

Figure 6: Recurrent causal relationships (identified for at least two years) that influence **continued publication patterns** related to non-English languages in the CL community, *e.g.,* scientist co-authorship PageRank effects maintaining non-English publication focus in 2014 and 2016. Black markers identify the effect, with line segments extending to the cause nodes, and distinct relationships are represented by varying colors.

ences not publishing on x in the next two years) for research related to non-English languages in the 2016-2018 time frame (see Figure 6). These might be explained by the impact of large-scale research programs and funding (note, we will empirically confirm or dispute this hypothesis as a part of our future work). For example, we find that these outcomes (whether researchers continue to publish research related to non-English languages in 2017-2020) align with the last few years (and program-wide evaluation events[7]) of the LORELEI (Low Resource Languages for Emergent Incidents) DARPA program[8].

The goal of the LORELEI program was "to dramatically advance the state of computational linguistics and human language technology to enable rapid, low-cost development of capabilities for low-resource languages", and resulted in several publications on such languages from performers *e.g.,* (Strassel and Tracey, 2016). "What is funded is published" may be an intuitive influence, but here we see qualitative evidence that funding could influence the causal mechanisms of the publication ecosystem — these signals are strong enough to be reflected in causal systems discovered using causal discovery algorithms in observational data. For *adopting* non-English as a research focus, we also see influence from the authors' country associations – *i.e.,* institution affiliations in China influence adopting non-English research (Fig. 7).

Table 3 illustrates a peak in the positive influence of publishing in a particular non-English language (*i.e.,* Arabic, which was one of the languages of interest for the LORELEI program) and continuing to publish on non-English languages. We see that the divergence of the causal relationships, and the persistence of authorship in non-English language research, illustrated in Figure 8, center around or peak in 2017 and begin to flip (causal forest estimates a negative effect of -0.55) in 2019.

5 Discussion and Conclusions

In this study, we identified and analyzed causal influences between the trends and publishing behavior on future research performed and published in the computational linguistic community. Adjusting for confounders related to publication properties extracted from publication text and metadata, author characteristics, and collaboration network proper-

[7] https://www.nist.gov/itl/iad/mig/lorehlt-evaluations

[8] https://www.darpa.mil/program/low-resource-languages-for-emergent-inciden

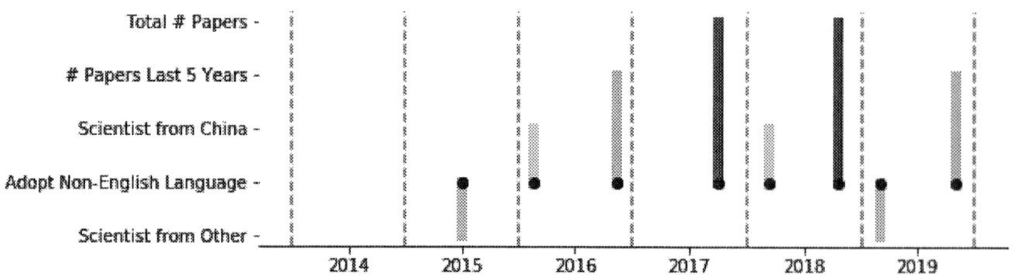

Figure 7: Recurrent causal relationships that influence **new publication patterns** related to non-English languages.Black markers identify the effect, with line segmnets extending to the cause nodes, and distinct relationships are represented by varying colors. Empty time windows indicate no recurrent relationships were discovered.

Publish on Arabic → Continue Publishing on non-English

Method	2014	2015	2016	2017	2018	2019
CF	0.04	0.03	0.28	0.56	0.40	-0.55
VAINE	0	0.20	0.43	0.51	0.13	0.06
Mean	0.02	0.12	0.36	0.54	0.27	0.00

Publish on Arabic → Stop Publishing on non-English

Method	2014	2015	2016	2017	2018	2019
CF	0.44	0.80	0.40	0.13	0.50	0.91
VAINE	0.81	0.71	0.45	0.20	0.82	0.91
Mean	0.62	0.75	0.42	0.16	0.66	0.91

Publish on Arabic → Increase Publications next year

Method	2014	2015	2016	2017	2018	2019
CF	-0.03	-0.03	0.31	1.8	0.23	-0.09

Table 3: Treatment effect estimates for the treatment *Publish on Arabic* for outcomes *Maintain non-English in the next two years* (above) and *Stop publishing on non-English in the next year* (below) by year, illustrating a peak in influence continuing to publish in 2017.

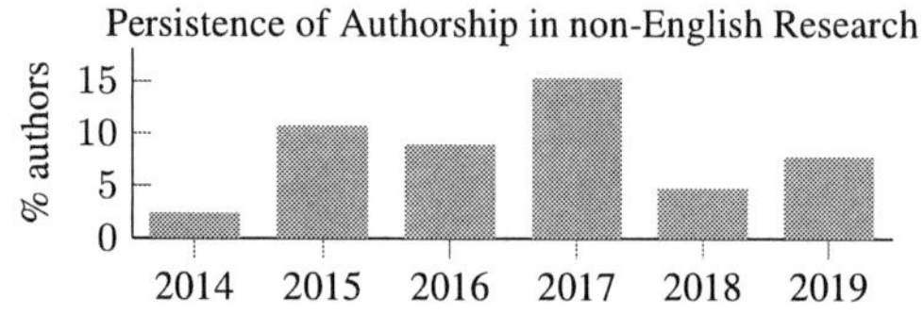

Figure 8: The percentage of authors who published on non-English languages in a given year, who also published on non-English languages in the following year.

ties, we examine the causal relationships that could potentially be driving scientist productivity and the adoption, maintenance, and retirement of methods, materials, and tasks referenced in publications, and how these dynamics evolve over time.

Our analyses show that publishing once on a specific task, application, or methodology has a causal influence that causes authors not to publish on the same approach in the following year e.g., robustness, interpretability etc. This is consistent across a significant number of the research methods, tasks, and application domains represented in our consolidated annotations.

There are several potential drivers of this causal relationship. First, publishing in the CL community, particularly in recent years, is extremely competitive. Acceptance rates are low and the number of submissions each year continue to grow – there is a lot of competition for few spots. This could also be reflective of the churn in novelty and state-of-the-art technologies: as one technology (*e.g.,* LSTMs) are replaced by a new SOTA methodology (*e.g.,* biLSTMs, or transformers), this naturally leads to the retirement of the previous methods, which we also see reflected in the findings presented in subsection 4.2. As we drive the field forward, we stop publishing on older methods, materials, and tasks because of novelty incentives or requirements to be accepted in top-tier venues.

Limitations A limitation of our current causal analysis approach is the restriction to ACL Anthology publication records only. As this dataset comprises only ACL venues, it does not guarantee inclusion of all possible publications from each author. For example, authors who publish in ACL venues may also publish in ICLR, NeurIPs, etc. Future work can address this limitation by augmenting the data set with supplementary collects from these venues (*e.g.,* using Google Scholar).

Another avenue of future work is to incorporate funding information directly in the analyses. As we have shown, there is evidence that funding has causal relationships with publication outcomes and expertise evolution, and may act as a confounder for other relationships. Future work will extract funding from full text PDFs (*e.g.,* from the acknowledgements section) in order to adjust for the effects of funding as a confounder, which may also be an impactful treatment to analyze.

Acknowledgements

This material is based on work funded by the United States Department of Energy (DOE) National Nuclear Security Administration (NNSA) Office of Defense Nuclear Nonproliferation Research and Development (DNN R&D) Next-Generation AI research portfolio and Pacific Northwest National Laboratory, which is operated by Battelle Memorial Institute for the U.S. Department of Energy under contract DE-AC05-76RLO1830. Any opinions, findings, and conclusions or recommendations expressed in this material are those of the author(s) and do not necessarily reflect the views of the United States Government or any agency thereof. We would like to thank Joonseok Kim and Jasmine Eshun for their assistance preparing data.

References

2008–2021. Grobid. `https://github.com/kermitt2/grobid`.

Andrés Abeliuk, Zhishen Huang, Emilio Ferrara, and Kristina Lerman. 2020. Predictability limit of partially observed systems. *Scientific reports*, 10(1):1–10.

Nazanin Alipourfard, Peter G Fennell, and Kristina Lerman. 2018. Using simpson's paradox to discover interesting patterns in behavioral data. In *Twelfth International AAAI Conference on Web and Social Media*.

Bryon Aragam and Qing Zhou. 2015. Concave penalized estimation of sparse gaussian bayesian networks. *The Journal of Machine Learning Research*, 16(1):2273–2328.

David Maxwell Chickering. 2002. Optimal structure identification with greedy search. *Journal of machine learning research*, 3(Nov):507–554.

Diego Colombo and Marloes H Maathuis. 2014. Order-independent constraint-based causal structure learning. *The Journal of Machine Learning Research*, 15(1):3741–3782.

Joseph Cottam, Maria Glenski, Yi Shaw, Ryan Rabello, Austin Golding, Svitlana Volkova, and Dustin Arendt. 2021. Graph comparison for causal discovery. *Visualization in Data Science 2021*.

Munmun De Choudhury and Emre Kiciman. 2017. The language of social support in social media and its effect on suicidal ideation risk. In *Proceedings of the International AAAI Conference on Web and Social Media*, volume 11.

Munmun De Choudhury, Emre Kiciman, Mark Dredze, Glen Coppersmith, and Mrinal Kumar. 2016. Discovering shifts to suicidal ideation from mental health content in social media. In *Proceedings of the 2016 CHI conference on human factors in computing systems*, pages 2098–2110.

Vincent Dorie, Jennifer Hill, Uri Shalit, Marc Scott, and Dan Cervone. 2019. Automated versus do-it-yourself methods for causal inference: Lessons learned from a data analysis competition. *Statistical Science*, 34(1):43–68.

Seyed Mirlohi Falavarjani, Hawre Hosseini, Zeinab Noorian, and Ebrahim Bagheri. 2017. Estimating the effect of exercising on users' online behavior. In *Proceedings of the International AAAI Conference on Web and Social Media*, volume 11.

Peter G Fennell, Zhiya Zuo, and Kristina Lerman. 2019. Predicting and explaining behavioral data with structured feature space decomposition. *EPJ Data Science*, 8(1):23.

Christian Fong and Justin Grimmer. 2016. Discovery of treatments from text corpora. In *Proceedings of the 54th Annual Meeting of the Association for Computational Linguistics (Volume 1: Long Papers)*, pages 1600–1609.

Santo Fortunato, Carl T Bergstrom, Katy Börner, James A Evans, Dirk Helbing, Staša Milojević, Alexander M Petersen, Filippo Radicchi, Roberta Sinatra, Brian Uzzi, et al. 2018. Science of science. *Science*, 359(6379).

Kata Gábor, Haifa Zargayouna, Davide Buscaldi, Isabelle Tellier, and Thierry Charnois. 2016. Semantic annotation of the ACL anthology corpus for the automatic analysis of scientific literature. In *LREC 2016*.

Amanda Gentzel, Dan Garant, and David Jensen. 2019. The case for evaluating causal models using interventional measures and empirical data. *Advances in Neural Information Processing Systems*, 32:11722–11732.

Daniel Gildea, Min-Yen Kan, Nitin Madnani, Christoph Teichmann, and Martín Villalba. 2018. The ACL anthology: Current state and future directions. In *Proceedings of Workshop for NLP Open Source Software (NLP-OSS)*, pages 23–28.

Robert Gunning et al. 1952. Technique of clear writing.

Grace Guo, Maria Glenski, ZhuanYi Shaw, Emily Salandha, Alex Endert, Svitlana Volkova, and Dustin Arendt. 2021. Vaine: Visualization and ai for natural experiments. *IEEE transactions on visualization and computer graphics*.

Ruocheng Guo, Lu Cheng, Jundong Li, P Richard Hahn, and Huan Liu. 2020. A survey of learning causality with data: Problems and methods. *ACM Computing Surveys (CSUR)*, 53(4):1–37.

Alain Hauser and Peter Bühlmann. 2012. Characterization and greedy learning of interventional Markov equivalence classes of directed acyclic graphs. *Journal of Machine Learning Research*, 13:2409–2464.

Daniel E Ho, Kosuke Imai, Gary King, and Elizabeth A Stuart. 2007. Matching as nonparametric preprocessing for reducing model dependence in parametric causal inference. *Political analysis*, 15(3):199–236.

Jake M Hofman, Amit Sharma, and Duncan J Watts. 2017. Prediction and explanation in social systems. *Science*, 355(6324):486–488.

Bas Hofstra, Vivek V Kulkarni, Sebastian Munoz-Najar Galvez, Bryan He, Dan Jurafsky, and Daniel A McFarland. 2020. The diversity–innovation paradox in science. *Proceedings of the National Academy of Sciences*, 117(17):9284–9291.

Diviyan Kalainathan and Olivier Goudet. 2019. Causal discovery toolbox: Uncover causal relationships in python.

Markus Kalisch, Martin Mächler, Diego Colombo, Marloes H. Maathuis, and Peter Bühlmann. 2012. Causal inference using graphical models with the R package pcalg. *Journal of Statistical Software*, 47(11):1–26.

Katherine Keith, David Jensen, and Brendan O'Connor. 2020. Text and causal inference: A review of using text to remove confounding from causal estimates. In *Proceedings of the 58th Annual Meeting of the Association for Computational Linguistics*, pages 5332–5344.

Emre Kiciman, Scott Counts, and Melissa Gasser. 2018. Using longitudinal social media analysis to understand the effects of early college alcohol use. In *Twelfth International AAAI Conference on Web and Social Media*.

David Lazer, Alex Pentland, Lada Adamic, Sinan Aral, Albert-Laszlo Barabasi, Devon Brewer, Nicholas Christakis, Noshir Contractor, James Fowler, Myron Gutmann, et al. 2009. Social science. computational social science. *Science (New York, NY)*, 323(5915):721–723.

Yi Luan, Luheng He, Mari Ostendorf, and Hannaneh Hajishirzi. 2018. Multi-task identification of entities, relations, and coreference for scientific knowledge graph construction. In *Proceedings of the 2018 Conference on Empirical Methods in Natural Language Processing*, pages 3219–3232.

Joris M Mooij, Jonas Peters, Dominik Janzing, Jakob Zscheischler, and Bernhard Schölkopf. 2016. Distinguishing cause from effect using observational data: methods and benchmarks. *The Journal of Machine Learning Research*, 17(1):1103–1204.

Michael Paul. 2017. Feature selection as causal inference: Experiments with text classification. In *Proceedings of the 21st Conference on Computational Natural Language Learning (CoNLL 2017)*, pages 163–172.

Judea Pearl. 2019. The seven tools of causal inference, with reflections on machine learning. *Communications of the ACM*, 62(3):54–60.

Judea Pearl and Dana Mackenzie. 2018. *The book of why: the new science of cause and effect*. Basic Books, New York City, NY.

Judea Pearl et al. 2009. Causal inference in statistics: An overview. *Statistics surveys*, 3:96–146.

Reid Pryzant, Dallas Card, Dan Jurafsky, Victor Veitch, and Dhanya Sridhar. 2020. Causal effects of linguistic properties. *arXiv preprint arXiv:2010.12919*.

Dragomir Radev and Amjad Abu-Jbara. 2012. Rediscovering ACL discoveries through the lens of acl anthology network citing sentences. In *Proceedings of the ACL-2012 Special Workshop on Rediscovering 50 Years of Discoveries*, pages 1–12.

Vineet K Raghu, Allen Poon, and Panayiotis V Benos. 2018. Evaluation of causal structure learning methods on mixed data types. *Proceedings of machine learning research*, 92:48.

Daniel Ramage, Christopher D Manning, and Daniel A McFarland. 2020. Mapping three decades of intellectual change in academia. *arXiv preprint arXiv:2004.01291*.

Margaret E Roberts, Brandon M Stewart, and Richard A Nielsen. 2020. Adjusting for confounding with text matching. *American Journal of Political Science*, 64(4):887–903.

Paul R Rosenbaum and Donald B Rubin. 1983. The central role of the propensity score in observational studies for causal effects. *Biometrika*, 70(1):41–55.

Emily Saldanha, Robin Cosbey, Ellyn Ayton, Maria Glenski, Joseph Cottam, Karthik Shivaram, Brett Jefferson, Brian Hutchinson, Dustin Arendt, and Svitlana Volkova. 2020. Evaluation of algorithm selection and ensemble methods for causal discovery.

Bernhard Schölkopf, Francesco Locatello, Stefan Bauer, Nan Rosemary Ke, Nal Kalchbrenner, Anirudh Goyal, and Yoshua Bengio. 2021. Toward causal representation learning. *Proceedings of the IEEE*, 109(5):612–634.

Amit Sharma, Jake M Hofman, and Duncan J Watts. 2015. Estimating the causal impact of recommendation systems from observational data. In *Proceedings of the Sixteenth ACM Conference on Economics and Computation*, pages 453–470.

Yishai Shimoni, Chen Yanover, Ehud Karavani, and Yaara Goldschmnidt. 2018. Benchmarking framework for performance-evaluation of causal inference analysis. *arXiv preprint arXiv:1802.05046*.

Karamjit Singh, Garima Gupta, Vartika Tewari, and Gautam Shroff. 2018a. Comparative benchmarking of causal discovery algorithms. In *Proceedings of the ACM India Joint International Conference on Data Science and Management of Data*, pages 46–56.

Mayank Singh, Pradeep Dogga, Sohan Patro, Dhiraj Barnwal, Ritam Dutt, Rajarshi Haldar, Pawan Goyal, and Animesh Mukherjee. 2018b. Cl scholar: The acl anthology knowledge graph miner. In *Proceedings of the 2018 Conference of the North American Chapter of the Association for Computational Linguistics: Demonstrations*, pages 16–20.

Peter Spirtes, Clark N Glymour, Richard Scheines, and David Heckerman. 2000. *Causation, prediction, and search*. MIT press.

Stephanie Strassel and Jennifer Tracey. 2016. Lorelei language packs: Data, tools, and resources for technology development in low resource languages. In *Proceedings of the Tenth International Conference on Language Resources and Evaluation (LREC'16)*, pages 3273–3280.

Julie Tibshirani, Susan Athey, Rina Friedberg, Vitor Hadad, David Hirshberg, Luke Miner, Erik Sverdrup, Stefan Wager, Marvin Wright, and Maintainer Julie Tibshirani. 2018. Package 'grf'.

Ioannis Tsamardinos, Constantin F Aliferis, and Alexander Statnikov. 2003. Time and sample efficient discovery of markov blankets and direct causal relations. In *Proceedings of the ninth ACM SIGKDD international conference on Knowledge discovery and data mining*, pages 673–678, New York City, NY.

Hal R Varian. 2016. Causal inference in economics and marketing. *Proceedings of the National Academy of Sciences*, 113(27):7310–7315.

Victor Veitch, Dhanya Sridhar, and David Blei. 2020. Adapting text embeddings for causal inference. In *Conference on Uncertainty in Artificial Intelligence*, pages 919–928. PMLR.

Adam Vogel and Dan Jurafsky. 2012. He said, she said: Gender in the acl anthology. In *Proceedings of the ACL-2012 Special Workshop on Rediscovering 50 Years of Discoveries*, pages 33–41.

Stefan Wager and Susan Athey. 2018. Estimation and inference of heterogeneous treatment effects using random forests. *Journal of the American Statistical Association*, 113(523):1228–1242.

Galen Weld, Peter West, Maria Glenski, David Arbour, Ryan Rossi, and Tim Althoff. 2020. Adjusting for confounders with text: Challenges and an empirical evaluation framework for causal inference. *arXiv preprint arXiv:2009.09961*.

Zach Wood-Doughty, Ilya Shpitser, and Mark Dredze. 2018. Challenges of using text classifiers for causal inference. In *Proceedings of the Conference on Empirical Methods in Natural Language Processing. Conference on Empirical Methods in Natural Language Processing*, volume 2018, page 4586. NIH Public Access.

Kui Yu, Jiuyong Li, and Lin Liu. 2016. A review on algorithms for constraint-based causal discovery. *arXiv preprint arXiv:1611.03977*.

A Appendix

We summarize the publication record encodings (treatments, outcomes, and covariates) used in our causal discovery and treatment effect estimation analyses in Table 4.

Treatment	Description
Publish on x	Binary encoding of whether x (one of our 50 research entities) was extracted from the publication's full text, using SpERT (Luan et al., 2018).
Scientist from c	Binary encoding of whether author is a scientist affiliated with country c (*i.e.,* author is associated with an insitution located in country c). There are six variations of this treatment, where c is one of the five countries wiht the greatest representation in ACL publications (the United States, China, Germany, Japan, France) or "Other".

Outcome	Description
Adopt x	Binary encoding of whether author will publish on x for the first time in the next calendar year.
Maintain x	Binary encoding of whether author previously published on x and has at least one publication on x in the following calendar year.
Retire/Pause x	Binary encoding of whether author previously published on x but has no publications on x in the following two calendar years.
Publication Increase Rate	The relative increase in the number of publications by author in the next calendar year, *i.e.,* $\frac{\#\ publications\ in\ year\ t+1}{\#\ publications\ in\ year\ t}$

Covariate	Description
# Papers	Total number of author's publications (cumulative since first publication).
# Papers (Last Year)	Number of author's publications within the last year.
# Papers (Last 5 Years)	Number of author's publications within the last five years.
# Co-authors	Number of co-authors linked to author in the collaboration network (by year).
Avg. # Papers Co-authored	Average paper count per co-author, *i.e.,* $\frac{\#Papers}{\#Co-Authors}$
Co-author Likelihood	Likelihood that a randomly selected co-author was a co-author on the publication, *i.e.,* $\frac{Avg.\#PapersCo-authored}{\#Papers}$
Centrality	Degree centrality of the author in the collaboration network, for the publication's calendar year.
Page Rank	Page rank of the author in the collaboration network, for the publication's calendar year.
Time Since First Paper	Number of years since the author's first publication in the ACL anthology.
Conference	Binary encoding of whether the paper is published in a conference (1) or journal (0).
# Authors	Publication's total number of authors.
Page Length	Page length of the publication's full text PDF.
# Words	Total number of words in the publication's full text.
Gunning Fog Index	Gunning Fog Index readability measure (Gunning et al., 1952) calculated using the publication text.

Table 4: Overview of Treatments (above), Outcomes (center), and Covariates (below).

It's quality and quantity: the effect of the amount of comments on online suicidal posts

Daniel M. Low
Harvard University & MIT
dlow@g.harvard.edu

Kelly L. Zuromski
Harvard University

Daniel Kessler
Harvard University
{kelly_zuromski,dtkessler}@fas.harvard.edu

Satrajit S. Ghosh
MIT & Harvard Medical School
satra@mit.edu

Matthew Nock
Harvard University
nock@wjh.harvard.edu

Walter Dempsey
University of Michigan
wdem@umich.edu

Abstract

Every day, individuals post suicide notes on social media asking for support, resources, and reasons to live. Some posts receive few comments while others receive many. While prior studies have analyzed whether specific responses are more or less helpful, it is not clear if the quantity of comments received is beneficial in reducing symptoms or in keeping the user engaged with the platform and hence with life. In the present study, we create a large dataset of users' first r/SuicideWatch (SW) posts from Reddit (N=21,274), collect the comments as well as the user's subsequent posts (N=1,615,699) to determine whether they post in SW again in the future. We use propensity score stratification, a causal inference method for observational data, and estimate whether the amount of comments —as a measure of social support— increases or decreases the likelihood of posting again on SW. One hypothesis is that receiving more comments may *decrease* the likelihood of the user posting in SW in the future, either by reducing symptoms or because comments from untrained peers may be harmful. On the contrary, we find that receiving more comments *increases* the likelihood a user will post in SW again. We discuss how receiving more comments is helpful, not by permanently relieving symptoms since users make another SW post and their second posts have similar mentions of suicidal ideation, but rather by reinforcing users to seek support and remain engaged with the platform. Furthermore, since receiving only 1 comment —the most common case— decreases the likelihood of posting again by 14% on average depending on the time window, it is important to develop systems that encourage more commenting.

1 Introduction

Suicide is among the leading causes of death in the US and worldwide and the second leading cause of death among youth, 10 to 34 years old (Fortgang and Nock, 2021). Despite a century of scientific research on suicide prevention, suicide rates are similar to what they were 100 years ago because suicide is still very hard to predict and treat (Fortgang and Nock, 2021; Bentley et al., 2020) and because many individuals at risk do not receive optimal treatment due to known perceived barriers such as stigma and cost (Mohr et al., 2010; Andrade et al., 2014). Instead of seeking professional help, many individuals seek support online from peers, which could have negative consequences including learning about suicide methods, receiving ineffective responses, and being subject to suicide contagion (Niederkrotenthaler et al., 2016; Colombo et al., 2016). Therefore, there is an urgent need to model and understand the effect of these responses.

1.1 Prior work

When analyzing the content and quality of peer responses to suicidal posts on social media, prior work has found that responses are generally positive (Naslund et al., 2016; Fu et al., 2013; Li et al., 2015; Jiang et al., 2020; O'dea et al., 2018), suggesting that peer responses may be helpful peer-delivered interventions. One study of the subreddit r/SuicideWatch (SW) found that posters rated the most helpful peer responses as including professional help suggestion (e.g., "Have you tried getting any professional help?"), life meaning (e.g., "Instead of reasons why not to, perhaps think of reasons to live. . . "), and relationship/loss support (e.g., "I am really sorry for your loss...") (Jiang et al., 2020). Another study found that online users in non-professional suicide forums tend to see reductions in the symptoms of their suicidal ideation when responses to their posts include constructive active listening, collaborative problem-solving, constructive advice, debunking of public suicide myths, alternatives to suicide, stories of lived experience, and recommendations of help services (Niederkrotenthaler et al., 2016). In Jiang et al.

Proceedings of CI+NLP: First Workshop on Causal Inference and NLP, pages 95–103
November 10, 2021. ©2021 Association for Computational Linguistics

(2020) the most frequent response type was asking questions (e.g., "What kinds of things in the past have you tried that have helped you cope before?"), compared to treatment and medication (e.g., "I recommend medication for anxiety"), which was both the least frequent and lowest-rated response in terms of perceived helpfulness. This finding aligns with studies on intervention messaging engagement (Owens et al., 2011; Whiteside et al., 2014), that rank question-form prompts, or prompts designed to initiate responses (e.g., "Do you want to talk?"), as among the most engaging.

Although there are relatively few studies examining the impacts of specific peer responses on suicidal posts, numerous other studies have highlighted messaging content features that lead to engagement among participants in online interventions. For example, prior work has found that people tend to be attracted to, and engage with, intervention-related messages that suggest they are cared about, show concern or caring for the individual, are personalized to them (even if personalization is automated), provide information on resources, and that others experiencing similar symptoms found helpful (Aguilera and Berridge, 2014; Whiteside et al., 2014). Furthermore, participants of such message-based interventions tend to engage with messaging that encourages help-seeking (e.g., "Sometimes family can be supportive during tough times") (Pisani et al., 2018), provides psychoeducational information (Jaroszewski et al., 2019; Murray et al., 2015) or that provides validation and normative feedback (e.g., "It's okay to feel angry") (Owens et al., 2011).

De Choudhury and Kiciman (2017) used stratified propensity score matching to estimate which ngrams make it more likely that users posting on 14 mental health subreddits (e.g., r/Depression, r/ptsd, r/mentalhealth) would later post on SW for the first time in comparison to those who never end up making the transition to this overall higher-severity subreddit. They modeled different ngrams in the comments as treatments (i.e., interventions on a given outcome), ngrams appearing prior were covariates, and posting on SW was the binary outcome.

While these studies have identified the distribution, quality, and potential effects of specific types of comments, it is not clear whether receiving more or less comments overall is helpful in keeping the user engaged.

1.2 Current study

SW posts receive 0 to many peer responses in the form of comments. Here we study the effect of receiving few or many replies to suicidal posts. We estimate the likelihood of posting again on SW as function of how many comments a post received. This could be thought of as estimating the treatment effect given a particular dosage in a randomized trial. There are multiple possible hypotheses:

- H0: The amount of comments is not associated with whether users will post on SW again.

- H1: Receiving more comments *decreases* the likelihood of posting again on SW. Plausible reason: receiving more comments is more helpful, that is, it reduces symptoms which would result in a decreased need to post in SW in the future. It could also indicate something very different; namely that receiving more non-professional responses is ineffective or harmful, and therefore users tend to not to use the forum in the future. If receiving more comments decreases the likelihood of posting again in SW (H1), it seems unlikely that this would be due to the effectiveness of peer responses from mostly untrained individuals. Helping reduce an individual's suicidal thoughts and behaviors (STBs) is very challenging and seems to require more substantial treatments such as cognitive behavioral therapy, mindful emotion awareness, generating cognitive flexibility, and emotion exposure (Bentley et al., 2020). Even when undergoing formal treatment, about half of individuals with depression relapse within 2 years of treatment (Steinert et al., 2014). Therefore, viewing responses as ineffective might be the most likely explanation to a decrease in returning to SW as users receive more responses.

- H2: Receiving more comments *increases* the likelihood of posting again in SW. Plausible reason: it seems comments would be reinforcing support-seeking behavior and not reducing symptoms, because if they were reducing STBs, then users would be less likely to post again. However, it is possible that users that post in SW again are returning to report signs of improvement, which we will will check by comparing the amount of mentions of STBs

	25%	50%	75%	max
Prior posts	0	3	15	4436
Subs. posts	1	9	43	9566
Subs. SW posts	0	0	1	235
Comm. per post	1	2	5	261

Table 1: Descriptive statistics per user. Minimum = 0 for all rows. SW: r/SuicideWatch; Subs.: subsequent; comm.: comments.

between first and second posts using custom lexicons.

2 Methods

2.1 Dataset

We obtained 24,401 SW posts from 2018 and 2019 from the Reddit Mental Health Dataset (Low et al., 2020). We then used the Reddit pushshift API [1] to download all posts by those users until 2021-07-20 (N=1,615,699). We removed users that had deleted their accounts, posts that were deleted by their users as well as posts removed by moderators. For every user, we located their first SW post (N=21,274 unique posts and users) and downloaded the corresponding comments (N=102,394) (see Table 1). First SW posts range from 2010-09-14 to 2019-04-21 and we know whether users posted again in SW or not until 2021-07-20, a minimum of 27 months, which we consider a large enough time window to estimate comments' effects on initial SW posts.

For 33% of users (N=6,954), posting on SW was their first time posting on Reddit, and 10% (N=2,176) posted on Reddit only once before. After their first SW post, 12% of users (N=2,482) posted in SW again within a week, and 36% of users (N=7,749) posted in SW again within a year (see Fig. 1). For our analysis, we chose the following time windows in days: 7, 14, 21, 30, 60, 90, 180, 365, because we expect effects from the amount of comments received to be most present sooner (e.g., 1 or 2 weeks) and then fade with larger time windows (e.g., 6 months, 1 year), when other factors may play a larger role regarding whether users post again.

20% of users (N=4,207) never posted on Reddit again. For some, death is a possible outcome given posts often describe imminent suicidal plans (e.g., "Hello, I keep it short because i will kill myself today. (...)"), but not posting again can also be related

N	Posts receiving N comments	Proportion
0	1777	0.08
1	5193	0.24
2	3689	0.17
3	2421	0.11
4	1725	0.08
5	1313	0.06
6	939	0.04
7	721	0.03
8	542	0.03
9	445	0.02
10+	2509	0.12

Table 2: Amount of posts with N amount of comments.

to not finding Reddit helpful or symptoms improving and not needing any further help. Therefore, not posting on Reddit again should be considered an ambiguous outcome in that it can be positive or negative. We removed post authors' replies from the count of comments received. Half the posts in SW receive up to 2 comments (see Table 2). Each comment is counted, even if they are from the same commenter.

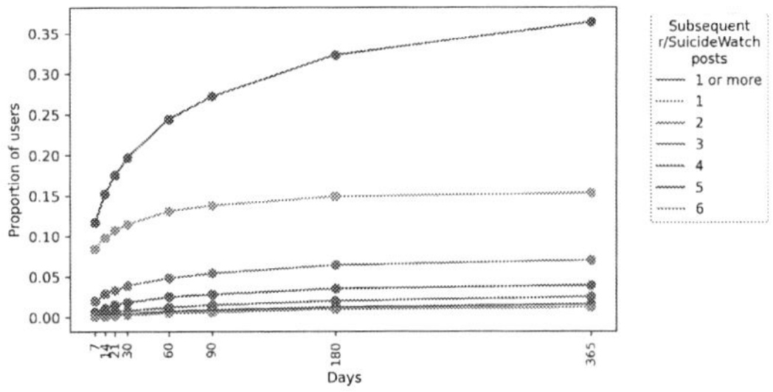

Figure 1: Proportion of users that post again in r/SuicideWatch.

2.2 Estimating the effect of comments through propensity score stratification

Given a causal model such as the one depicted in Fig. 2, we can infer the causal effect of treatment. Whether a user will re-post on SW again depends not only on the amount of comments they received (the treatment) but also on the severity and content of their post (e.g., more severe posts may capture more suicidality which would make it more likely to post again on SW), which in turn may also influence how many comments they will receive. In an ideal setting, treatment is randomized so that the treatment assignment mechanism is ignorable

[1] https://github.com/pushshift/api

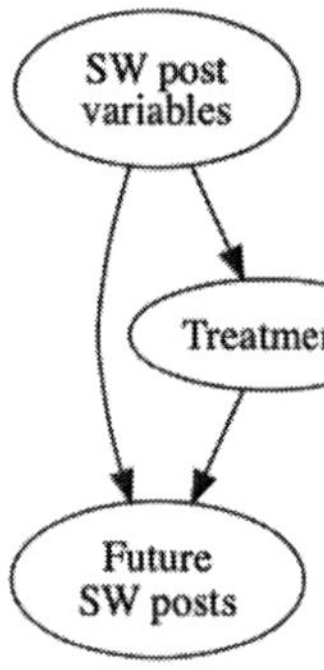

Figure 2: A directed acyclic graph of the model with Treatment (T; indicator variable of N comments), Outcome (Y; discrete variable of how many times the user posted in SW in the future) and Confounders (C; 48 linguistic variables extracted from the SW post). We expect the content of the post to influence the amount of comments received (T) and the likelihood to post in SW again (Y). SW: r/SuicideWatch.

and independent of counterfactual outcomes. In observational settings, however, treatment is not randomly assigned. Under the causal model in Fig. 2, treatment assignment is ignorable given the extracted linguistic variables because exposure to treatment is no longer confounded by post characteristics. In this case, the propensity score, the probability of treatment exposure given the observed covariates, is the basis for adjusting for confounding (Lunceford and Davidian, 2004):

$$\hat{e}(C) = P(T = 1|C)$$

where T is treatment (here, for simplicity, it is a binary indicator) and C is the vector of confounders. Under the causal model, $T \perp\!\!\!\perp C|\hat{e}(C)$, so that individuals from either treatment group with the same propensity score are "balanced". The treatment indicates receiving a certain amount of comments; therefore, we built one model per treatment from 1 to 10+ comments, and each treatment is compared to receiving 0 comments. We next discuss how we exploit the causal model to estimate the treatment effect using propensity score stratification.

We used the *dowhy v0.6* package implementation of propensity score stratification (Sharma et al., 2019). The analysis used the following steps: (1) train a logistic regression classifier with L2 penalty to predict T from C. For every post, compute the propensity score based on the estimated logistic regression model; (2) based on the score, stratify (i.e., rank scores so that high propensity scores of treated and untreated are in the same stratum or subgroup of similar samples, and split evenly with at least 11 samples per strata); (3) compute the per stratum average treatment effect (ATE) as the weighted average of outcome differences per strata; (4) estimate the overall ATE by a weighted sum of the differences of sample means across strata where the weight is proportional to the number of observations falling in each stratum. See Lunceford and Davidian (2004) for technical details.

To validate estimates, we include two methods from the *dowhy* package: (1) data subset refuter: we make sure estimates do not change in comparison to the mean estimate run on multiple subsets of the data (similar to cross-validation); (2) placebo treatment refuter: randomly assign a covariate as a treatment and re-run the analysis, the estimate of which should be close to 0 with a high p-value (e.g., above 0.05).

2.3 Feature extraction

To capture the content of the post, we extracted 39 Linguistic Inquiry and Word Count (LIWC; Pennebaker et al., 2015) variables including anxiety, anger, sadness, personal pronouns, and swearing. These were chosen because they reflect emotional and psychological processes. Nine additional lexicons were created to capture different subtypes of suicidal thoughts and behaviors (active, passive, self-harm) as well as stressors (domestic stress and violence, substance use, financial stress, and mental health; see Appendix A.1 for details).

3 Results

3.1 The effect of amount of comments on future SW posts

Receiving 1 comment *decreased* the likelihood of posting on SW again by 14% on average across the time windows. As comments increase, so does the likelihood of posting on SW (increasing the likelihood up to 16% on average), providing evidence for hypothesis H2, especially up until 5 comments and again with 9 or more comments (see Fig. 3). The mean changes in likelihood over time windows (and range) for the different amount of comments are 1: -14% [-23% – -8%]; 2: -13% [-21% – -8%]; 3: -6% [-9% – -4%]; 4: 0% [-3% – 1%]; 5: 8% [1% – 13%]; 6: 7% [-2% – 28%]; 7: -4% [-9% – -1%]; 8: -1% [-12% – 8%]; 9: 6% [-5% – 11%]; and 10+: 16% [0% – 27%].

To validate these estimates, using validation

method 1 (data subset refuter), we found the mean error between (a) the original estimate and (b) the mean estimate (and standard deviation) made after multiple re-runs using subsets of the data increases with larger time windows: 7 days: 0.003 (0.016); 14 days: 0.001 (0.019); 21 days: 0.002 (0.023); 30 days: 0.002 (0.022); 60 days: 0.02 (0.059); 90 days: 0.021 (0.062); 180 days: 0.044 (0.124); 365 days: 0.054 (0.154). Therefore, it seems the effect of comment dosages is not captured in such large time windows (i.e., whether a user posts in SW within 180 or 365 days is affected less by past comment experience). Furthermore, all estimates were validated by method 2 (placebo treatment refuter) as randomly assigning a confounder as a treatment resulted in effects near 0 with p-values >= 0.37. Overall, it is important to note that *smaller* time windows may have less precision given there have been less cases of one of the outcomes (reposting in SW) since it is more likely to post in SW as more time passes (see Fig. 1), while *larger* time windows may have less precision since the effect of the decision to post in SW again may be influenced less by the amount of comments received a long time ago.

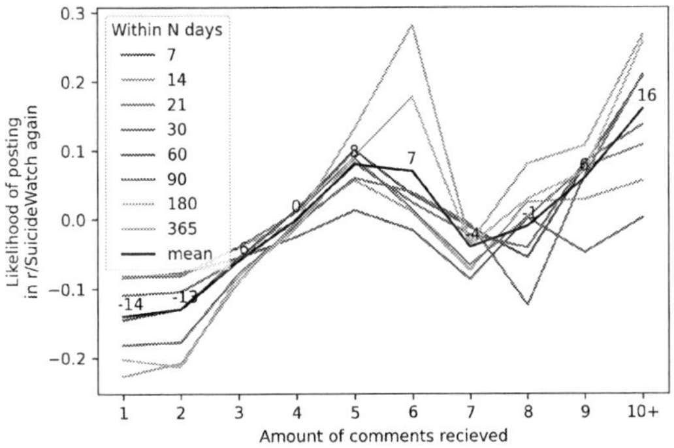

Figure 3: Likelihood of posting in r/SuicideWatch as function of the amount of comments (dosage) received within different time windows. Mean percentage values are displayed.

We checked whether the second time a user posts in SW, variables capturing suicidality reduced as a function of the amount of comments received. In Fig. 4 we show the difference in suicidality general lexicon values between each user's second and first post. The whiskers are set at the 5 and 95 percentiles; therefore 90% of the changes are near 0. This indicates that language about suicidality, as approximated by lexicons, remain relatively the same the second time they post for 90% of users. See Appendix A.2 for similar results using other variables.

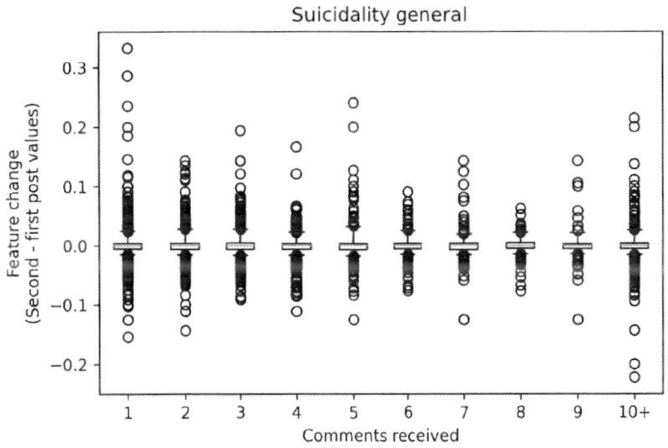

Figure 4: Boxplots showing differences in lexicon values between each user's second and first post. Variable values do not change considerably as 90% within-participant differences remain near 0.

4 Discussion

Non-professional online support groups for suicide are often considered dangerous in that untrained peers may invalidate emotions or inspire more suicidal thoughts and behaviors (Niederkrotenthaler et al., 2016). However, prior research on Reddit has shown responses are generally positive (Jiang et al., 2020). This may be due to strict moderation that removes responses containing guilt-tripping (e.g., one SW guideline asks to report "abuse or 'tough love' including any guilt-tripping like 'suicide is selfish' or 'think of your loved ones'"), pro-suicide comments, or descriptions of suicide methods. The question remains whether a few comments is enough to keep the user engaged with peers and whether responses actually reduce symptoms indefinitely.

A positive outcome after a suicidal post would be that either the comments decrease the poster's suicidal ideation or that the user engages by responding to comments and returning when symptoms persist. We estimated the effect of dosing comments on the likelihood of posting in SW again after having posted for the first time. In the case of receiving a single comment, first-time SW users are 14% less likely on average to post again on SW (range: 23% – 8%). The plausible explanation is that the user did not receive enough support and was not reinforced to use the platform again. As users received more comments they are more likely to post in SW again, supporting hypothesis 2 (H2) at least up until 5 comments and again for 9 or more comments. Receiving 4-8 comments had mean likelihoods closer to 0, which would mean first-time SW posters are equally likely to return.

Given how difficult treating suicidal thoughts and behaviors has shown to be (Bentley et al., 2020), it is likely that positive peer responses may only provide in-the-moment reduction given effective treatment for STBs include cognitive behavioral therapy, mindful emotion awareness, generating cognitive flexibility, emotion exposure and learning skills that prevent crises for when therapy is discontinued (Bentley et al., 2020). Therefore, positive comments on Reddit that include validating emotions, providing resources towards more professional help such as crisis hotlines, and keeping the user socially supported (Jiang et al., 2020) should result not in less likelihood of returning but rather in re-engaging with the platform when or if symptoms return. Furthermore, out of the users posting on SW a second time, it does not seem to be the case that users are generally returning to express signs of improvement; we found measures of suicidality concerns (as approximated through custom lexicons) remain similar between first and second posts (see Fig. 4 and Appendix section A.2).

Keeping users engaged on a platform is extremely important. STBs can be chronic and have very different longitudinal trajectories, with one study finding the median onset for suicidal ideation occurs 1 to 5 years prior to attempting (Millner et al., 2017). Furthermore, taking into account the type of ideation as we did in this work (active vs. passive vs. self-harm) seems to be key for more accurate estimation given more active STBs where individuals describe planning future attempts (Millner et al., 2017). Furthermore, it is also worth considering how many samples are available for estimation. Compared with trying to estimate the effects of specific ngrams (i.e., the content of comments), estimating effects of the amount of comments as was done here will tend to have many more samples for a more accurate estimation (e.g., the amount of times "it gets better" is responded is likely lower than the amount of posts receiving 1 to 10+ comments).

4.1 Limitations and future work

There are several limitations resulting from the model's assumptions. For instance, there are multiple unobserved confounders that prevent us from claiming the comments causally affect subsequent posting behavior (e.g., life crises or stressors, psychiatric or psychological treatments); however, the fact that individuals return to SW would likely indicate that they found it useful somewhat independent of unobserved confounders. Therefore, it is important to try to understand variables that make users post again even if we cannot know why they may have worsened or improved. Furthermore, the stable unit treatment value (SUTVA, i.e., that user's outcomes are affected only by the treatment they receive and not by treatments other users receive) may be violated given possible network effects between posters receiving comments (e.g., reading other posts and comments may affect posting or re-posting behavior). Our current implementation does not provide confidence intervals for estimates nor the distribution for propensity scores, which will be important future work. Additional covariates could include the user's post frequency, amount of posts before first post to SW, and age of the account. Using nonproprietary features instead of LIWC could help reproducibility. Additional future work can include looking into which confounder variables seem to be most important in driving the effect. Ultimately, surveying SW users could help better determine why users decide to return or disengage with the platform.

4.2 Conclusion

We provide empirical evidence that receiving few comments decreases the likelihood of posting on SW again by 14% on average when receiving 1 comment, which is concerning given it is the most common case (24% of SW posts). Receiving more comments increases the likelihood of using SW again by 16% on average when receiving 10+ comments. Receiving many comments can be considered a positive treatment by keeping users engaged with peer-support and hence with life. It is therefore critical to better promote peer responses and develop systems to reinforce SW posters to return and seek resources.

Acknowledgements

DML was supported by a RallyPoint Fellowship and National Institute on Deafness and

Other Communication Disorders T32 training grant [5T32DC000038-28]. KLZ was supported by National Institute of Mental Health grant K23MH120439. The work was supported by a gift to the McGovern Institute for Brain Research at MIT. MN receives publication royalties from Macmillan, Pearson, and UpToDate. He has been a paid consultant in the past year for Microsoft Corporation, the Veterans Health Administration, Cerebral, and for a legal case regarding a death by suicide. He is an unpaid scientific advisor for Empatica, Koko, and TalkLife.

References

Adrian Aguilera and Clara Berridge. 2014. Qualitative feedback from a text messaging intervention for depression: benefits, drawbacks, and cultural differences. *JMIR mHealth and uHealth*, 2(4):e3660.

Laura Helena Andrade, J Alonso, Z Mneimneh, JE Wells, A Al-Hamzawi, G Borges, E Bromet, Ronny Bruffaerts, G De Girolamo, R De Graaf, et al. 2014. Barriers to mental health treatment: results from the who world mental health surveys. *Psychological medicine*, 44(6):1303–1317.

Kate H Bentley, Shannon Sauer-Zavala, Kimberly T Stevens, and Jason J Washburn. 2020. Implementing an evidence-based psychological intervention for suicidal thoughts and behaviors on an inpatient unit: Process, challenges, and initial findings. *General hospital psychiatry*, 63:76–82.

Gualtiero B Colombo, Pete Burnap, Andrei Hodorog, and Jonathan Scourfield. 2016. Analysing the connectivity and communication of suicidal users on twitter. *Computer communications*, 73:291–300.

Munmun De Choudhury and Emre Kiciman. 2017. The language of social support in social media and its effect on suicidal ideation risk. In *Proceedings of the International AAAI Conference on Web and Social Media*, volume 11.

Rebecca G Fortgang and Matthew K Nock. 2021. Ringing the alarm on suicide prevention: a call to action. *Psychiatry*, pages 1–4.

King-wa Fu, Qijin Cheng, Paul WC Wong, and Paul SF Yip. 2013. Responses to a self-presented suicide attempt in social media. *Crisis*.

Adam C Jaroszewski, Robert R Morris, and Matthew K Nock. 2019. Randomized controlled trial of an online machine learning-driven risk assessment and intervention platform for increasing the use of crisis services. *Journal of consulting and clinical psychology*, 87(4):370.

Meng Jiang, Brooke A Ammerman, Qingkai Zeng, Ross Jacobucci, and Alex Brodersen. 2020. Phrase-level pairwise topic modeling to uncover helpful peer responses to online suicidal crises. *Humanities and Social Sciences Communications*, 7(1):1–13.

Ang Li, Xiaoxiao Huang, Bibo Hao, Bridianne O'Dea, Helen Christensen, and Tingshao Zhu. 2015. Attitudes towards suicide attempts broadcast on social media: an exploratory study of chinese microblogs. *PeerJ*, 3:e1209.

Daniel M Low, Laurie Rumker, Tanya Talkar, John Torous, Guillermo Cecchi, and Satrajit S Ghosh. 2020. Natural language processing reveals vulnerable mental health support groups and heightened health anxiety on reddit during covid-19: Observational study. *Journal of medical Internet research*, 22(10):e22635.

Jared K Lunceford and Marie Davidian. 2004. Stratification and weighting via the propensity score in estimation of causal treatment effects: a comparative study. *Statistics in medicine*, 23(19):2937–2960.

Alexander J Millner, Michael D Lee, and Matthew K Nock. 2017. Describing and measuring the pathway to suicide attempts: A preliminary study. *Suicide and Life-Threatening Behavior*, 47(3):353–369.

David C Mohr, Joyce Ho, Jenna Duffecy, Kelly G Baron, Kenneth A Lehman, Ling Jin, and Douglas Reifler. 2010. Perceived barriers to psychological treatments and their relationship to depression. *Journal of clinical psychology*, 66(4):394–409.

Melanie CM Murray, Sara O'Shaughnessy, Kirsten Smillie, Natasha Van Borek, Rebecca Graham, Evelyn J Maan, Mia L van der Kop, Karen Friesen, Arianne Albert, Sarah Levine, et al. 2015. Health care providers' perspectives on a weekly text-messaging intervention to engage hiv-positive persons in care (weltel bc1). *AIDS and Behavior*, 19(10):1875–1887.

John A Naslund, Kelly A Aschbrenner, Lisa A Marsch, and SJ Bartels. 2016. The future of mental health care: peer-to-peer support and social media. *Epidemiology and psychiatric sciences*, 25(2):113–122.

T Niederkrotenthaler, M Gould, G Sonneck, S Stack, and B Till. 2016. Predictors of psychological improvement on non-professional suicide message boards: content analysis. *Psychological medicine*, 46(16):3429–3442.

Bridianne O'dea, Melinda R Achilles, Mark E Larsen, Philip J Batterham, Alison L Calear, and Helen Christensen. 2018. The rate of reply and nature of responses to suicide-related posts on twitter. *Internet interventions*, 13:105–107.

Christabel Owens, Paul Farrand, Ruth Darvill, Tobit Emmens, Elaine Hewis, and Peter Aitken. 2011. Involving service users in intervention design: a participatory approach to developing a text-messaging intervention to reduce repetition of self-harm. *Health Expectations*, 14(3):285–295.

James W Pennebaker, Ryan L Boyd, Kayla Jordan, and Kate Blackburn. 2015. The development and psychometric properties of liwc2015. Technical report.

Anthony R Pisani, Peter A Wyman, Kunali Gurditta, Karen Schmeelk-Cone, Carolyn L Anderson, and Emily Judd. 2018. Mobile phone intervention to reduce youth suicide in rural communities: field test. *JMIR mental health*, 5(2):e10425.

Amit Sharma, Emre Kiciman, et al. 2019. DoWhy: A Python package for causal inference. https://github.com/microsoft/dowhy.

Christiane Steinert, Mareike Hofmann, Johannes Kruse, and Falk Leichsenring. 2014. Relapse rates after psychotherapy for depression–stable long-term effects? a meta-analysis. *Journal of Affective Disorders*, 168:107–118.

Ursula Whiteside, Anita Lungu, Julie Richards, Gregory E Simon, Sarah Clingan, Jaeden Siler, Lorilei Snyder, and Evette Ludman. 2014. Designing messaging to engage patients in an online suicide prevention intervention: survey results from patients with current suicidal ideation. *Journal of medical Internet research*, 16(2):e42.

A Appendix

A.1 Feature extraction

We used the following LIWC features: word count, personal pronouns, 1st person singular pronouns, negations, comparisons, interrogatives, affective processes, anxiety, anger, sadness, family, friends, insight, causation, discrepancy, tentative, certainty, perceptual processes, body, health, sexual, ingestion, achievement, power, reward, risk, past focused, present focused, future focused, work, leisure, home, money, religion, death, informal, swear words, question markers, exclamation marks. We also built custom lexicons to count tokens in posts and normalized the counts by the posts's word count (see Table 1 for examples). Lexicons were created based on most frequent ngrams in r/SuicideWatch, r/Lonely, and r/PersonalFinance, and a glossary from the US National Institute on Drug Abuse [2]. STB general included tokens that could not be strictly classified into the other STB lexicons. Mental health included words related to common non-STB disorders, symptoms, and complaints. Lexicons are freely available within the code [3].

[2]`https://www.drugabuse.gov/drug-topics/commonly-used-drugs-charts`

[3]Code and lexicons: `https://github.com/danielmlow/playbook_comments`

Lexicon	Tokens
STB general	suicid, shitty life, i deserve to die, crisis hotline, wasting space
STB active	jump into traffic, kill myself, commit suicide, hang myself
STB passive	don't want to wake up, wish i was never born, thinking about death, i'm ready to go
STB self-harm	cut myself, slit my wrists, burn my, self harm
Mental health	hospitalized, psychiatr, stress, insomnia, worried, xanax
Loneliness and isolation	lonely, no one cares, i miss my, any friends, quarantine, am single
Domestic stress and violence	divorc, violence, husband, single parent, push, scream, fight
Financial stress	my credit, loan, rent, mortgage, bills, salary, job, poverty, evict
Substance use	clean, rehab, sober, relaps, withdraw, 12 step, adderal, alcohol, hangover, cocaine

Table 1: Examples of custom lexicons. STB: suicidal thoughts and behaviors.

A.2 Differences between first and second post

See Figures A.1, A.2, and A.3 for within-user differences for different suicidality variables.

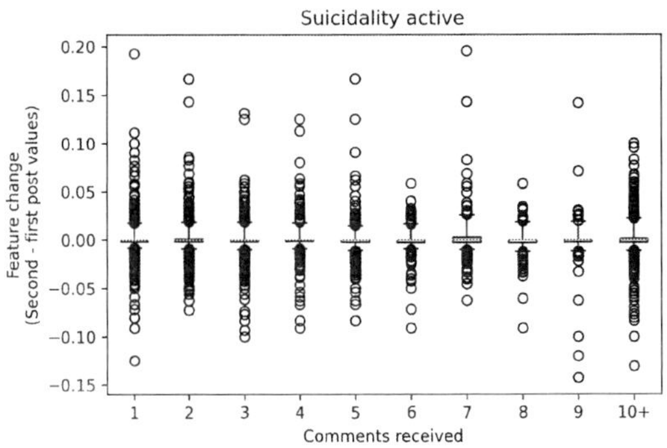

Figure A.1: Boxplots showing differences in lexicon values between each user's second and first post. Variable values do not change considerably as 90% within-participant differences remain near 0.

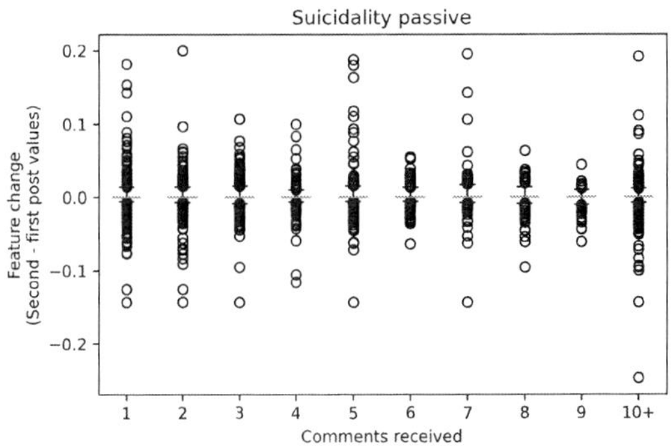

Figure A.2: Boxplots showing differences in lexicon values between each user's second and first post. Variable values do not change considerably as 90% within-participant differences remain near 0.

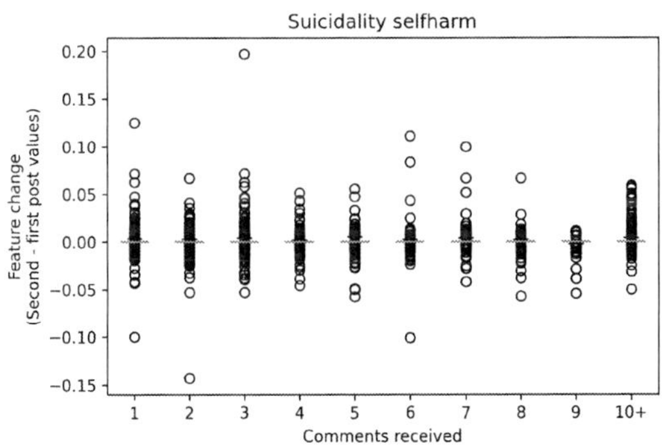

Figure A.3: Boxplots showing differences in lexicon values between each user's second and first post. Variable values do not change considerably as 90% within-participant differences remain near 0.

Association for Computational Linguistics
209 N. Eighth Street
Stroudsburg, Pennsylvania 18360

ISBN 978-1-7138-9187-1

CURRAN ASSOCIATES INC.
proceedings.com